New York University Institute of Philosophy

Determinism and Freedom in the Age of Modern Science

Determinism and Freedom

IN THE AGE OF MODERN SCIENCE

A philosophical symposium

edited by SIDNEY HOOK

NEW YORK UNIVERSITY PRESS

WASHINGTON SQUARE

ISBN 0-8147-0195-7

The contents of this volume comprise the Proceedings of the first annual New York University Institute of Philosophy, held at Washington Square, New York, February 9 and 10, 1957.

Introduction

(From the welcoming address to participants in the first New York University Institute of Philosophy)

In behalf of New York University it gives me great pleasure to welcome the participants to this the first meeting of the New York University Institute of Philosophy. A university exists to achieve many purposes. But however varied its purposes, the spirit of the university is found at its best only where men are found thinking together. Thinking together is something more than explicit teaching and learning, although it may be that, too. It is a process of mutual stimulus and response in which our minds become clearer, even when they are not altered by the give and take of intellectual exchange. It is a process whose outcome determines whether our ideas —most of them held with equal initial conviction—are firm principles or only familiar prejudices. Sometimes thinking together is not only a dialogue that contributes to conceptual clarification and self-understanding but a common voyage of intellectual discovery. Even when discoveries are made by a solitary thinker, they are not seldom influenced by the funded results of previous thinking together.

The New York University Institute of Philosophy has invited not only distinguished philosophers from other leading universities to these deliberations but representatives of other disciplines. This expresses a unity or convergence of *interest* on common problems, not a unity of *doctrine* or *point of view*. In a world where specialization tends to make every scholar in the university an expert and none able to understand or talk to his colleague, opportunities for intellectual co-operation should be encouraged.

I therefore hope that this series of meetings will be the first of a long line of similar proceedings contributing to the enrichment of intellectual life in America.

Carroll V. Newsom
President, New York University

Contents

Part II   Determinism in Modern Science

Part III   Determinism and Responsibility in Law and Ethics

Part IV   Discussion

Preface

The New York University Institute of Philosophy is an experiment designed to further fruitful discussion in philosophy. The annual regional meetings of the American Philosophical Association perform an excellent and indispensable professional function. But because of the large number of persons involved, the broad scope of the programs, and the adherence to fixed time schedules—natural limitations of all gatherings of this kind—it seems desirable to multiply opportunities for free and sustained interchange of views. Toward this end we therefore resolved to try something new: to select one philosophical topic or theme for intensive discussion by a small group of philosophers and other scholars and thinkers deeply concerned with it, and willing to explore it together around a long seminar table. We hope our action will inspire similar efforts in other regions of the country.

Our great problem was to keep the number of participants within reasonable compass without making invidious distinctions. No inference is to be made as to a philosopher's eminence or professional qualification to analyze the theme under discussion on the basis of his absence from this Institute. For obvious reasons geographical considerations played a large role. Nonetheless we hope to establish a revolving membership for our Institute so that before long all philosophers with a strong interest in the themes under discussion and within easy traveling distance from New York City will on one or another occasion join us as participants in the Institute.

On the other hand, the choice of a theme for our first Institute was not very much a problem. "Determinism and Freedom" is not only a perennial philosophical issue but seems today to be moving once more into the forefront of intellectual concern. For example, almost contemporary with our Proceedings, the January 1957 issue of *Mind* contains two long articles on the subject, and the issue before that includes a piece in which it is argued that the entire notion of "moral responsibility" is moribund and should be extruded from vocabulary of intelligible expressions.[1] Our theme was selected long before these and similar articles appeared.

Not only professional philosophers but also our colleagues in other fields are astir over the issue. Three converging tendencies of thought have contributed to a revival of interest in the question of determinism and freedom.

The first is political and social. Whereas in the past the extension of the deterministic philosophy in the natural sciences was hailed as a support of human freedom because it increased man's power of control over nature, today belief in determinism in the social sciences and social affairs is feared by many because it increases the power of men to control other men. Some individuals confess that it is not only Orwell's scientifically controlled *1984* that causes their hackles to rise in fear but even the picture of comparatively sunny communities like that drawn in Skinner's *Walden II*. In some quarters this reaction has gone so far that even the term "planning" and the notion of "a planned society," which a short generation ago was the hallmark of a rational social philosophy, are viewed with suspicion as suggesting, if not evidencing, a conspiracy against human freedom.

The second reason for a revival of interest in our theme is that

[1] W. I. Matson, "On the Irrelevance of Free Will to Moral Responsibility, and the Vacuity of the Latter," *Mind* (October 1956).

in the very stronghold of traditional determinism, the natural sciences, the field in which determinism celebrated its greatest triumph, the belief in the doctrine or postulate of universal determinism seems to have been surrendered in an effort to understand the world of subatomic behavior. The actual relevance of these glad tidings to the momentous issues of human freedom and responsibility remains to be established. But in the writings of several eminent scientists it has been eloquently proclaimed.

The third reason for the *actualité* of our theme derives from growth of interest in modern psychology, psychiatry, and psychoanalysis in all their scientific and mythological forms. The apparent upshot of the acceptance of determinism in explaining the human psyche is the belief that the more we learn about a man's past history, the less he seems responsible for his present behavior. This conclusion has affected thinking and practice in law, pedagogy, and social work, and has produced something of a revolution in penology. Sometimes its proponents rather inconsistently blame us for blaming Hitler and Stalin for the crimes they voluntarily committed, on the ground that since Hitler and Stalin were once babies—hard as it is to imagine—they must have inherited or acquired the complexes and obsessional drives that caused them to do what they couldn't help doing. Even when pruned of inconsistency, this argument threatens to produce a revolution in moral theory by asserting that the concept of moral responsibility is completely vacuous.

The strategy of our discussion is to begin with an analysis of the general concept of determinism, to proceed to the notion of determinism in physics, and to conclude with a discussion of freedom and responsibility in law and ethics.

The papers of the readers and selected commentators are here reproduced substantially in the form in which they were presented to the Institute. Most of the other comments by participants in the Institute are elaborations of comments and criticisms made after the papers were presented. Some of the comments are a result of post-Institute reflection on the spirited give and take among the participants, which technical difficulties prevented us from reproducing in their entirety.

Sidney Hook
New York University

PART I   Determinism in Philosophy

1. The Case for Determinism

Brand Blanshard, Yale University

I am a determinist. None of the arguments offered on the other side seem of much weight except one form of the moral argument, and that itself is far from decisive. Perhaps the most useful thing I can do in this paper is explain why the commoner arguments for indeterminism do not, to my mind, carry conviction. In the course of this explanation the brand of determinism to which I am inclined should become gradually apparent.

But first a definition or two. Determinism is easier to define than indeterminism, and at first glance there seems to be no difficulty in saying what one means by it. It is the view that all events are caused. But unless one also says what one means by "event" and "caused," there is likely to be trouble later. Do I include among events not only changes but the lack of change, not only the fall of the water over the cataract's edge, but the persistence of ice in the frozen river?

The answer is "Yes." By an event I mean any change or persistence of state or position. And what is meant by saying that an event is caused? The natural answer is that the event is so connected with some preceding event that unless the latter had occurred the former would not have occurred. Indeterminism means the denial of this. And the denial of this is the statement that there is at least one event to which no preceding event is necessary. But that gets us into trouble at once, for it is doubtful if any indeterminist would want to make such an assertion. What he wants to say is that his decision to tell the truth is undetermined, not that there is no preceding event necessary to it. He would not contend, for example, that he could tell the truth if he had never been born. No, the causal statement to which the indeterminist takes exception is a different one. He is not saying that there is any event to which some namable antecedents are not necessary; he is saying that there are some events whose antecedents do not make them necessary. He is not denying that all consequents have necessary antecedents; he is denying that all antecedents have necessary consequents. He is saying that the state of things just before he decided to tell the truth might have been exactly what it was and yet he might have decided to tell a lie.

By determinism, then, I mean the view that every event A is so connected with a later event B that, given A, B must occur. By indeterminism I mean the view that there is some event B that is not so connected with any previous event A that, given A, it must occur. Now, what is meant here by "must"? We cannot in the end evade that question, but I hope you will not take it as an evasion if at this point I am content to let you fill in the blank in any way you wish. Make it a logical "must," if you care to, or a physical or metaphysical "must," or even the watered-down "must" that means "A is always in fact followed by B." We can discuss the issue usefully though we leave ourselves some latitude on this point.

With these definitions in mind, let us ask what are the most important grounds for indeterminism. This is not the same as asking what commonly moves people to be indeterminists; the answer to that seems to me all too easy. Everyone vaguely knows that to be undetermined is to be free, and everyone wants to be free. My question is rather, When reflective people accept the indeterminist view nowadays, what considerations seem most cogent to them? It seems to me that there are three: first, the stubborn feeling of freedom, which seems to resist all dialectical solvents; second, the conviction that natural science itself has now gone over to the indeterminist side; and, third, that determinism would make nonsense of moral responsibility. The third of these seems to me the most important, but I must try to explain why none of them seem to me conclusive.

One of the clearest heads that ever devoted itself to this old issue was Henry Sidgwick. Sidgwick noted that, if at any given moment we stop to think about it, we always feel as if more than one course were open to us, that we could speak or be silent, lift our hand or not lift it. If the determinist is right, this must be an illusion, of course, for whatever we might have done, there must have been a cause, given which we had to do what we did. Now, a mere intuitive assurance about ourselves may be a very weak ground for belief; Freud has shown us that we may be profoundly deceived about how we really feel or why we act as we do. But the curious point is that, though a man who hates his father without knowing it can usually be shown that he does and can often be cured of his feeling, no amount of dialectic seems to shake our feeling of being free to perform either of two proposed acts. By this feeling of being free I do not mean merely the freedom to do what we choose. No one on either side questions that we have that sort of freedom, but it is obviously not the sort of freedom that the indeterminist wants, since it is consistent with determinism of the most rigid sort. The real issue, so far as the will is concerned, is not whether we can do what we choose to do, but whether we can choose our own choice, whether the choice itself issues in accordance with law from some antecedent. And the feeling of freedom that is relevant as evidence is the feeling of an open future as regards the choice itself. After the noise of argument has died down, a sort of intuition stubbornly remains that we can not only lift our hand if we choose, but that the choice itself is open to us. Is this not an impressive fact?

No, I do not think it is. The first reason is that when we are making a choice our faces are always turned toward the future, toward the consequences that one act or the other will bring us, never toward the past with its possible sources of constraint. Hence these sources are not noticed. Hence we remain unaware that we are under constraint at all. Hence we feel free from such constraint. The case is almost as simple as that. When you consider buying a new typewriter your thought is fixed on the pleasure and advantage you would gain from it, or the drain it would make on your budget. You are not delving into the causes that led to your taking pleasure in the prospect of owning a typewriter or to your having a complex about expenditure. You are too much preoccupied with the ends to which the choice would be a means to give any attention to the causes of which your choice may be an effect. But that is no reason for thinking that if you did preoccupy yourself with these causes you would not find them at work. You may remember that Sir Francis Galton was so much impressed with this possibility that for some time he kept account in a notebook of the occasions on which he made important choices with a full measure of this feeling of freedom; then shortly after each choice he turned his eye backward in search of constraints that might have been acting on him stealthily. He found it so easy to bring such constraining factors to light that he surrendered to the determinist view.

But this, you may say, is not enough. Our preoccupation with the future may show why we are not aware of the constraints acting on us, and hence why we do not feel bound by them; it does not explain why our sense of freedom persists after the constraints are disclosed to us. By disclosing the causes of some fear, for example, psychoanalytic therapy can remove the fear, and when these causes are brought to light, the fear commonly does go. How is it, then, that when the causes of our volition are brought to light volition continues to feel as free as before? Does this not show that it is really independent of those causes?

No again. The two cases are not parallel. The man with the panic fear of dogs is investing all dogs with the qualities—remembered, though in disguised form—of the monster that frightened him as a child. When this monster and his relation to it are brought to light, so that they can be dissociated from the Fidos and Towsers around him, the fear goes, because its appropriate object has gone. It is quite different with our feeling of freedom. We feel free, it was suggested, because we are not aware of the forces acting on us. Now, in spite of the determinist's conviction that when a choice is made there are always causal influences at work, he does not pretend to reveal the influences at work in our present choice. The chooser's face is always turned forward; his present choice is always unique; and no matter how much he knows about the will and the laws, his present choice always emerges out of deep shadow. The determinist who buys a typewriter is as little interested at the moment in the strings that may be pulling at him from his physiological or subconscious cellars as his indeterminist colleague, and hence feels just as free. Thus, whereas the new knowledge gained through psychoanalysis does remove the grounds of fear, the knowledge gained by the determinist is not at all of the sort that would remove the grounds for the feeling of freedom. To make the persistence of this feeling in the determinist an argument against his case is therefore a confusion.

The second reason, I suggested, why so many thoughtful persons remain indeterminists is that they are convinced that science has gone indeterminist. Well, has it? If you follow Heisenberg, Eddington, and Born, it has. If you follow Russell, Planck, and Einstein, it has not. When such experts disagree it is no doubt folly for the layman to rush in. But since I am discussing the main reasons why people stick to indeterminism, and have admitted that the new physics is one of them, I cannot afford to be quite prudent. Let me say, then, with much hesitation that, as far as I can follow the argument, it provides no good evidence for indeterminism even in the physical world, and that, if it did, it would provide no good evidence for indeterminism in the realm of will.

First as to physical indeterminism. Physicists now tell us that descriptive statements about the behavior of bodies are really statistical statements. It was known long ago that the pressure that makes a football hard is not the simple quality one feels in pushing something: it is the beating on the inner surface of the football of millions of molecular bullets. We now know that each of these bullets is a swarm of atoms, themselves normally swarms of still minuter somethings, of which the proton and the electron are typical. The physicist admits that the behavior of an enormous mass of these particles, such as a billiard ball, is so stable that we may safely consider it as governed by causal law. But that is no reason, he adds, for assigning a like stability to the ultimate particles themselves. Indeed, there is good reason, namely the principle of indeterminacy, for saying that they sometimes act by mere chance. That principle tells us that whereas, when we are talking about a billiard ball, we can say that it has a certain momentum and direction at point *B* as a result of having a certain momentum and direction at point *A*, we can never say that sort of thing about an electron. Why? Because the conditions of observation are such that, when they allow us to fix the position exactly, they make it impossible to fix the momentum exactly. Suppose that we can determine the position of a moving particle with more accuracy the shorter the wave length of light we use. But suppose that the shorter the wave length, the more it interferes with the momentum of the particle, making it leap unpredictably about. And suppose there is no way of determining the position without in this way leaving the momentum vague, or of determining the momentum without leaving the position vague. It will then be impossible to state any precise law that governs the particle's movement. We can never say that such-and-such a momentum at point *A* was necessarily followed by such-and-such a momentum at point *B*, because these statements can have no precise meaning, and can be given none, for either antecedent or consequent. Hence to speak any longer of nature as governed ultimately by causal laws—i.e., statements of precise connection between antecedent and consequent— is simply out of the question.

This argument, as Sir David Ross has pointed out, may be interpreted in different ways. It may be taken to say that, though the particle does have a certain position and momentum, we can never tell, definitely and for both at the same time, what they are. Many interpreters thus understand the theory. But so taken, there is of course nothing in it to throw the slightest doubt on the reign of causality. It is merely a statement that in a certain region our knowledge of causal law has limits. Secondly, the theory might be taken to mean that electrons are not the sort of things that have position and momentum at all in the ordinary sense, but are fields, perhaps, or widespreading waves. This, too, has no suggestion of indeterminism. It would not mean that general statements about the nature and behavior of electrons could not be made, but only that such statements would not contain references to position and momentum. Thirdly, the theory might mean that, though these particles do have a position and a momentum, the position or momentum is not definitely this rather than that. Even laymen must rise at this point and protest, with all respect, that this is meaningless. Vagueness in our thought of a position makes sense; vagueness of actual position makes none. Or, finally, the argument may mean that, though the particle does have a definite position and momentum, these cannot even in theory be correlated with anything that went before. But how could we possibly know this? The only ground for accepting it is that we do not know of any such correlates. And that is no reason for denying that any exist. Indeed, to deny this is to abandon the established assumption and practice of science. Science has advanced in the past precisely because, when things happened whose causes were unknown, it was assumed that they had causes nevertheless. To assume that a frustration of present knowledge, even one that looks permanent, is a sign of chance in nature is both practically uncourageous and theoretically a *non sequitur*.

But let us suppose that the Eddingtonians are right and that what has been called "free will among the electrons" is the fact. Would that imply indeterminism in the realm that most nearly concerns us, the realm of choice? I cannot see that it would. The argument supposed to show that it would is as follows: Psychical processes depend on physical processes. But physical processes are themselves at bottom unpredictable. Hence the psychical processes dependent on them must share this unpredictability. Stated in the abstract, the argument sounds impressive. But what does it actually come to? We are told that, even if there is inconstancy in the behavior of single particles, there is no observable inconstancy in the behavior of masses of them; the particles of a billiard ball are never able to get together and go on a spree simultaneously. Eddington admitted that they might, just as he admitted that an army of monkeys with a million typewriters might produce all the books in the British Museum, but he admitted also that the chances of a billiard ball's behaving in this way were so astronomically remote that he would not believe it if he saw it.

The question of importance for us, then, is whether, if acts of choice are dependent on physical processes at all, they depend on the behavior of particles singly or on that of masses of particles. To this there can be but one answer. They depend on mass behavior. An act of choice is an extremely complex process. It involves the idea of one or more ends, the association of that idea with more or less numerous other ideas, the presence of desires and repulsions, and the operation of habits and impulses; indeed, in those choices for which freedom is most demanded, the whole personality seems to be at work. The cortical basis for so complex a process must be extremely broad. But if it is, the great mass of cells involved must, by the physicist's admission, act with a high stability, and the correlated psychical processes must show a similar stability. But that is what we mean by action in accordance with causal law. So, even if the physicists are right about the unstable behavior of single particles, there is no reason whatever for translating this theory into a doctrine of indeterminism for human choice.

We come now to the third of the reasons commonly advanced in support of indeterminism. This is that determinism makes a mess of morality. The charge has taken many forms. We are told that determinism makes praise and blame meaningless, punishment brutal, remorse pointless, amendment hopeless, duty a deceit. All these allegations have been effectively answered except the one about duty, where I admit I am not quite satisfied. But none of them are in the form in which determinism most troubles the plain man. What most affronts him, I think, is the suggestion that he is only a machine, a big foolish clock that seems to itself to be acting freely, but whose movements are controlled completely by the wheels and weights inside, a Punch-and-Judy show whose appearance of doing things because they are right or reasonable is a sham because everything is mechanically regulated by wires from below. He has no objections to determinism as applied by physicists to atoms, by himself to machines, or by his doctor to his body. He has an emphatic objection to determinism as applied by anyone to his reflection and his will, for this seems to make him a gigantic mechanical toy, or worse, a sort of Frankenstein monster.

In this objection I think we must agree with the plain man. If anyone were to show me that determinism involved either materialism or mechanism, I would renounce it at once, for that would be equivalent, in my opinion, to reducing it to absurdity. The "physicalism" once proposed by Neurath and Carnap as a basis for the scientific study of behavior I could not accept for a moment, because it is so dogmatically antiempirical. To use empirical methods means, for me, not to approach nature with a preconceived notion as to what facts must be like, but to be ready to consider all kinds of alleged facts on their merits. Among these the introspectively observable fact of reflective choice, and the inference to its existence in others, are particularly plain, however different from anything that occurs in the realm of the material or the publicly observable or the mechanically controlled.

Now, what can be meant by saying that such choice, though not determined mechanically, is still determined? Are you suggesting, it will be asked, that in the realm of reflection and choice there operates a different kind of causality from any we know in the realm of bodies? My answer is: Yes, just that. To put it more particularly, I am suggesting (1) that even within the psychical realm there are different causal levels, (2) that a causality of higher level may supervene on one of lower level, and (3) that when causality of the highest level is at work, we have precisely what the indeterminists, without knowing it, want.

1. First, then, as to causal levels. I am assuming that even the indeterminist would admit that most mental events are causally governed. No one would want to deny that his stepping on a tack had something to do with his feeling pain, or that his touching a flame had something to do with his getting burned, or that his later thought of the flame had something to do with his experience of its hotness. A law of association is a causal law of mental events. In one respect it is like a law of physical events: in neither case have we any light as to *why* the consequent follows on the antecedent. Hume was right about the billiard balls. He was right about the flame and the heat; we do not see why something bright and yellow should also be hot. He was right about association; we do not understand how one idea calls up another; we only know that it does. Causality in all such cases means to us little if anything more than a routine of regular sequence.

Is all mental causation like that? Surely not. Consider a musician composing a piece or a logician making a deduction. Let us make our musician a philosopher also, who after adding a bar pauses to ask himself, "Why did I add just that?" Can we believe he would answer, "Because whenever in the past I have had the preceding bars in mind, they have always been followed by this bar"? What makes this suggestion so inept is partly that he may never have thought of the preceding bars before, partly that, if he had, the repetition of an old sequence would be precisely what he would avoid. No, his answer, I think, would be something like this: "I wrote what I did because it seemed the right thing to do. I developed my theme in the manner demanded to carry it through in an aesthetically satisfactory way." In other words, the constraint that was really at work in him was not that of association; it was something that worked distinctly against association; it was the constraint of an aesthetic ideal. And, if so, there is a causality of a different level. It is idle to say that the musician is wholly in the dark about it. He can see not only *that* B succeeded A; as he looks back, he can see in large measure *why* it did.

It is the same with logical inference, only more clearly so. The thinker starts, let us say, with the idea of a regular solid whose faces are squares, and proceeds to develop in thought the further characteristics that such a solid must possess. He constructs it in imagination and then sees that it must have six faces, eight vertices, and twelve edges. Is this association merely? It may be. It is, for example, if he merely does in imagination what a child does when it counts the edges on a lump of sugar. This is not inference and does not feel like it. When a person, starting with the thought of a solid with square faces, deduces that it must have eight vertices, and then asks why he should have thought of that, the natural answer is, Because the first property entails the second. Of course this is not the only condition, but it seems to me contrary to introspectively plain fact to say that it had nothing to do with the movement of thought. It is easy to put this in such a way as to invite attack. If we say that the condition of our thinking of B is the observed necessity between A and B, we are assuming that B is already thought of as a means of explaining how it comes to be thought of. But that is not what I am saying. I am saying that in thinking at its best thought comes under the constraint of necessities in its object, so that the objective fact that A necessitates B partially determines our passing in thought from A to B. Even when the explanation is put in this form, the objection has been raised that necessity is a timeless link between concepts, while causality is a temporal bond between events, and that the two must be kept sharply apart. To which the answer is: Distinct, yes; but always apart, no. A timeless relation may serve perfectly well as the condition of a temporal passage. I hold that in the course of our thinking we can easily verify this fact, and, because I do, I am not put off by pronouncements about what we should and should not be able to see.

2. My second point about these causal levels is that our mental processes seldom move on one level alone. The higher is always supervening on the lower and taking over partial control. Though brokenly and imperfectly rational, rational creatures we still are. It must be admitted that most of our so-called thinking moves by association, and is hardly thinking at all. But even in the dullest of us "bright shoots of everlastingness," strands of necessity, aesthetic or logical, from time to time appear. "The quarto and folio editions of mankind" can follow the argument with fewer lapses than most of us; in the texts of the greatest of all dramas, we are told, there was seldom a blot or erasure; but Ben Jonson added, and no doubt rightly, that there ought to have been a thousand. The effort of both thought and art is to escape the arbitrary, the merely personal, everything that, casual and capricious, is irrelevant, and to keep to lines appointed by the whole that one is constructing. I do not suggest that logical and aesthetic necessity are the same. I do say that they are both to be distinguished from association or habit as representing a different level of control. That control is never complete; all creation in thought or art is successful in degree only. It is successful in the degree to which it ceases to be an expression of merely personal impulses and becomes the instrument of a necessity lying in its own subject matter.

3. This brings us to our last point. Since moral choice, like thought and art, moves on different causal levels, it achieves freedom, just as they do, only when it is determined by its own appropriate necessity. Most of our so-called choices are so clearly brought about by association, impulse, and feeling that the judicious indeterminist will raise no issue about them. When we decide to get a drink of water, to take another nibble of chocolate, to go to bed at the usual hour, the forces at work are too plain to be denied. It is not acts like these on which the indeterminist takes his stand. It is rather on those where, with habit, impulse, and association prompting us powerfully to do X, we see that we ought to do Y and therefore do it. To suppose that in such cases we are still the puppets of habit and impulse seems to the indeterminist palpably false.

So it does to us. Surely about this the indeterminist is right. Action impelled by the sense of duty, as Kant perceived, is action on a different level from anything mechanical or associative. But Kant was mistaken in supposing that when we were determined by reason we were not determined at all. This supposition seems to me wholly unwarranted. The determination is still there, but, since it is a determination by the moral necessities of the case, it is just what the moral man wants and thus is the equivalent of freedom. For the moral man, like the logician and the artist, is really seeking self-surrender. Through him as through the others an impersonal ideal is working, and to the extent that this ideal takes possession of him and molds him according to its pattern, he feels free and is free.

The logician is most fully himself when the wind gets into his sails and carries him effortlessly along the line of his calculations. Many an artist and musician have left it on record that their best work was done when the whole they were creating took the brush or pen away from them and completed the work itself. It determined them, but they were free, because to be determined by this whole was at once the secret of their craft and the end of their desire. This is the condition of the moral man also. He has caught a vision, dimmer perhaps than that of the logician or the artist, but equally objective and compelling. It is a vision of the good. This good necessitates certain things, not as means to ends merely, for that is not usually a necessary link, but as integral parts of itself. It requires that he should put love above hate, that he should regard his neighbor's good as of like value with his own, that he should repair injuries, and express gratitude, and respect promises, and revere truth. Of course it does not guide him infallibly. On the values of a particular case he may easily be mistaken. But that no more shows that there are no values present to be estimated, and no ideal demanding a special mode of action, than the fact that we make a mistake in adding figures shows that there are no figures to be added, or a right way of adding them. In both instances what we want is control by the objective requirements of the case. The saint, like the thinker and the artist, has often said this in so many words. I feel most free, said St. Paul, precisely when I am most a slave.

We have now dealt, as best we can in a restricted space, with the three commonest objections to determinism. They all seem to admit of answers. To the objection that we always feel free, we answer that it is natural to feel so, even if we are determined, since our faces are set toward results and not toward causes, and the causes of present action always elude us. To the objection that science has gone indeterminist, we answer that that is only one interpretation of recent discoveries, and not the most plausible one, and that, even if it were true, it would not carry with it indeterminism for human choice. To the objection that determinism would reduce us to the level of mechanical puppets, we answer that though we are puppets in part we live, as Aristotle said, on various levels. And so far as causality in reflection, art, and moral choice involves control by immanent ideal, mechanism has passed over into that rational determinism that is the best kind of freedom.

2. Making Something Happen

Max Black, Cornell University

I

You are thirsty, but there is a glass of beer within easy reach; you stretch out your hand, bring the glass to your lips, and drink. Here is what I call a *perfectly clear case* of making something happen. When you brought the glass nearer, that was a perfect instance of what all of us *call* "making something happen."[1] But of course many other simple actions would serve just as well: closing a window, opening a drawer, turning a doorknob, sharpening a pencil. Any

[1] Or rather a clear case of "moving a glass." The expression "making something happen" is introduced for brevity in referring to similar cases. The first part of the paper investigates a class of transitive verbs, like "moving," "breaking," "opening," "upsetting," etc., indicated by the blanket expression "making something happen." When the expression "making something happen" occurs, the reader may usually imagine the more specific expression "moving a glass" substituted—with the understanding, however, that the discussion is intended to apply indifferently to an entire class of similar expressions.

number of perfectly clear cases can be found of making something happen.

The following is not a clear case of making something happen. On hearing the opening of this paper, a member of the audience leaves the room, to be found later in the nearest saloon. To establish that my remarks *made* him leave the room would require a specific investigation. Evidence could be obtained for or against the view that talk about drinking had *made* the hearer leave; until such evidence had been provided, the final verdict would remain in doubt.

In the case of the thirsty man reaching for the glass, an investigation to determine whether or not he really did move the glass would be out of place. There would be an absurdity in saying that evidence could be provided for or against the view that he had moved the glass; or in saying that whether he had made anything happen was a hypothesis. It would be absurd to say that there was a question whether he had moved the glass, and that the answer would be undecided until further evidence had been weighed.

For what could be the goal of the supposed investigation? If somebody is not already satisfied that the familiar episode *is* a case of what we ordinarily call "making something happen," it is inconceivable that further empirical evidence would satisfy him. The supposed investigation would have no terminus; criteria would be lacking by which to judge the relevance and strength of testimony.

I am trying to affirm something noncontroversial and hence acceptable in advance of any philosophical analysis or commitment. I am contending that we do all treat simple episodes like the one I described as perfectly clear cases of making something happen.

We do in fact recognize the absurdity of a supposed attempt to *find out* whether the drinker had made the glass move. Suppose I were to say to somebody, "You saw that man reach out for that glass of beer just now—well, *find out* whether he moved the glass." I have no doubt that a layman would be dumfounded and quite at a loss to know what could be meant. A sufficient reply would be: "Surely, we *saw* him move the glass." If I insisted that I wanted *evidence* that the drinker had moved the glass, my interlocutor might begin to suspect the situation was abnormal—for this would be one way of making sense of my demand. Suppose we were suddenly to see the glass of beer levitate and fly like a homing pigeon straight to the drinker's mouth! Then we might rub our eyes and begin to wonder whether the man in the armchair had really moved the glass the first time. We might then plausibly suspect ourselves in some magician's establishment, well stocked with trick devices for making objects move in extraordinary ways. This would be a fantastically abnormal situation. In describing the case of the thirsty drinker I wished to present a situation that was *normal,* one whose description was intended to exclude monstrosities and miracle.

I was therefore taking for granted that the person concerned was neither hypnotized nor walking in his sleep nor obeying a neurotic compulsion to reach for the glass nor acting in response to threats. And I was assuming that the glass of beer was an ordinary vessel, having no concealed magnet or other special devices and subject to no remote physical or mental controls. In short, I was taking for granted that the exemplary situation was a perfectly familiar, ordinary case. If a situation were not of this familiar sort, it might be necessary to investigate and find out whether the man concerned really had made something happen.

So far, I have been contrasting a perfectly clear case of making something happen with cases in which an investigation would be in order. The latter we might call *problematic* cases. A second kind of contrast could be made between a perfectly clear case and a *borderline* case.

Suppose you jogged my hand, so that my elbow knocked against the glass and spilled its contents. Did *I* spill the glass, or did *you* in fact do it? Both answers are plausible. We are inclined to say something like, "I spilled the beer all right, but you made me do it, so really *you* spilled it." Here the presence of the qualification "really" in *"really* you spilled it" is a sign that criteria for the use of the expression "making something happen" are no longer precise and determinate. We would not teach a child what "making something happen" means by citing this kind of case or a case in which somebody's involuntary gesture displaced an object. Similarly, we would not teach somebody the meaning of "orange" by showing color patches that most of us should hesitate to label either orange or yellow.

The uncertainty here is not due to lack of information and could not be removed by any empirical investigation. Uncertainty of application is a feature of our uses of "orange" and can be removed only by *stipulation*. Our use of the expression "making something happen" is infected by similar uncertainty. Only I should wish to deny that any such uncertainty of application is to be found in the clear case that I began by describing.

Indeed, if anybody were to show genuine hesitation about using the expression "making something happen" in the situation described, that would be evidence that he did not really *understand* that expression. If I were teaching a foreigner how to use that English expression, a test of my success would be his unhesitating identification of the exemplary situation as a case of making something happen. (Of course, he must also hesitate in borderline cases.) Should the pupil waver in the clear case, we might try to find out whether he suspected some hidden mechanism or trick device, i.e., whether he mistakenly took the situation to be abnormal. But if he convinced us that he fully understood our description of the familiar case, yet still did not know whether to say that something had been made to happen, we could be sure that efforts to teach him the uses of the English expression had not yet succeeded.

I have said that the case of the thirsty drinker is a perfectly clear one of making something happen, leaving no room for further empirical investigation—a case neither "problematic" nor "borderline." I want to add now that the episode is also a *paradigm* for application of the phrase "making something happen." That it is a paradigm is closely connected with its being a perfectly clear case; yet to call it a "paradigm" is to say something new.

Suppose we are faced with something that is *not* a clear case of making something happen, and wish to decide whether or not to apply the expression. A natural recourse would be to compare the doubtful case with some perfectly clear case, with a view to finding sufficient similarity or dissimilarity to arrive at a correct decision. By treating the clear case as a *standard* we can base our decision to use or withhold the expression upon *reasons*: we appeal to the clear case to resolve doubt. It follows, therefore, that no reason can be given why the clear case itself should bear the identifying label in question. There is nothing besides itself to which the clear case can be compared—nothing else to serve as a standard. The absurdity of asking that reasons be given for using the clear case as a standard would be just like that of trying to give reasons why the standard meter rod is counted as one meter in length, or a standard color sample is accepted as "red." Should someone demand reasons in defense of calling my exemplary instance a case of making something happen, the best I could do by way of reply would be to say: "That's what I *call* 'making something happen.'" Now here I am not offering a genuine reason, but repudiating the demand for a reason. The retort "That's what I call 'making something happen'" is a way of showing how I use the expression. In making that retort I show that I treat the instance as a paradigm. But showing is not arguing, and brandishing a paradigm is not offering a reason.

The case of the thirsty drinker differs from that of the meter rod in one important respect. The expression "one meter long" is formally defined in terms of a standard measure, so that those who understand how the expression is used know that a dispute about the correctness of any attribution of metric length would ultimately have to be resolved by appeal to a known and identifiable standard of comparison. But there is no formal definition of "making something happen," and of course no permanent and identifiable situations to serve as standards of comparison. We have a wide range of choice in exhibiting "perfectly clear cases," and they are not preserved in official bureaus of standards. Nevertheless, we do appeal to them in case of doubt—our choice of just *those* situations as acceptable standards being a feature of our use of the expression in question. Instead of the unique arbiter, we have, as it were, a reserve of available judges, any of which indifferently can serve to remind us of our linguistic conventions. Pressed to give reasons, we eventually stop at situations of which we can say no more than, "That's what I *call* such-and-such." Our choice of halting places shows which instances we in fact treat as paradigms. In calling my exemplary situation a paradigm for the use of the expression "making something happen," therefore, I am claiming that it is useful as a standard for the correctness of application of the expression in question.

Paradigm cases also serve as standards of reference when we pass from primitive uses of an expression to other uses derived by resemblance, analogy, and metaphorical extension. Uses of "making something happen" and cognate expressions are strikingly various;

yet the paradigm helps to illuminate all such uses. The exemplary instance, or sufficiently similar alternatives, functions as a prototype for the derivative uses of "making something happen." We refer to it in testing the plausibility of analogy and metaphor.

As we pass from the homespun language of "making something happen" to the more sophisticated language of "cause" and "effect," the influence of the paradigm remains powerful. We continue to model descriptions of cases remote from the prototypes on the simpler primitive cases, often by using metaphors literally applicable only to those clear cases. In order to understand clearly what we mean by "cause" and "effect" we must labor to understand what we mean by the precausal langage in which the more sophisticated vocabulary is embedded.

If my exemplary situation is a clear case (a paradigm, a prototype) of making something happen, it follows that it would be nonsensical to speak of there being any possible *doubt* whether something was made to happen. This remains true, no matter how much the original description of the situation might be augmented or elaborated by scientific explanation, provided only that the additional information did not conflict with the original assumption of "normality." A scientist might explain why the pressure of the fingers required the glass to change position without slipping through the hand; another scientist might offer elaborate explanations of the physiology of thirst; a psychologist might connect your present thirst with childhood deprivation. But such accounts, informative as they might be, would have no tendency to discredit the correctness of the use of the expression "making something happen." They could not do so, because the description of the paradigm case is complete. If the description left gaps to be filled by scientific data as yet unknown, none of us would be able to use the expression "making something happen" correctly. The expression would be a blank check drawn on an uncertain future.

My chief contention, so far, is the commonplace one that it is perfectly certain that persons do sometimes make something happen. It might be unnecessary to insist on anything so obvious, had not philosophers sometimes claimed to have arguments to show that it is logically impossible for anything to be a cause, since the notion of a cause is self-contradictory. Now, to make something happen is to cause something to happen. It is certain therefore that the notion of a cause is not self-contradictory.

II

Once we are satisfied that we have identified and sufficiently described a paradigm for the use of a given expression, we can proceed to look for features and criteria of application. That is to say, we can ask, "What is it about this clear case that we treat as relevant in using it as a standard of comparison?" Sometimes the search for criteria leads nowhere: to the question, "What is it about this clear case of red that makes us call it 'red'?" there is no answer. But sometimes a demand for criteria can be met. If the question is raised about our paradigm case of making something happen, it can elicit a set of relevant features, some trite and uninteresting, but others surprisingly at variance with accepted analyses of causation. I shall list some of these features and comment on a few of them. In order to save time, I shall refer to the person who moved the glass as "*P*." I shall call the object moved "*O*," its motion "*M*," and the action performed by the agent "*A*."

The following assertions about the episode seem to me plainly true:

1 What happened was made to happen by *P*.
2 What he made happen was a *motion* of *O* (i.e., *M*).
3 *P* made this happen by *doing* something (moved his hand to *O*, clasped it, and brought it back to him).
4 In doing *A*, *P* was acting *freely* (was not in anyway being forced or constrained to do *A*).
5 *A* occurred throughout the time that *M* was occurring.
6 *M* (the motion of *O*) would not have occurred unless *A* had occurred.
7 When *A* occurred, *M* had to occur.

If we used the accepted terminology of discussions of causation, we could roughly summarize the foregoing seven points by saying that the cause was a *free act* of a person, the effect was a *motion* of an inanimate object, the cause and effect were *cotemporal* (operative through the same time interval), and the effect was a *necessary consequence*. (We might add that the cause and effect were spatially contiguous, in a way too obvious to detail.)

I shall now comment on some of these points.

The agent acted freely. The contrast to be made here is with forced or constrained action; and, again, with action as an intermediary. If *P* had been compelled by physical coercion or by threats, we should confidently say he had not acted freely; there might be more hesitation about saying the same if he had acted because asked to do so, or if he had expected to receive some reward, or had some other ulterior motive. But neither coercion nor inducement was present in our paradigm case: *P* took the glass because he "just wanted to." If he had any motive at all, it may have been that he was thirsty, but he might equally well have had no antecedent and separable thirst. There would be no harm in saying the act was unmotivated—which is not to say it was irrational or unintelligible. On the other hand, the presence in other cases of a distinct and separable motive prior to the act would not disqualify an episode as a clear case of making something happen. Neither presence nor absence of a separable motive functions as a clear-cut criterion.

It may provoke surprise and an accusation of anthropomorphism that the presence of a person is insisted on as a feature of the paradigm. But the insistence is necessary. A candid examination of causal language will show that our prototypes involve persons. Certainly the word "make" strongly suggests a maker; and we find it not at all unnatural to substitute "make" for "cause." If this be anthropomorphism, we must make the best of it.

To return to our illustration. Not only is it true that the agent acted freely: we are entitled, I think, to add that the very same situation is a clear case and a paradigm for acting freely. This means, as I previously explained, that it would be logically absurd to demand an investigation as to whether the agent acted freely; it also means that there could be no doubt that he had acted freely, nor any further reason to show that he had so acted.

Now, if this is so, it follows that so far from there being a radical conflict between the notion of causation and freedom, as many philosophers have insisted, the two notions, or their informal progenitors, are logically inseparable. Our paradigmatic conception of causing something to happen is a conception of somebody *freely* making something happen. So anything having a tendency to show that the agent was not acting freely, but responding to constraint, duress, or ulterior inducement, would immediately have a tendency to show that *he* was not the cause but merely an instrument or an intermediary between the true cause and its effects.

It also follows that no scientific elaboration of the antecedents of the paradigmatic episodes could destroy their character as paradigms of acting freely, and so causing something to happen. No physiological or psychoanalytical explanation of the unconscious cause, if any, of *P's* moving *O* can have the least tendency to discredit our calling his act a case of freely making something happen. Of course the case would be altered if such scientific elaboration led us to view his act as pathological, but this outcome was excluded by our description of the paradigm.

The effective action lasted throughout the motion it produced. It has been a truism for writers on causation that the cause must *precede* the effect. And certainly there would be a logical absurdity in supposing that the cause might succeed its effect. But our paradigm has cause and effect occurring together. It might be objected that the initiating action, *A,* began before the motion, *M,* it produced. But it would be easy to define the action as lasting for exactly the same period of time as the motion generated; we must therefore allow that sometimes cause and effect can be simultaneous or cotemporal. This will not render the causal relation symmetrical, as might be feared; the desired asymmetry is here ensured by the fact that the cause is a *free action* while the effect is not an action at all but the motion of an inanimate body. And when one person acts on another, so that one action is contiguous and cotemporal with another action, we can still immediately identify the cause as that action of the two that was *free*. If John pushes James, John acts freely, but James doesn't; and conversely, if James was moving of his own free will, John didn't push him.

Now cotemporality of cause and effect is not a mere peculiarity of "prescientific" thinking; it is a commonplace of causal description at scientific levels, as philosophers have occasionally noticed. The moon's gravitational pull lasts as long as the tide it produces; difference of temperature registers throughout the period that thermometric expansion occurs; a catalyst continues to act during the chemical reaction it is influencing; and so on, for any number of similar cases. There is some reason to regard the principle of strict priority of the cause as a metaphysical prejudice. And, like other metaphysical prejudices, it can be opposed by equally powerful metaphysical prejudices of opposite tendency.

The induced motion would not have occurred but for the action that produced it. As it stands, this formula is incorrect. It is untrue to say the glass would not have moved as it did unless P had made it do so, for if P had not moved it some other person might have done so. What we mean, of course, is that the glass would not have moved *by itself:* that is, if P had not performed action A, or some other action resulting in O's moving, the glass would have remained stationary. In short, had A not occurred, the glass would not have moved, though all other features of the setting remained unchanged. One might perhaps say that A is *conditionally necessary* for the occurrence of M. Or again: the occurrence of A included *some* of the necessary conditions for M to occur.

In speaking of this feature of the paradigm I have used a "counterfactual." I said that, in the presence of certain contextual factors, M would not have occurred but for A's occurrence. Alternatively: if A had not occurred (other things remaining unchanged), M would not have occurred. Now such a statement is a so-called "counterfactual." Some contemporary philosophers have found this notion troublesome—possibly because they have failed to explain satisfactorily how a counterfactual conditional could be verified. Yet the notion "would not have happened unless" is as primitive and unproblematic as the notion "making something happen." Both are applicable in the same circumstances, long before any question of scientific terminology arises. There are accordingly relatively direct and unsophisticated ways of establishing such a claim as: The glass would not have moved unless somebody had moved it. In making such an assertion we do, in fact, simply rely on our commonplace knowledge that when nobody is "doing anything" the glass stays put, and that when somebody does "do something" of a certain sort the glass moves. It would, however, be a mistake to say that the statement "The glass would not have moved by itself" had the same meaning as "Glasses do not move when left alone"; for the two statements are made in different contexts and have different uses, even though the procedure of verifying them may sometimes be identical.

When pushed, the glass had *to move.* Certainly it is natural to say this, and there must be some sense in which it is true. No doubt mythology plays a part: there is a discernible inclination to think of the moving object as animate—a manikin, helpless in our grasp, "having no choice" but to move. But good sense remains when mythology has been discarded. We need only remind ourselves of the circumstances in which we say that an object acted on by an external force does *not* have to move. We say so when the given force is insufficient to produce the desired motion. If I push my cat gently, Hodge may or may not move, though if he does I shall say he did *because* I pushed him; but if I push hard enough, Hodge *has* to move. Again, a penny tossed into the air *has* to come down again, but it does not *have* to come down tails. Here and elsewhere, the relevant contrast is between what sometimes happens and what invariably happens. To generalize: we say that *M had* to happen when *A* happened, only if *M* would always ensue, given an unchanged setting and the same concomitant. Using a phrase parallel to one introduced earlier, we might call *A conditionally sufficient* for *M.* Alternatively, we might say that *A* is a part of a certain sufficient condition for the occurrence of *M.*

In this cursory examination of some features of a paradigm of making something happen, I have had little occasion to refer to any "constant conjunction" between producing action and induced motion. The omission has been deliberate. The assertion "*P* made *M* happen by doing *A*" does not mean the same as "If *P* were to repeat actions sufficiently like *A,* then, other things being equal, motions sufficiently like *M* would invariably ensue." If the analysis were correct, the original causal statement would include as part of its meaning a generalization whose verification would need repeated observation and an induction upon an indefinite number of situations resembling the original situation. The original statement ("*P* made something happen, etc.") is so far from being verifiable by inspection that a lengthy inquiry would be needed to establish its truth. (It is as if we had to perform a long inductive inquiry into the behavior of meter rods before we could use a given meter rod to measure a given object.) But I think the truth of the matter is much simpler: in order to be sure that *P* made *O* move, we need only look. The verifying situation is right before our eyes. To establish conclusively that *P* did make O move, we need only be sure that *P* did do such-and-such, and that *O* was moving thus-and-thus meanwhile.

I do not say we should be right in maintaining that *A* made *M* happen whenever an action and a cotemporal motion are contiguous. In using the language of "making something happen" we take for granted that the episode in view has a special and appropriate character. Should we be challenged to specify these conditions in full detail, we should eventually have to talk about constant conjunctions; and in deciding in unusual, unfamiliar, or abnormal settings whether the use of causal language is appropriate, prolonged inductive investigations might be needed. But such investigation would establish the *presuppositions* for the proper use of causal language, not the meaning of the assertions made by means of such language.

Consider the following analogy: If I say, "Jones just made the move 'pawn to king four,' " a full and sufficient verification of my assertion is that Jones shifted a characteristically shaped piece of wood from a certain place on a chessboard to another place. Yet this is only part of the story. I would not say that Jones had made the move if he knew nothing of the game and was merely moving the piece at random; nor would I say so if he knew how to play chess but was amusing himself by replaying some master's game—or was composing a chess problem. In using the language of chess I take for granted the institution of chess-playing and a host of related facts. Before I can teach anybody how to use the language of chess, I must acquaint him with this background of presuppositions. But once the background has been established, I do not refer to it each time I announce somebody's move.

There is a general background also for talking about "making things happen." The subject could not be dealt with properly by anybody ignorant of a host of familiar facts about motions of human bodies, obstructions and resistances offered by other bodies, the dependable behavior of relatively permanent solid objects, and so on. But when we say, "Jones moved the glass," we do not refer to these uniformities or to the remainder of the background of presuppositions. When we say, "Jones moved the glass," we draw a line around an episode whose relevant features are directly observable. An informal causal statement is a straightforward report. Stripped of its background of presupposition, it would have the simple form, "While *P* did *this, that* happened."

There is a sense, therefore, in which "*P* made *M* happen by doing *A*" can be said to mean the same as "While *P* did *A*, *M* happened" —the sense in which both statements would be verified by the same state of affairs. But there is also an important sense in which the two are strikingly different—because they imply different presuppositions and are connected with diverse linguistic practices.

A full account of the linguistic practices connected with the vocabulary of "making something happen" would be lengthy and complicated. One obvious connection is with the language of imperatives. When we order somebody to do something, we envisage his making something happen. If our language contained no provision for isolating causal episodes, we could issue no orders, give no commands. And the same could be said for recipes, plans of operation, and other features of linguistic transaction. All that part of our life concerned with getting things done, or with anticipating and controlling the consequences of our actions, uses the language of "making things happen" and is inconceivable without it.

Another connection is with moral language. To say that somebody made *M* happen is to hold him responsible for it; it can be a prelude to the assignment of praise or blame, punishment or reward. And the further connections with ethical practices are equally obvious. To state the point negatively: a language containing no provision for linking persons with events for whose occurrence they were held responsible would be one in which moral judgments as we now know them would be impossible.

III

So far I have been considering primitive cases of making something happen. But we also talk about "making something happen" in an enormous variety of derivative situations. Some of the ways in which these related uses are connected with the paradigm are fairly obvious. I have been confining myself to cases where some person causes a *motion*. But it is very natural to extend the language to cases where the agent produces a cessation of motion, i.e., where the motion would not have ceased but for the person's intervention Or, again, it is equally natural to talk of "making something happen" when what is produced is a *qualitative* change. And so we pass, by easy transitions, from the material realm to that of the affections and sentiments. We talk of making somebody laugh, of making somebody reconsider, or making somebody happy—without always realizing how far we have strayed from the prototypes.

Criteria for the use of causal language can also shift in other ways. For instance, we commonly speak of intermediaries as causes. If I make a billiard ball move in such a way as to set another in motion, I can think of the impinging billiard ball as the causal agent. Here we discard the criterion of the human agent, allowing the motion of an inanimate object to count as that which "makes something happen." It is easiest to make this type of transition when the new field of application most plainly resembles the original paradigm. We freely attribute causal efficiency when some motion can be made to look like the motion of a human body. So we find no difficulty in conceiving of "forces" that push or pull, bend, or squeeze, but experience extreme discomfort in trying to imagine "action at a distance." The idea of a body "impressing" an external force is altogether natural, but we cannot understand how one body can "attract" another without being joined to it by an unbroken chain of physical intermediaries.

Anybody with a logician's desire for clear-cut distinctions may well be exasperated by the lack of systematic principle in these patterns of analogical and metaphorical extensions of causal language. A search for a common denominator in this kaleidoscope of applications leads at best to "universal conjunction" or the even vaguer notion of "predictability." But such abstract and simplified formulas fail to do justice to the actual uses of "cause" and its cognates. It would be more to the point to ask what role the language of causation plays—to inquire into the purposes served by passing from the homespun language of "making things happen" to the more abstract language of causation.

A partial answer might be that the language of causation seems most fitting when we are concerned with the effective production, prevention, or modification of events. Roughly speaking, an event X is most plainly eligible as a possible cause of another event Y, if we can manipulate X in such a way as to modify Y. A cause is something that we can or might be able to control. But we invoke causes also when we are interested in explaining something rather than controlling it. And as our accepted patterns of explanation become more complex, our notion of a cause becomes correspondingly more elusive, until it threatens to vanish altogether into the abstract conception of a law, a parameter, a boundary condition, or some combination of all of these. As scientific modes of investigation develop, the language of cause tends to its own supersession.

But this is not a special quirk or weakness of the language of causation. It happens regularly and characteristically in the transition from ordinary language to scientific terminology. Dominating my discussion throughout has been the notion that the vocabulary of "cause" and its informal progenitors is indigenous to ordinary language—the language of practical affairs and common-sense observation or understanding. The vocabulary of causation can be adapted to a scientific context, but the sophistication it suffers proves ultimately fatal. Scientific insight is the death of causal conceptions. But this does not mean there is anything amiss with the language of causation when employed in its proper settings. To say the opposite would be as implausible as to hold that the supersession of words like "hot" and "cold" in favor of the scientific terminology of thermometry shows that there is something wrong, or in need of correction, in the prescientific uses of thermal words.

IV

I have been arguing that "cause" is an essentially schematic word, tied to certain more or less stable criteria of application, but permitting wide variation of specific determination according to context and the purposes of investigation. Now, if this is so, any attempt to state a "universal law of causation" must prove futile. To anybody who insists that "nothing happens without a sufficient cause" we are

entitled to retort with the question, "What do you *mean* by 'cause'?"
It is safe to predict that the only answer forthcoming will contain
such schematic words as "event," "law," and "prediction." These,
too, are words capable of indefinite further determination according
to circumstances—and they are none the worse for that. But universal statements containing schematic words have no place in rational
argument. The fatal defect of determinism is its protean capacity to
elude refutation—by the same token, its informative content is negligible. Whatever virtues it may have in encouraging scientists to
search for comprehensive laws and theories, there can be no rational
dispute about its truth value. Many of the traditional problems of
causation disappear when we become sufficiently clear about what
we mean by "cause" and remind ourselves once more of what a
peculiar, unsystematic, and erratic notion it is.

3.   Determinism and Novelty

William Barrett, New York University

Most of what I shall have to say in this comment will be directed at
Professor Blanshard's paper. This is not to be taken as a judgment
on the relative merits of the two foregoing papers. Professor Black
has suggested a very interesting paradigm by which to explore the
question of determinism, and it would be fruitful to examine the
question wholly within the framework he sets. But since in most
matters I am, I think, in agreement with him, and since the function
of the commentator seems to be not so much to applaud in agreement as to join battle in debate, I shall be concerned principally with
Professor Blanshard's contribution.

    Professor Blanshard has presented an admirably clear, candid,
and persuasive paper in defense of the determinist position. On a
subject like this, which has been so long discussed that nothing new

is likely to be said, it is good to get a paper that performs a real act of simplification, that clears the ground of clutter, and so suggests the possibility of taking up the old beat-up problem with some degree of freshness.

Let us begin on the prephilosophical level of everyday life. Determinism is a position repugnant to most people. Why is this? The reasons, Professor Blanshard says, are our stubborn feeling of freedom and the belief that "determinism would make nonsense of moral responsibility." Here he omits, I think, one of the main motives in the rebellion against determinism, not only on the part of ordinary people but also of those modern philosophers who have been most vigorously opposed to the determinist position: namely, the desire for freshness, novelty, genuine creation—in short, an open rather than a closed universe. Such is the main impulse in the criticism of determinism by philosophers like Peirce, James, Bergson, Whitehead, and Dewey.

It is worth while in this connection to recall the story by the Italian poet Leopardi about the Almanac Vendor. The vendor appears under a window hawking his wares, crying out that he has good predictions to sell for the year ahead. A man leans out of the window and engages him in conversation: How long has the vendor been selling almanacs and making this same cry? "Twenty years, Excellency." And if he had the chance of living over any one of those years? "No, Excellency, certainly not; not for all the money in the world." Here the man who sells predictions would not care, as a human being, to have those predictions true in detail. The point of the story is that even a good year—had we to live it over again with every detail fixed beforehand—would stifle us with boredom: our food would taste dull to our palate, our most spontaneous talk sound as uninspired as the playback of a tape-recorded conversation, and our words of love would sound hollow because we should know beforehand the precise moment of fatigue when they would expire.

For my own part, I find the traditional concepts of free will extremely tenuous and rarefied in the face of my experience of people and the concrete situations of life, and from that point of view I could swallow determinism without too much trouble. Indeed, on the prephilosophical level my conviction tends rather toward the old primitive notion of fate, Moira, of Homer and the tragic poets; but

Homeric Moira is a very different thing from Newtonian or neo-Newtonian determinism, and my recoil from the latter is due to its dreary prospect of a stale and routine world from which surprise and genuine novelty may ultimately be banished.

But to come now to the philosophical level. Here, too, determinism seems to me to make very good sense, for it isolates the central issue: namely, the question of the predictability of phenomena, and moreover predictability in detail. For determinism predictability in general is not enough: it has to assert (and prove, if it can) predictability down to the last detail—lock, stock, and barrel, and even down to the last scratch on the barrel. Anything less than this, and the thesis of determinism must crumble. Determinism cannot afford to leave any loose ends lying around. Small and great are inextricably linked in the happenings of nature and history; and unpredictable detail might trigger an enormous explosion, and empires and battles do sometimes hang on a straw.

Professor Blanshard presents a very much simplified schema for examining the determinist assertion: "Given A, B must occur." Such simplification allows us to cut to the core of the matter. Professor Blanshard generously waives the question of what "must" means here, and proposes that we can go on with the discussion without settling it. I am sorry I cannot quite accept his generosity. So far, as I can see, the empirical evidence for determinism lies in the fact that some phenomena can be predicted, and the "must" in Professor Blanshard's schema therefore has to be understood in connection with predictability. Determinism is surely not a priori; not only is its denial conceivable by us, but it has actually been proposed as sober theory by scientists. Such scientific proposals may, in the end, turn out to be unwarranted by the facts, but the mere fact that they are seriously made and utilized for purposes of explanation should suffice to show that determinism itself is not founded on any a priori necessity. My discussion will therefore present an altogether different intellectual perspective from Professor Blanshard's, for it will turn centrally on the notion of predictability.

With the problem thus shifted, its nature changes considerably. We should be engaged in a painstaking examination of those regions of experience where we have established predictability, of the regions where we have not, and of the likelihood of our extending predictability to these latter regions. A good deal of very antiquated dialectic would promptly fall by the wayside. This may be laying very rough hands on determinism, but it has been dealing so long in the I.O.U.'s and promissory notes of hypotheticals—*if* all conditions are given (when they so obviously can't be); *if* we knew everything (when we so obviously never shall), etc., etc.—that at long last we may be pardoned for demanding cash or cutting off trade. Recasting the problem thus, we must also attempt to make the deterministic schema more specific by applying it to some definite models (in the mathematical sense of this last term). When Professor Blanshard lays down as the schema of determinism "Given *A, B* must occur" I am unclear about his meaning, not only because of the ambiguity of "must" but because I am unsure of the range of values to which *A* and *B* must apply. Suppose we substitute for *A* and *B* the following: Given the nineteenth century, the twentieth century must occur—that is, exactly in the form it does, down to the last detail; or: Given the first millennium of the Christian period, the second must follow exactly as it did. Such theses are, to my mind, too staggeringly vast to prove or disprove. Clearly some contraction of the range of variables is called for.

Accordingly, I should like to make some speculations about the question of predictability in connection with four specific fields: (1) mathematics; (2) physics; (3) intellectual and artistic creation; (4) history, in the sense of individual and relatively circumscribable events in time. Obviously within the scope of these brief remarks I can hope only to indicate, at most, certain issues that have a different weight for me and for Professor Blanshard, or at least lead my mind in a different direction from his.

1. *Mathematics.* Gödel, as is well known, has established the incompleteness of mathematics. What this means, in more human and concrete terms, is that mathematicians, as long as they remain creative, will always be exposed to the possibility of unpredictable surprises. Of Gödel's result itself, a mathematician of my acquaintance remarked: "Mathematicians didn't foresee any result like that. In fact, if you had asked them beforehand, they would have said that just the opposite would turn out to be the case." Of course, there is the distinction between the psychological and the logical, and the surprises, after we have understood them, turn out to be logically

inevitable. To be sure, to be sure; but it may be questioned whether from a human and practical point of view this will make much difference, since mathematicians, as a consequence of Gödel's discovery, will have to face 2,500 years from now a possibility of shock and surprise like that experienced by the Pythagorean brotherhood at the discovery of irrationals—which, according to one tradition, cost the discoverer his life at the hands of the outraged brotherhood.

The point becomes stronger if we consider Gödel's result a little more specifically. A Gödel formula is a perfectly constructible formula in elementary arithmetic; syntactically interpreted, this formula says that it itself is not provable. But it is not impossible—and this, thanks to Gödel himself—that a worker in number theory, operating with minimal formalization and maximal use of the devices of analysis, as is usually done, and not at all following the syntactical model, might come up with a demonstration, a long chain of formulas, at the end of which would be a Gödel formula. Not only is it unpredictable that this will not occur; it is unpredictable how, when, and where it will occur, if it does—for if all this were predictable, we should have produced the proof before it was produced. What would have happened here would be merely that a contradiction would have turned up in classical mathematics. Such a contradiction, of course, would not be catastrophic; mathematics, like life itself, thrives on contradiction and is fructified thereby; mathematicians would simply get busy plugging the leak so that the vessel could continue its voyage—a voyage that, as a result of Gödel's work, now shows itself to be over an ocean that is shoreless.

The determinist tends to think that the advance of a science always means an advance in predictability. Sometimes, however, an advance brings about a situation of disorder rather than order. Mathematics after Gödel is, so to speak, in a state of greater disorder than before him. We have to think of it less as a tightly organized monarchy dependent on some central court and more as a federation of states, sometimes with rather fluid and overlapping borders—borders at which conflict and contradiction may occur.

In bringing up mathematics for consideration I am of course deliberately raiding the classical citadel of necessity. After centuries of Platonism, we seem compelled at last—and by the results of the mathematicians themselves—to construe mathematics as a human enterprise, one that has, therefore, a thoroughly human future with the unpredictable possibilities that such a future involves.

2. *Physics.* Here Professor Blanshard has delightfully cleared the air by suggesting that it is all a question of which physicist one reads. I shall not debate with him the relative consensus among physicists, especially of the younger generation, though I think it favors my side; rather, I should like to accept his point and push it one step further. The reports that come to the layman these days from the physical laboratories are so rich and teasing to the imagination—with their talk of left-handed and right-handed neutrons, antimatter, and the rest—that perhaps we had better let physics alone for the present and not try to draw any philosophical conclusions from it. The change might be welcome to the physicists themselves: physics will be just physics and not something else. Certainly it has ruled the roost long enough on this philosophic question of determinism, so that it may now be time for a change. Physics now seems in such a state of upheaval that the whole science provides a good example of unpredictability; the new theoretical synthesis of all recent findings, if and when it comes, is unpredictable now. But these are matters for the physicists at tomorrow's session, when they will perhaps tell us something very different.

But Professor Blanshard does not seem to me to assess quite fairly the damage done to his position by the indeterministic leanings of modern physics, for these do at least make questionable what has hitherto been the main prop of determinism. The physical model (as in the case of Laplace's demon) has hitherto been the chief model of all deterministic thinking. Despite Heisenberg, Professor Blanshard tells us, nature in itself *may* be deterministic. To which we can only answer: then again, it *may not* be. "May be" sounds very curious issuing from the lips of a determinist; and when he is forced to the minimal assertion that determinism, after all, *may be true*, he is already trafficking in contingency. Behind the screen of appearances God may be in his heaven and every detail in nature in its place in accordance with unalterable law; but if we, by the natural laws themselves, are to live always on the hither side of the screen, we shall have to leave God's prospect to God and not hanker for something beyond our own human limitations. Professor Blanshard will find my view here, as throughout, incurably anthropocentric—to which charge I plead guilty—but I see no other center when we are talking about the possibilities of human knowledge.

3. *Artistic and intellectual creation.* Here we pass from hypothetical considerations of unpredictibilities that lie at the fringes of knowledge to actual cases of unpredictability.

There is the famous case of Poincaré's perceiving the solution of a mathematical problem that had agitated him for months at the moment he set foot on the bus at Coutances. The mathematician himself could not have foreseen this event: he would already have had to possess the solution to this problem, together with the psychological knowledge when, where, and how this solution would come to him—an obvious contradiction. But if Poincaré could not have foreknown the event, neither could anyone else; for no one else had carried that problem as far as he. We cannot imagine a superpsychologist or superpsychoanalyst, armed with an impossibly complete knowledge of Poincaré's unconscious, predicting this event, for this psychologist, too, would already have to know the solution to the mathematical problem. Of course, there remains the possibility of foreknowledge by the Divine Mind, or by his secular surrogate, the demon of Laplace, but I think we have to renounce such figments once and for all and recognize that if we are talking about prediction we have to have in mind some possible *human* being, representative of some body of *human* knowledge, who is going to make the prediction. To be sure, one must distinguish between unpredictable in fact and unpredictable in principle; but predictions do not float in the air by themselves; they are made by human beings, and if there is no conceivable human being who can make the prediction, then we have to say (as in the present case) that we are dealing with something unpredictable in principle.

Even if we consider the fictitious picture of the mind of the creative genius dismembered into all its mental atoms (if there be such), does the possibility of prediction present itself? The best empirical study on this subject that I know happens to be the work of a literary scholar: it is *The Road to Xanadu,* by J. L. Lowes, a dissection of Coleridge's "Ancient Mariner" and, principally, "Kubla Khan." The latter poem, "Kubla Khan," is a rare thing in the history of literature, since it comes closer than any other work to being a purely spontaneous and unconscious creation. Coleridge tells us that he woke from a nap with the whole poem in his mind and immediately began to write it down just as it had come to him in his sleep; there came a knock at the door, announcing that mysterious and forever unknown visitor, a neighbor from Porlock; Coleridge talked with him for some minutes, then returned to his desk to finish transcribing the dream; but it had completely vanished, and we are left with the teasing fragment of "Kubla Khan" as it is—in its own way, however, perfectly complete as a poem. Around 1900 some early notebooks of Coleridge's turned up on the literary market and were edited by German scholars. Armed with a hindsight knowledge of the two poems, Lowes read through all the books that had fed Coleridge's imagination.

Now, Lowes did find that a great number of Coleridge's images and even some of his phrases could be traced back to his earlier reading, particularly of travel books. Suppose, for argument's sake, that we could trace every image and phrase back to such antecedent reading. There would still remain the selection, fusion, and transformation of these in the poem. The poem is as unmistakably by Coleridge as any of his relatively more conscious creations; only *he* could have written it. Our hypothetical superpsychoanalyst could not have predicted the dream without writing the poem; but this, of course, no one could do but Coleridge. Hindsight does not remove the fact of unpredictability; if it succeeds in tracing certain elements back to some antecedent source, it nonetheless leaves us with the realization that it would have been impossible to foresee how, when, where, and why these elements would come together. In short, the enumeration of antecedents can at best give us only the necessary but never the sufficient conditions of a creative act. The introduction of the unconscious as an explanation does not help the determinist at all. Far from it: for the unconscious, when it is truly creative, is far more unpredictable than the conscious mind.

Indeed, artists repeatedly testify that when they sit down to their job they themselves cannot predict the work that will be produced. The psychological examples usually cited by determinists reflect the more monotonous and routine aspects of our behavior, as if to reinforce their general picture of the world as a vast and dreary machine. Professor Blanshard is not of this kidney; he wisely refers to a "causality of a higher level in the psychical realm." But something very odd happens to the word "necessity" when he refers to "aesthetic necessity" as a *vis a tergo* producing the unpredictable work, and I cannot see that the term here has any resemblance to the meaning it has in physics or in general deterministic schema he advanced earlier.

4. *History.* If in the previous sections, I have merely given indications of points, here—because of limitations of space—I shall be able to give only indications of indications.

So far as I can see, recent historians (except the Marxists) have become much more cautious, far more inclined to qualify, in asserting determinism on any large scale in their works. Determinism in history seems largely the historicism of the nineteenth century; it is ideological rather than scientific, and its technique is to impose, at the dictates of its ideology, large simplifying patterns in place of the actual chain of events. Anyone who wants a good example of this method might compare Trotsky's *History of the Russian Revolution,* a work composed thoroughly in accord with the nineteenth century ideology of Marxism, with the treatment of the Russian Revolution in Sidney Hook's *The Hero in History.* If you read Trotsky's work carefully, you will notice that it abounds in metaphors drawn from physics—the pressure and explosion of gases, the fusion of metals, etc.—all intended to convey a feeling of inevitable historic processes carried to their foreordained conclusion. Actually, continual apologizing is engaged in behind the scenes, because none of the café-intellectual Marxists of 1914 predicted that the Revolution would break out in Russia, and indeed their predictions pointed quite to the contrary. If we approach the facts in a more critical and scientific spirit, without an ideological *parti pris,* then I think we must conclude with Hook that the Revolution could not have taken place without the individual figure of Lenin. And, of course, the introduction of human personality multiplies the factors of chance beyond the determinist's ability to press them into any one of his ready-made schemes.

But the issues of history can perhaps be brought into sharpest relief with a consideration of our position now, in mid-twentieth century, as we face the future. This historical future is thoroughly problematic and uncertain. Will Russia or the United States be victorious? Or perhaps a third force? Will Communism conquer in the twentieth century? When will the next war break out? When will the first bomb be dropped? With such questions as these we face a future as unknown to us as the events of the next millennium were to an intelligent Greek of Thucydides' time, who must have felt—such, at least, is our impression from reading what has been called the first of modern histories—that the world would change, that it would become very different from what it was now, though in ways that could not be foreseen. Two thousand four hundred years have not made the least impression on unpredictability here.

Such questions about the future bring us back to the prephilosophical level from which this comment took off, the level at which, as individuals, we all live and die. On this level we encounter a vast, shaggy, amorphous mass of unpredictability on which our knowledge has made very little impression. Billions of dollars trade hands annually in games of chance; people are anxious about their future, and fortune-tellers ply a prosperous trade (there are currently eleven astrologers in the Classified Telephone Directory—a curious juxtaposition of ancient and modern); and where primitive peoples scanned the skies for signs and portents, we do so for unidentified aircraft, missiles, or flying saucers. Modern civilization has stabilized social life and enormously increased predictability in certain areas, but in another sense it has also enormously increased the total quantity of contingency and distributed it to other focal points in the body social.

Of course this final litany of contingency is not intoned as proof—only as a reminder to the determinist that the spheres in which determinism has so far been established are restricted. When Professor Blanshard concludes by saying that he has dealt with the three commonest objections to determinism, he seems to have forgotten the simplest, most direct, and, to my mind, most overriding objection: that as a total thesis determinism simply remains to be proved.

PART II   Determinism in Modern
Science

1.   Determinism in Modern Science

Percy W. Bridgman, Harvard University

Anyone who is inclined to define science as the consensus of competent scientists may well pause for second consideration when he contemplates the present state of opinion in physics with regard to the question of determinism as it is presented by quantum mechanics. Seldom in the history of physics (and for the purposes of this exposition I shall take the "science" of my title to be pretty nearly equivalent to physics) has there been such a radical difference of fundamental outlook between the acknowledged leaders. The so-called "official" or "orthodox" attitude is that of Niels Bohr and Heisenberg and Max Born. But it is well known that during their lifetimes Planck, who laid the foundations of the theory, and Einstein, who very early developed some of its most important physical consequences, were irreconcilably opposed to the official point of view. The intensity of Einstein's opposition amounted almost to intransigence. Among those living today, de Broglie, who first had the fundamental insights of wave mechanics, and whose first intuitive attitude was akin to the more traditional classical attitudes of Planck and Einstein, was bludgeoned into twenty-five years of unwilling acceptance of the official doctrines by Bohr's apparently irrefutable logic, but has recently kicked over the traces again with his glimpse of a possible way of refuting Bohr's argument. And it is well known that Schrödinger, who gave wave mechanics its mathematical form, has from the beginning been more or less of an *enfant terrible,* refusing to accept such orthodox concepts as quantum jumps. There is a host of other names not so closely connected with the historical beginnings of the subject. In this country Henry Margenau at Yale is well known to have unorthodox points of view. David Bohm, also unorthodox, has had a considerable following recently. In 1953 he wrote a widely used book in which certain departures from the orthodox view were suggested, and these have been further developed and accentuated in recent writings. "Strife About Complementarity,"[1] a lively article by Mario Bunge, paints a vivid picture of the present conflict of interests, viewpoints, and temperaments.

The point at issue in all the discussions is itself somewhat fuzzy. Such terms as "determinism," "causality," "natural law," "prediction" turn up almost inevitably. These terms are all connected in some way with the point or points at issue, in spite of the fact that they are not fully equivalent and that differences among them can be clearly specified if one wants to make one's analysis meticulous enough. I shall not find it necessary for the purposes of this exposition to attempt to sharpen distinctions to the point of emphasizing all recognizable differences among terms, but shall be able to use them in a more or less intuitive common-sense fashion. In addition to the four crudely synonymous terms mentioned above, some other terms, without which the discussion never gets very far, turn up: for example, "reality," "subjective," "objective." It is more difficult to find the meaning of these terms than of the first four; one often has to try to reconstruct the meaning by observing the use of the term in context, which is unsatisfactory and may result in a multiplicity of meanings. One may safely comment, however, that when

[1] *Brit. Jour. Phil. Sci.,* May 1955.

such terms begin to occur the discussion is heading away from the narrow limits of concern with the experimental findings of the laboratory toward something vaguer and more general, which, for want of a better description, we may characterize as "philosophical." In fact, it is difficult to keep the discussion from entering the field recognized as philosophy, and men like Bohr and Heisenberg and Born do not hesitate to use the word "philosophical" in connection with their own speculations.

However marked the failure of consensus with regard to the philosophical aspects of physics, there is no such failure with regard to the experimental situation in the laboratory. Everyone is agreed that it is possible to set up in the laboratory experimental systems in which events occur that we are at present completely unable to predict. This is another way of saying that we can establish no unique causal connection between the event and other events or situations, which is another way of saying that up to the present we have been able to formulate no law of nature according to which the given event follows from other things. This again may be described by saying that, as far as we can now see, the event is undetermined. Whether or not the existence of such undetermined events is closely connected with what the philosopher understands by determinism and indeterminism, we do not need to examine. There are doubtless valid distinctions to be made here, but for our purposes we need not elaborate them.

The relevant experimental situations in which there is such consensus are usually situations in the "microscopic" world of electrons and individual quantum events. A typical example would be the interference pattern produced by a slender beam of light passing through a system of slits. The pattern ordinarily seen is a pattern of light and dark bands with smooth gradations from light to dark. But if the intensity of light is made very low, the smooth pattern breaks down into a pattern of individual spots, which mark the arrival of individual photons of light and the excitation of individual grains of the photographic emulsion. The place and time of occurrence of any individual spot in this pattern are at present absolutely unpredictable. It is not necessary, however, that the unpredictable event should be on the microscopic scale; it would be possible so to couple a disintegrating speck of some radioactive compound to an atomic bomb as to blow up a city at an absolutely unpredictable time. Such an unpredictable situation on the scale of daily life, however, seems always to involve some reaching down into the "microscopic" and bringing it up to the scale of daily life.

There is, then, no disagreement about the experimental situation; disagreement begins with our interpretation of the significance of the experimental facts, and in the program for future action that we draw up in its light. There is in the first place the question of how best to talk about the experimental situation as we now have it. This involves in particular how best to devise a mathematics for describing the present experimental situation with its at present unresolved fuzziness. Here again I think there is consensus that the present mathematical machinery of wave mechanics is competent to handle adequately all the phenomena at present experimentally accessible —involving the reactions of atoms, molecules, electrons, and photons—that it was constructed to handle. From one point of view this is all the physicist is concerned with, and we might dismiss all the disagreement as being outside the realm of physics and therefore of no proper concern to the physicists. But physicists are obviously concerned. Physics is finding itself forced into a position where it is increasingly concerned with problems outside the realm of its traditional activity and verging toward "philosophy."

The mathematical machinery, then, is generally accepted. Bohr and Schrödinger would make the same calculations to find, for example, how two hydrogen atoms combine to form a hydrogen molecule. Differences arise in interpreting the mathematics, which means perhaps that the question is how we shall best talk about what we do when we use the mathematics. It is to be anticipated that we shall have difficulties in finding how best to talk about what we do, for the world of newly discovered happenings is a strange and paradoxical world in which the customary patterns according to which ordinary events behave are no longer found. The first major step in interpretation was taken by Max Born, who pointed out that the psi function of Schrödinger's wave equation, an equation that had already been successfully used in handling atomic phenomena, could be described in terms of probabilities. Specifically, in a problem dealing, for example, with electrons, the square of the psi function at any place determines the probability that an electron will be found at that place. The recognition of this possible interpretation of the psi function, which is fundamental to the "orthodox" attitude toward wave mechanics as formulated by Bohr and Heisenberg, is everywhere regarded as remarkable intuitive insight on Born's part.

There was a great advantage in an interpretation in terms of probability because the mathematical machinery for handling probability had been developed by mathematicians for its own interest and had been previously applied by physicists to such problems as the kinetic theory of gases and the statistical interpretation of the second law of thermodynamics, which made understandable the universal degradation of energy. At the same time it must be recognized that the fundamental role ascribed to probability is one of the reasons why there is no consensus on the significance of wave mechanics. For in spite of the fact that there is agreement as to the use of statistical analysis in practical situations—all competent persons would agree on how to draw up a table for a life insurance company or how to bet in a complicated gambling game—there is no agreement as to what probability "really" is, and the matter is still controversial.

Let us now turn to a more detailed examination of the different points of view. First consider the orthodox interpretation of Bohr and Heisenberg, which is probably that accepted by the majority of physicists. In this interpretation the Heisenberg uncertainty relations and Bohr's principle of complementarity play a leading role. According to the Heisenberg principle there is a correlation between the fuzziness of a position measurement and the fuzziness of a velocity measurement such that when one fuzziness becomes less the other becomes greater in proportion. It follows that it is at present impossible to make measurements that will permit the accurate calculation of the position of a particle at some future time. In this sense, therefore, the future position of the particle is not determined, and the particle in its motion is not subject to causality. This situation is often described by saying that it is not possible to make simultaneous measurements of position and velocity with sufficient precision to predict the future position (or velocity)—the implication being that for some reason "position" and "velocity," although "really there," are not accessible to us simultaneously. Bohr cannot insist too strongly that this is not a legitimate way of talking; that, if "in principle" position and velocity cannot be known simultaneously, then the object cannot simultaneously "have" position and velocity. We can, however, choose which it is to "have" by our choice of the measuring instrument. A great deal of Bohr's analysis has been devoted to a detailed consideration of the greatest variety of different methods of measurement and to showing in detail that the fuzziness described by Heisenberg's principle is a consequence of the reaction between the measuring instrument and the object being measured. It was an essentially new insight for the physicist that the act of acquiring knowledge itself disturbs the object of knowledge. The further fact that the disturbance so introduced is uncontrollable as far as we can now see is fundamental to the structure of wave mechanics.

Bohr's principle of complementarity, which is one of the chief bones of contention, may be described as a working out of the consequences of seriously accepting all the implications of the statement that a body cannot simultaneously have position and velocity. We can use either method of description as we choose, but having made our choice we must abandon use of the other. The principle has more general applications than just to position and velocity; the chief consequence is that if we choose to describe a system in conventional terms of space and time we must renounce the possibility of describing it in causal terms, or if we choose to describe it in causal terms we must renounce describing it in terms of space and time. Involved in all this, in a way that is perhaps not always very explicitly evident, is the insight that, since an object never occurs naked but always in conjunction with an instrument of measurement or the means by which we acquire knowledge of it, the concept of "object," as something in and of itself, is an illegitimate one. Acceptance of this insight with all its implications is obviously going to react strongly on our idea of "reality," and many of the objections to the orthodox view arise precisely from unwillingness to accept the altered view of "reality."

What is Bohr's own attitude toward his orthodox doctrine? I can only guess, of course, but I think it safe to say that, if in the future experimental detail is discovered of which we now have no inkling, by means of which it would be possible to predict the individual photons in an interference pattern, Bohr would simply accept the fact, as would every scientist, and recognize that the present wave mechanics, as a method of dealing with the complete physical situation, would have to be abandoned. For practical purposes of calculation within the appropriate range, however, wave mechanics could be retained, just as Newtonian mechanics has its range of application even after the formulation of relativity theory. But just as relativity theory forced a conceptual revolution, so I think discovery of at present unsuspected experimental detail would force a conceptual revolution in Bohr's point of view, and I believe that Bohr would be the first to recognize this. The question of Bohr's private opinion as to the probability of the discovery of new kinds of experimental facts is another matter. One may guess that he considers the probability rather remote, or he would not have spent so much time and thought on elaborating his present position.

The possibility of the discovery of new experimental facts that would invalidate present quantum theory has often been discussed. A roughly equivalent formulation is to ask whether there may not be "concealed parameters" in addition to those we now know and in terms of which we can adequately describe present experimental knowledge. In this connection there is an often quoted analysis by von Neumann, which seems to be generally accepted as rigorous, to the effect that it is not permissible to suppose that there may be "concealed parameters" of such a kind that the principle of causality would be saved by their introduction, because the present quantum symbolism has no place for such new parameters, which could not be introduced without sacrificing the successful account of experiment that we now achieve with our present parameters. In this analysis "causal" is understood with the usual connotation of the physicist as being the sort of complete causality that is inconsistent with Heisenberg's relation. Von Neumann's argument does not apply to such an emasculated definition of causality as is satisfied with a psi function causally controlled. I digress here to remark on an apparent inconsistency with a pronouncement of Poincaré's, in the days when Planck's h was still new, to the effect that no system whatever, no matter how strange its behavior, can be peremptorily declared inconsistent with classical mechanics if one admits the possibility of sufficiently complicated concealed parameters. For one can, if necessary, imagine concealed inside each weirdly behaving atom, or elsewhere, a robot with written instructions to act exactly as the atom actually does. A robot, we may assume, is a classically functioning mechanism. The joker is that the concealed mechanisms reproducing the supposedly unmechanical behavior must be completely isolated from outside contact or access, so that there is no method whatever by which their existence can be established, and for all practical purposes we are dealing with a pure verbalism.

The question of Bohr's personal attitude is, after all, more or less beside the point. We need not accept any more of Bohr's opinions on the "philosophical" questions involved here than are necessarily implicit in what Bohr has done in distinction to what he has said. It seems to me that what Bohr has done, essentially, is, in the first place, to take seriously the thesis that we shall never discover experimental detail that will restore causal control to atomic events and the insight that nothing occurs except as part of a larger whole; and, in the second place, to try to develop a logically consistent way of thinking about what we find. I am not sure Bohr would maintain that he had devised a system of thought logically watertight in all conceivable aspects, but I think we can see that he has gone a long way toward success and that the problem he has set himself is one that cannot be ignored.

One can describe the problem Bohr has set himself in another equally noncommittal way: namely as the problem of devising a method of talking about the presently known experimental situation that will emphasize the occurrence of events we cannot predict.

It seems to me that most of the criticisms of Bohr arise from unwillingness to accept the conditions of the problem Bohr has effectively set himself. Perhaps part of the unwillingness arises from failure to appreciate the purely formal aspects of the problem of devising methods of thinking about a hypothetical physical situation. Regarding the problem in this formal light, one should be able to attack it purely as an intellectual exercise. But I believe the unwillingness actually involves many other factors, some of them recognizably emotional. The reason people will not see the problem in a purely formal light is that the hypothetical state of affairs basic to the problem is so much at variance with their conventional and traditional pictures of what the experimental situation must be that they will have none of it, and even refuse to speculate how they might act if it actually existed. The repugnance of different persons to accept the possibility that the world is actually constructed according to the hypothesis of orthodox quantum theory varies greatly and may involve considerations closely approaching the religious. This is perhaps most strikingly shown by Einstein, who could not bring himself to accept the idea that chance plays a fundamental role in the scheme of things, and who passionately exclaimed, *"Der Herr Gott würfelt nicht"* ("The Lord God does not throw dice"). Einstein's repugnance led him so far that, instead of postulating that there might be experimental facts not yet discovered, which is a perfectly tenable position and all that he needed, he was convinced that no theory giving a fundamental place to probability could be logically consistent, and he spent a great deal of time trying to point out logically untenable aspects of quantum theory, always to be patiently refuted by Bohr.

Many alternatives for the orthodox interpretation have been proposed, especially recently. I have neither the time nor the competence to attempt to specify them in detail and to classify them. There is an illuminating paper on this aspect of the situation by Professor Margenau in *Physics Today*.[2] I shall content myself with some very general comments.

There are in the first place those who maintain that it is possible to save the causality principle. A classified grouping together the various interpretations that attempt to maintain the causality principle would cut across the lines of classification proposed by Professor Margenau; he himself would be found in this class, although in his own classification he stands alone. The causality principle is usually saved by transferring its sphere of operation from concrete individual events to the probabilities in terms of which the theory describes the statistics of many occurrences of the individual event. This is possible because the psi function of wave mechanics, which describes the statistics, satisfies a definite differential equation, and therefore unfolds in an orderly and predictable way with time. The psi function may therefore be said to be causal in the sense that its future distribution is determined by its present.

Now, no one can deny that the psi function satisfies an equation according to which it unfolds systematically in time; the question is,

[2] **7**, 6–13, 1954.

Why do those who save the causality principle in this way regard this behavior of the psi function as pertinent or significant, and why do they regard this way of saving the causality principle with so much satisfaction? No one who maintains the causality principle by this method would claim that the individual event, such as the single photon in an interference pattern, thereby becomes causally determined. We are here in the presence of a dilemma, for, inspite of the fact that we apparently must give up causality for individual atomic events, it is obvious that there is some sort of regularity here, since the apparently haphazard individual photons somehow build themselves into a regular pattern when there are a great many of them. What is behind this regularity? The fact of the regularity may be formally described by saying that there are *laws* of statistical behavior, although there are not laws for individual events. But how can this be? How can individual events, each of which is completely haphazard, combine into regular aggregates unless there is some factor of control over their combination into aggregates, and what kind of control can there be over a haphazard event?

The situation is almost unthinkable with the ordinary connotations of our words. It becomes rationally less repugnant, perhaps, if we can rediscover on another level the regularity that we have lost on the level of individual events. This I think accounts for some of the satisfaction of those who emphasize that the psi function, which describes the statistics of physical situations, is itself not subject to chance, but is controlled by an equation as deterministic as the equations of classical physics. Such a causality is, however, but a poor ghost of the robust causality of the classical conception, which ascribes a cause (and an effect also) to *every* event. I believe, however, that there is a deeper undercurrent in the thinking of such people than merely the desire to recover a moiety of rationality; they feel that they can now say, "The world is *really* deterministic and causal, after all, in spite of superficial appearances to the contrary." Such a feeling usually carries the further consequence that the psi function is ascribed an "objective reality," for what is the use of a really determined world if the thing that is determined is not real?

This brings up the whole question of the meaning of "reality," a term that has undergone a surprising renascence in the usage of physicists after a period of conscious abstention. The word is freely used by Schrödinger and de Broglie, and even Max Born uses it on occasion. As would be expected, there is no clean-cut specification of the meaning of "reality." One is often left to infer the meaning by observing the usage, as when an author says, "Everyone would agree that such-and-such a situation is real." I have yet to see, however, an attempt at a definition of reality that would justify one in saying that a probability is objectively real.

Here we encounter one of those situations in which, in spite of long discussion, there is not even yet consensus, for there still are different schools of thought with regard to probability. There arc some who maintain that individual concrete events "have" a probability, and that it is possible to find what this probability is. Professor Margenau is one of these, and his conception of probability is basic to his interpretation of wave mechanics. He defines his probability in terms of frequency, and he obtains the probability of a specific event by observing its frequency of occurrence. I think he would say that any actual observation of frequency can give only a rough value for the probability, because of the finite size of the sample, but that nevertheless it is good enough for practical purposes. Now, to me—and here I enter controversial territory—any such view of probability that allows one to say—and to attempt to prove that he is right when he says it—that the probability of some concrete event is some specific number rests simply on poor observation and poor reporting of what he does when he applies the probability concept to some concrete situation. What can one possibly do to show that there was a one-sixth chance that a particular throw of a die would yield a three when the actual throw has been made and yields a three? It seems to me that the meaning of probability must be found in another sphere of activity. Inspection of what we do leads, I believe, to a view of probability expressed by Max Born as follows: "Chance can be understood only in regard to expectations of a subject."[3] Elsewhere, however, he says that probability must be recognized to have some "objective" reference because we successfully apply probability to objective situations. This sort of tenuous second-hand objectivity, however, is apparently not what Professor Margenau and others have in mind.

We return to the question of the frame of mind of those who are

[3] *Proc. Roy. Soc.,* **66,** 503, 1953.

so firmly resolved that there shall be an underlying order that they are satisfied to find it even in a probability. It appears to me that their views often have some pretty deep emotional roots. Many men apparently crave a friendly universe, one in which they can feel themselves at home at least to the extent that they can believe the universe intrinsically understandable by the human mind. Because a universe without underlying regularities would not be understandable, simply owing to the method of functioning of the human mind, there follows the resolution that there shall be regularities.

A slightly different twist is given to this point of view by the German philosopher Ernst Cassirer in his book *Determinism and Indeterminism in Modern Physics*,[4] recently translated into English, with an introduction by Professor Henry Margenau. For Cassirer the domain of natural law is not the domain of objective things but of cognitions; natural laws are defined by the ordering of cognitions that they make possible. For him the causal relation is epistemologically necessary. He says:

> We find the essential significance of the causal relation, if interpreted in a critical rather than a metaphysical sense, to be that it contains a statement not immediately about things but about experience, by which and in virtue of which alone things, as objects of knowledge, can be given us. It expresses something about the content of empirical knowledge.[5]

If one reads between the lines, particularly in the early part of the book, where Cassirer says in one place, "*Ignorabimus* is the only answer that science can give to the question of the essence and origin of consciousness,"[6] I think one is justified in believing that Cassirer displaces the domain of law and causality from the physical to the mental world because of his belief in the existence of a mental world inaccessible by the methods of science.

Whether or not this is a fair evaluation of Cassirer's attitude, I think that one cannot read the many writings of physicists on this question without feeling that they, too, have injected something nonphysical into the situation. This is usually unconscious, perhaps, but may break forth into articulate expression, as in the following quotation from Schrödinger:

[4] Trans. by O. Theodor Benfey (New Haven: Yale University Press, 1956).
[5] *Ibid.*, p. 114.
[6] *Ibid.*, p. 5.

. . . there is a tendency to forget that all science is bound up with human culture in general, and that scientific findings, even those which at the moment appear the most advanced and esoteric and difficult to grasp, are meaningless outside their cultural context. A theoretical science, unaware that those of its concepts considered relevant and momentous are destined eventually to be framed in concepts and words that have a grip on the educated community and become part and parcel of the general world picture—a theoretical science I say, where this is forgotten, and where the initiated continue musing to each other in terms that are, at best, understood by a small group of fellow travellers, will necessarily be cut off from the rest of cultural mankind; in the long run it is bound to atrophy and ossify.[7]

There is more in a similar vein; one point of particular emphasis is that the physicist should not allow to forget his organic connection with the past. Now, some of the implications of Schrödinger's attitude can be unhesitatingly accepted; nearly everyone would agree that society as a whole has a vital stake in the scientific enterprise and that therefore it is desirable to find the means for disseminating as widely as possible an appreciation of the nature of science and a knowledge of its factual findings. But it seems to me that other and wider implications are unmistakable—the implication that it behooves the scientist in his theoretical constructions to cast his thinking into idioms of his times and his culture. In some ways this is a most surprising admonition. I had supposed everyone recognized that as a matter of fact the theories of the scientist are colored by contemporary culture, but that this was nevertheless something to be regarded as undesirable, although unavoidable because rooted in human frailty. I had supposed that the ideal of the theorist was to erect a structure determined as far as possible by the facts themselves functioning autonomously, and that, if he could discern that his structure was being influenced by the intellectual fashion of the times, scientific integrity demanded that he resist as far as he could. I am old-fashioned enough to be shocked at the suggestion that the scientist should cut his cloth to the general intellectual fashion of his times, but I very much fear that Schrödinger has put his finger on a change in the intellectual atmosphere of the scientist. I find it hard, in reading the recent discussions of causality and determinism, to

[7] *Brit. Jour. Phil. Sci.,* **3,** 109, 1952.

resist the impression that many of the debaters were influenced by extrascientific considerations. This influence is evident even in the work of Max Born, who says, in combating Schrödinger's thesis that it is waves and not particles that are fundamental, "I think Scrödinger's suggestion is impracticable and against the spirit of the time."[8] This is perhaps unfair to Born, who may have been throwing back into Schrödinger's teeth his demand that the theorist be aware of his cultural background, but nevertheless one could wish that Born had not said it.

Among writers of less scientific stature than Born the influence of extrascientific factors is unmistakable. This is particularly evident in Mario Bunge's paper "Strife About Complementarity."[9] The burden of Bunge's paper is that physicists are at last awakening from the "dogmatic slumber" in which they have accepted "the official philosophy of quantum theory, which is essentially of a positivistic character" and are embarking instead on "new, realistic, rationalistic, and deterministic trends." It seems to me that there is too little argument in the paper and too much name-calling. It is assumed that the reader will react negatively to such epithets as "positivistic" and "empiristic" and positively to "realistic," "deterministic," and "scientific materialism." The assumption that the reader will react in the expected way to these epithets and that it is desirable that he should so react obviously does not have its origin in any purely scientific experience. In particular it seems to me that a strong odor of Marxian dialectic is detectable here.

Bunge lists four axioms "underlying every scientific endeavor and confirmed by its failures and successes": (a) nature and every one of its parts is inexhaustible, actually as well as potentially; (b) nature is an interconnected whole, so that the complete specification of a single object would require the complete specification of the whole universe; (c) knowledge is as inexhaustible as its objects; (d) we are limited to a finite number of variables, whereas the complete specification of every bit of matter would presumably require an infinite number of variables. It is not quite clear what is meant by calling these "axioms." The meaning cannot be that all scientific workers do as a matter of fact follow these axioms, for Bunge's con-

8 *Guthrie* lecture, p. 507.
9 *Brit. Jour. Phil Sci.*, May 1955.

tention is that the orthodox interpretation of quantum mechanics does not follow these axioms and therefore cannot be correct. Neither can "axiom" be used in the sense of mathematical postulate analysis, where an axiom is a formally accepted preliminary to a deduction of the logical consequences concealed in the axiom. Surely no one would maintain that the physicist is any more restricted than the mathematician in setting up any system of axioms that he pleases and deducing the consequences. "Axiom" must mean something else; its usage indicates that it ought to be described, rather, as a precept or maxim that "should" guide the scientist. We may well ask, Whence comes the authority claimed for these precepts? Surely it does not come from any scientific experience but from something extrascientific, something that is never formulated and can only be guessed at.

Considering the axioms in detail, one can have little objection to the first, if it is to be taken as advising the theorist that he would do well to leave room in his thinking for the discovery of at present unknown facts; but it is to be rejected if it suggests that it is illegitimate for the physicist to speculate what the consequences would be if there were no new facts to be discovered, which I think is essentially what Bohr has done. The second axiom, that nature is so interconnected that the complete specification of a single object would require the complete specification of the whole universe, is in the spirit of the old Newtonian mechanics, which could set up a formula giving numerically the gravitational interaction of any two objects in the universe, no matter how small or how remote from each other. But this axiom is completely divorced from any possible experience and furthermore violates the spirit of the first axiom, because it effectively says that nature is so constituted that there is no minimum interaction below which one object has no effect on another, and in so saying presumes to dictate the structure of future experience. Not only this, but it is inconsistent with the structure of our present experience, for one of the consequences of Planck's discovery of h is precisely that it showed that there are, as a matter of fact, minimum interactions. I remember my own almost audible relief when I saw that in discovering the existence of h Planck had absolved me of the necessity of believing that the slightest motion of an atom on this earth really has some effect on every atom in Sirius, an idea that always seemed to me absurd to the point of grotesqueness. I never was willing to push mathematics so far or to take it so seriously. Yet the Newtonian view is the one to which the classical conception of causality would lead one.

Bunge's other two precepts, (c) and (d), may be taken in the same spirit as the first in so far as they are not truisms, namely as offering advice as to the direction that theory may take in order to be probably profitable, but in no sense as setting limits to the direction that it *must* take. I have doubtless devoted a disproportionate amount of space to Bunge's paper, but it does seem to me to offer an illuminating example of what may happen when we allow ourselves to be unduly influenced by extrascientific considerations.

The attentive reader can perhaps detect an undercurrent of disapproval in my ascription of extrascientific motives to those who are led by their desire for a friendly universe to demand determinism and to repudiate probability as an ultimate. The same repudiation, however, may arise from considerations not necessarily emotional at all. One of the fundamental drives of the scientist is to find explanations for the things around him. If one accepts probability as ultimate, he has, by the very definition of probability, given up the possibility of explanation. I would concede that one has a perfect right not to give up the possibility of explanation except in the very last resort, and to follow as long as he can a program of theorizing that envisages the ultimate possibility of finding some sort of "explanation." It seems to me that it is in this spirit that de Broglie has returned, in his most recent book, to a further examination of the consequences of assuming a sort of ghost mathematics back of the recognized mathematics of wave mechanics—a mathematics in which most of the present results are reproduced but that retains a place for possible causality.

I should now like to present the conclusions to which I myself have come. There have been several guiding insights: In the first place, the so-called microscopic world, which is commonly thought to be the arena of quantum theory, is really nothing but the altered world of our own macroscopic experience—altered because we have learned new sorts of macroscopic manipulations such as constructing microscopes or Wilson cloud chambers or Geiger counters. It is consequently to be expected that the roots of the difficulties revealed to us by quantum theory are already present in the sphere of ordinary life and should be discoverable by acute enough analysis. Secondly, the process of acquiring information or knowledge in any physical situation must interfere with and to some extent alter the system about which we wish to acquire information. This means that no object can ever be strictly isolated and considered in and for itself, but must be treated as a part of a larger system in which at least the instrument by which we acquire knowledge is included. It is further made plain that aspects of a situation about which we have no actual or potential knowledge can be of no concern. Such aspects can only be talked about, and then not without concealed self-contradiction. Finally, our ultimate concern is with events or happenings rather than things. With a background of this sort it seems to me that we can face the world as revealed to us by quantum theory without feeling that it does not make sense.

Take in the first place the consideration that the object of knowledge is not to be separated from the instrument of knowledge. Two extreme limiting cases are to be recognized: the instrument is very small compared with the object, and the object is very small compared with the instrument. Since *we* are in the last resort the instrument for acquiring knowledge, the two limiting cases are: objects large compared with us and objects small compared with us, or, in other words, simply large and small objects. Now, it seems to me to make sense to suppose that a small instrument can find out more about a large object than a large instrument can find out about a small object. The small instrument can explore the large object bit by bit in a way impossible for a large instrument with a small object. It also seems to me to make sense to suppose that more perfect knowledge of the large object would make possible more effective ways of dealing with it. In particular, I think it makes sense to find that we can predict the future behavior of a large object but not that of a small object. This is merely another way of saying that it makes sense that causality should fail for small objects. As part of the same picture, the Heisenberg uncertainty relation does not outrage my feeling of what makes sense. Of course these very vague general considerations can give no hint of the mathematical form of the Heisenberg relation or of the existence of Planck's h— this must come from the detailed analysis of the actual experiments.

As another example, consider the often quoted paradox that an electron has no individuality or identity. The paradox disappears if one no longer thinks of an electron as an "object," but as an aspect of what happens in particular kinds of physical situation—including in the physical situation all the instrumentation by which the electron is detected or measured. Under such conditions it need make no more sense to ask whether the electron we now observe is the "same" as the electron we observed a moment ago than to ask whether the wind that now cools our cheek is the same as the wind that blew yesterday. The paradox disappears even from such statements as that we can "choose" whether the electron is to have position or velocity. The electron in and by itself does not "have" either position or velocity; these pertain to what happens in the whole situation, including the instrumentation. We can set up a "position situation" or a "velocity situation" as we please by suitably arranging the apparatus. There is surely nothing paradoxical here.

I think quantum mechanics makes sense, and I think that the fact that it does make sense and hangs together logically means, among other things, that a law of causality or a deterministic structure for the universe or an underlying continuity as distinguished from discreteness is not, as has often been maintained, a necessary prerequisite to rational thought. But whether quantum mechanics will survive is a different question, a question to which the answer rests with experiment. There is no present indication that experiment will decide against it. I would like to suggest, however, two directions in which I think future experiment might look for at present undiscovered structure.

The first has to do with the significance of the successful use of the mathematical apparatus of statistics and probability. In this mathematical apparatus we had a ready-made tool admirably adapted to dealing qualitatively with situations characterized by vagueness or experimental uncertainty or inaccuracy. The experimental check so far leaves nothing to be desired; nevertheless all our experimental checks have been of a rather special kind in that they have been confined to regions of high probability density. I should like to see developed an experimental method for dealing more in detail with regions of low probability density. What inspires this suggestion is my lifelong repugnance to such statements as that of Bertrand Russell, that if we only wait long enough we shall certainly see a pail of water freeze on the fire. This may be conceded to be a rigorous consequence of the mathematics, but to me it is utterly incredible as a statement of physical fact. I would propose the question: Can phenomena be found anywhere corresponding even remotely to Russell's freezing of water on a fire? A more conservative proposal would be the investigation of the fluctuations of fluctuation phenomena.

The second direction in which I would look for new types of experimental evidence is suggested by our so-called freedom to decide whether the electron shall have position or velocity. My question is: What are the limitations on the time at which we have to decide which it shall be? Ordinarily we make our choice long in advance; we set up a position apparatus or a velocity apparatus and then wait to catch an electron in it. But what happens if we make our choice after we have caught our electron? Specifically, imagine an interference apparatus in which an electron passes through one hole, presently meets a first screen with two holes, and still later impinges on a second screen, where it forms part of an interference pattern. If there had been only one hole in the first screen we would have got a pattern entirely different from that obtained with a two-hole screen. My question now is: What happens if we change from a one-hole screen to a two-hole screen (or vice versa) *after* the electron has passed the first hole and while it is in transit to the first screen? The same sort of experiment might even more instructively be performed with light quanta rather than with electrons. The general problem might be to study in closed systems the fine structure of macroscopic propagation phenomena that occur in times less than the time required by light to travel across the system. Such experiments have not yet been accessible to technique, but I am told that they soon will be. They might throw light on such problematic questions as the supposed instantaneous collapse of the psi function when new information is acquired at any point of a system.

Finally, I should like to suggest what seems to me a limitation on all quantum theoretical analysis or, for that matter, on the criticisms of that analysis. It has been a new insight, at least for the physicist, that the object of knowledge is not to be separated from the instrument of knowledge. This has often been expressed by saying that an analysis of the role of the observer is necessary to an understanding of quantum theory. Here the observer is identified with the instrument of knowledge. It is well recognized that there is no sharp dividing line between the instrument of knowledge and the object of knowledge, and that for different purposes the line may be drawn at different places. Thus it may be drawn at the photographic plate on which some event is recorded, or at the retina of the eye of the experimenter who examines the plate, or at the neural processes in the brain produced by the events at the retina. Wherever we draw the line, we eventually end with knowledge. Seldom, if ever, does the physicist ask what the nature of this knowledge is, because for his purposes he does not need to. If one wants a specific description of what the physicist's purposes are, the answer can be found by examining what he does with his quantum theory: his use of it, for the most part, is limited to the atomic events he manipulates in his laboratory. But for purposes wider than those of the physicists, in particular for the purpose of acquiring the fullest possible understanding, we cannot forgo asking what this knowledge is that for the physicist is the end product. Here we obviously enter a field of great vagueness. From one point of view a question has no meaning if we cannot formulate what sort of an answer we should be willing to accept, and it must be admitted that it is not easy to formulate the conditions that should be satisfied if we are to feel that we had an understanding of the nature of knowledge. But I think that our groping quest may nevertheless have some direction. What gives me most disquietude here, and what I think quantum theory ignores in spite of its ostensible concern with the observer, is the simple observation that knowledge never occurs except in conjunction with a nervous system that has itself been subjected to a most elaborate preconditioning. Furthermore, the nervous system is itself a physical system of a complexity so formidable that we are only beginning to have an inkling of how it functions. It seems to me that we cannot permanently be satisfied with an analysis that purports, as does quantum theory, to reduce to understandability the functioning of the ultimate structural units of the universe, when that understandability itself demands the cooperation of superstructures of as yet unfathomed complexity.

It seems to me that when we take full cognizance of the fact that we cannot get away from our nervous systems, we shall recognize intellectual limitations that we at present ignore. With such a background I would say to those who think quantum theory does not make sense that it at least makes sense that it should not make sense.

2. The Relativity of Determinism

Milton K. Munitz, New York University

The lack of consensus in current discussions about determinism in modern science, as Professor Bridgman has made amply clear, is not in any way due to a disagreement either about the experimental facts or about the mathematical calculations employed in various formulations of physical theory. Professor Bridgman ascribes the defense of a deterministic view on the part of some writers to extrascientific motives of a specifically emotional sort, involving, among other things, a longing for a "friendly universe," one in which regularities are pervasively present. In briefly setting out his own views he has indicated why it makes sense to say, not that the universe is unfriendly, but that causality, as he puts it, "should fail for small objects." Professor Bridgman, it would seem, finds a universe in which there is some objective element of indeterminism one in which he finds himself perfectly at home.

Now, whether or not emotional considerations are relevant factors in either accepting or rejecting a determinist view, there is another basis of approach, to which Professor Bridgman alludes, that is of greater moment. He remarks that "we cannot forgo asking what this knowledge is that for the physicist is the end product." This is precisely the important kind of question to raise. It indicates at once that what we are concerned with is a *philosophical* question. Unfortunately, for Professor Bridgman this means, as he says, that at this point we "enter a field of great vagueness." Perhaps so.

But whether or not the issue of determinism is vague in principle *because* it is a philosophical one, this issue, in so far as there is one, is not in any case *internal* to science; nor is it to be settled on emotional grounds. (I say "in so far as determinism is an issue" because the term is sometimes used in a purely technical sense as a label for the specific type of differential equations and their solutions in classical Newtonian mechanics; analogously, the equations of modern quantum mechanics, different in certain crucial respects, are called "indeterministic.") The issue of determinism is more nearly indicated by the problems that arise when one tries to decide whether to agree with Professor Bridgman when he says: "a law of causality or a deterministic structure for the universe or an underlying continuity as distinguished from discreteness is not . . . a necessary prerequisite to rational thought." This type of question cannot be settled simply by consulting the above-mentioned "technical" meanings of determinism as used to label certain types of equations in physics. If settled at all, the issue of determinism is one to be resolved by trying to clarify the cognitive status of various types of statements in science, and among them a type of statement of which the principle of indeterminacy is a particularly intriguing example. It is the complex of differences in the *philosophy* of science, not *in* science, that emerges here and that helps us focus on the point where controversy genuinely arises.

Perhaps I can best bring out my main point if I call attention to what at first sight might seem to Professor Bridgman and others a somewhat strange coupling of his own views with that of a philosopher-scientist who, as he has reminded us, has taken an almost intransigent view, wholly opposite to his own, with respect to determinism: namely Einstein. I would suggest that Professor Bridgman, like many other "indeterminists," has more in common with determinists like Einstein, from one philosophical point of view, than is sometimes recognized. What they have in common, indeed, is of more interest and importance than their differences. In order to support this way of approaching the question, I should like to suggest in barest outline what seems to me at least one other entirely different way of looking at the matter, one that serves as a major alternative to this first type of philosophy. There is no question here of course of trying to *prove* the superiority of one philosophy of science over another. At best, what we may hint at is the manner in which certain difficulties and controversies dissolve when we shift our perspective in a sufficiently fundamental way. The thesis I am proposing, in short, is that the whole controversy between determinism and indeterminism as it is customarily formulated is not finally to be settled by taking sides and showing the overwhelming merits of one of them. It is to be "settled" by taking seriously a philosophy of science in which the terms "determinism" and "indeterminism" not only undergo radical change, but in doing so, require *all* scientific knowledge involving the use of theory to be deterministic.

Various terms are at hand by which we may label these rival philosophics. Karl Popper, for example, has recently suggested the terms "essentialism" and "instrumentalism" as suitable ones, while the terms "realism" and "conventionalism" may be preferred by others. Since, however, I wish to stress that one whole group of views, whether "determinist" or "indeterminist," has reference to what are alleged to be the structural features of *events* or *situations* or *objects* as "disclosed" by scientific inquiry, I shall refer to this approach as basically "ontological." According to the other approach, "causality," "determinism," "necessity," "predictability," and other associated terms have to do primarily with the connections between *statements,* which represent what is or is not present in the *inference patterns* of the scientist. This I shall call the "logical" approach.

Einstein's lifelong opposition to those who regarded quantum physics as pointing to an element of genuine indeterminism or unpredictability among some of nature's events was based on a profound belief in what he thought of as the intelligibility of the universe. It was not simply that he thought, for example, that the program of field physics to which he devoted all his energies would be more successful as a heuristic device for achieving better predictions or explanations, or that it was simply a more "congenial" point of view. Rather, he looked on nature in Spinozistic terms and referred to his Spinozism as his "religion." He thought of nature, to use his own favorite metaphor, as rather like a puzzle. The scientist tries to fit the pieces together or obtain solutions to his queries by seeking the *uniquely* correct way of specifying what the structure is. Einstein believed the program of field physics to hold out the promise of eventually realizing this goal to a superior degree in comparison with any other. Einstein's dissatisfactions with quantum physics arose from the conviction that its conceptual foundations were essentially incomplete, that because of its statistical character quantum theory referred to "ensembles of systems and not to individual systems."

If one is going to criticize such a view philosophically, one can perhaps best begin by showing that the "root metaphor" on which it rests—that nature is like a puzzle with a unique solution—is really one that turns out to be cramping rather than liberating in its implications. Real puzzles are constructed *by* men *for* men, and we know in advance that there is a favored solution. But why think of nature as a puzzle? Men, being curious or troubled, *find problems* in nature, and in their religious moments they may even wish to dwell on an element of ineffable mystery connected with it. Given the problems that scientists encounter and *pick out,* they can offer a variety of possible answers. But why need we assume that there is some *one* supremely satisfactory way of dealing with these problems? Einstein's philosophy, one might say, is the outcome of projecting into the allegedly antecedent and independent structure of facts what is at bottom a favored view but still only *one* of many possible theoretical views of things. His realistic rationalism is the result of reifying the conceptualizations of a legitimate yet limited perspective into the necessities of things and events. The successes of the special and general theory of relativity in yielding explanations and predictions of a more adequate sort than those provided by earlier or rival theories—these the working physicist recognizes and gladly welcomes without having to subscribe to the ontologism of Einstein's philosophy of science. Such a working physicist may rightfully insist on the use of quantum physics, even if in its conceptual basis it is wholly different from what Einstein would think of as desirable. And again he would do so on the simple pragmatic ground that it is successful in its predictions and explanations to a sufficiently high degree to warrant his use of it. But need there be any logical incompatibility in using side by side the wholly different techniques of inference or different analogical modes of viewing things that constitute the foundations of these various theories? Not, he may say, if we do not commit ourselves in advance to the belief that nature has *a* structure that will yield its secrets to one and only one of these formulations. This is another way of saying that we have no compelling reason to believe that the *theories* with which the physicist works are, or aim to be, true, that they would disclose to us, as Galileo put it, "the language in which the Book of Nature is written." For nature is not really like a book written in a language at all. Hence nature is neither logical nor illogical, neither mathematical nor nonmathematical, neither rational nor irrational, and so neither determined nor undetermined. These predicates apply only to statements in human discourse, and the way in which such statements fit or not into certain accepted patterns of inference, patterns that in the case of empirical science are set up by men for dealing with the facts of observational experience.

Now, unlike Einstein's, Professor Bridgman's orientation to physics is primarily that of an experimentalist, and this fact controls his interpretation of what is contained in the distinctive ideas of quantum physics. If we examine the manner in which he expounds and illustrates the main principles of this physics, it becomes clear that he reads them as basically experimentally verifiable reports of what is found in the laboratory. First, Professor Bridgman tends to equate the physicist's process of acquiring *knowledge* with the process of acquiring *information* through the use of appropriate instrumentation. It makes sense, he argues, on the submicroscopic as well as on the macroscopic level that the very process of acquiring information (knowledge) should interfere in some way with the "objects" whose "traits" are being examined, so that a more comprehensive perspective would include this very interaction itself in all its complexity, extending even so far as the still undisclosed intricacies of the human nervous system. Secondly, Heisenberg's principle of uncertainty is taken to describe the relation of relative fuzzinesses in the measurements, experimentally arrived at, of the velocity and position of subatomic particles. Finally, Professor Bridgman interprets what we are to understand by such a phrase as the "individuality of the electron" as not referring to some object existing in itself apart from the observer's interaction with "it," but as a more complex situational event. "The electron," he says, "in and by itself does not 'have' either position or velocity; these pertain to what happens in the whole situation, including the instrumentation."

Granted the obvious importance of the experimentalist's instrumentation in obtaining information as a necessary and relevant ingredient in the process of obtaining knowledge of the physical world, it seems to me that the stress Professor Bridgman gives to the virtual identification of information and knowledge slurs over certain important distinctions between the roles of theory and observation. Now, theory is primarily a matter of conceptual construction, having, as all thought must, a neurological base; but to speak of this element in knowledge as interacting with the object seems to me somewhat queer and indeed confusing. It results from trying to put under the heading of apparatus what is actually not apparatus at all. Moreover, this way of approaching the matter has a further and perhaps more serious consequence. One assumes that theory is at best only a report of what one finds in experiment. The fact is, however, that Heisenberg's principle, for example, is *not* a report of what one discovers as a result of trying to perform certain measurements. It is, instead, a defining element of quantum *theory,* and so, among other things, a way of specifying what for the purposes of the theory is to be regarded as a "particle." This is not the "particle" of traditional mechanics, since, even on the level of theory, there is no possibility of simultaneous specification to any desired degree of accuracy of both its position and velocity. What we have here, then, is a part of a different and, in some ways, more complex set of theoretical ideas by means of which it is attempted to provide explanations and predictions for observed or observable facts. Similarily, what is referred to as an "electron" or "photon" is not an object of direct observation, but represents in summary fashion, a whole schema of interpretational devices and inferential techniques of theory that are brought to bear in thinking or reaching conclusions about observational materials. Professor Bridgman, it seems to me, though appearing to rely exclusively on what one finds in the laboratory, is actually letting in a good deal in the way of constructive theory and is thus perhaps giving a greater ontological weight to the terms of theory—as if these corresponded to some structural features of physical events—than need be done. He finds indeterminism in the universe not really because the measurements of the laboratory force this interpretation, but because he is willing to accept the orthodox interpretation of quantum theory as describing the alleged structure of certain physical events. In displaying this confidence in orthodox quantum theory, he is expressing, I suspect, the same type of confidence in what theory can accomplish as Einstein, although the specific ontology, to be sure, is different.

Now, instead of letting the reifications of one's ontological approach to scientific theory come in through either the front door or the back door, one might say, in the present context of discussion, that quantum theory is as deterministic as classical physics, or indeed as any theory, by its very nature, is bound to be. This means simply that a specific theory, whatever its conceptual tools or analogical base, offers us a way, distinctive to itself, of making inferences *from* certain observationally identifiable facts *to* others, and of interpreting what those experimental facts are. Any conclusions reached in accordance with the rules of inference specified by the theory are logically determined. Thus the principle of indeterminacy, among others, is part of a total physical theory that in its functioning provides determined results of a type *it* is competent to reach. If it proves successful in dealing with observational facts, it is not because "causality fails for small objects" but because man's creative intellectual ingenuity has found one more means for dealing effectively through his inferences with the data of his experience.

3. The Case for Indeterminism

Alfred Landé, Ohio State University

Professor Bridgman has painted a lively picture of the strife about determinism. It is a strife not so much about empirical facts as about the interpretation of facts. Many consider determinism the only rational interpretation—if not an aprioristic category of the mind. They would admit indeterminacy in modern physics only as a temporary expedient adapted to our present incapacity to predict microphysical events, an incapacity that may be overcome by future technical developments. In opposition to this view I agree with Bridgman when he said: "it makes sense that causality should fail for small objects." But I would go even further and maintain that, irrespective of any possible future technical developments, determinism does not and never will make sense,[1] in particular when applied to those random-like situations we know from games of chance. The question is, of course, whether there are true games of chance, i.e., random-like situations that are irreducible to concealed causes *in principle*. In this argument about principles it makes little difference whether the random-like situations are those encountered in atomic experiments, in dice games, or in the games insurance companies play with their clients. Therefore I shall have to extend our topic from determinism in *modern* science to natural science in general. My excuse for this deviation is Bridgman's own declaration: "It is to be expected that the roots of the difficulties revealed to us by quantum theory are already present in the sphere of ordinary life, and should be discoverable by acute enough analysis." Let us therefore analyze an example taken from ordinary life.

Imagine a game of balls dropped through a chute onto a knife edge. The angle of aim a may be adjusted by a screw, and the knife edge may be sharp or slightly rounded. If the chute is aimed at the right (left) of center, all balls will drop to the right (left). Experience shows, however, that between right- and left-hand aim there is always a small but *finite* range Δa of aim within which an experimentally adjusted angle a leads neither to all balls dropping to the right nor to all balls dropping to the left but rather to both r- and l-balls occurring at a certain frequency ratio. The latter varies from $100 : 0$ to $0 : 100$ when the aim is shifted from the right to the left of the small range Δa. Primitive persons and other indeterminists will interpret this as a sign of uncertainty, of blind fate, with *one* and the same cause capable of being followed by *two* different effects, r or l. Determinists will say, however: "The distribution of the r- and l-results only *appears* to be erratic. Actually each individual result has its particular deterministic cause, be it a small deviation of the angle of aim, or a small perturbation of the ball on its flight." (Similarly, although insurance companies count on their frequency tables, each

---

[1] Cf. the critique of determinism by K. R. Popper, *Brit. J. Philos. Science* **1**, Nos. 2 and 3.

individual "accident" is not an accident but has its particular cause.)

I submit, however, that the hypothesis of (concealed) individual causes behind individual effects *r* or *l* does *not* explain the essential point of the observed situation in a deterministic fashion. When the determinist ascribes the present final event *r* to an *r*-producing chain ... *r r r* reaching back into the infinite past, he merely shifts the problem *r*- and *l*-events to *r*- and *l*-chains and, further, to the beginning of those chains, if they have a beginning. We must ask him now for a deterministic explanation of the strange empirical observation that those chains, or initial conditions, occur again and again at a definite frequency ratio and, furthermore, why even the fluctuations away from the average occur at a rate conforming with the mathematical theory of random as though by a pre-established harmony between fact and theory. It is this *pre-established harmony* that calls for explanation. Referring to the infinite past, and saying that this harmony has always prevailed, is an evasion rather than a deterministic explanation. A stubborn determinist may defend his cause, however, by means of the following argument: "Once upon a time there was a *demon* who knew his mathematical random theory and who deliberately went out to deceive the observer. He first initiated two *r*-chains, then an *l*-chain, then four *r*-chains; then realizing that he had given too much preponderance to *r*-chains, he thereupon started five *l*-chains in a row, cleverly arranging the whole sequence with averages and fluctuations so that a present-day scientist might be lured away from the true deterministic faith." There seems indeed to be only the following alternative: *Either* the observed random-like distributions of final events or chains or initial conditions in games of chance represent a basic and irreducible trait of nature. *Or* statistical distributions only feign an appearance of random, when in reality there is, or has been, concerted deterministic action. Either a *deus ex machina* or no deterministic explanation at all. Since deceitful demons have no place in scientific theories, I have reluctantly joined the party of indeterminacy pure and simple. But I concede, that it is a party of renunciation with a purely negative creed. Most of my partisans, including myself, suffer from a guilt complex that draws us toward our old infatuation, determinism. This infatuation *may* have its roots in a feeling of being ourselves demons who can deliberately start deterministic chains. In other words, it *may* be that we believe in strict determinism because we feel we have free will—a somewhat paradoxical psychological hypothesis. But as a scientist who observes games of chance, and who is unwilling to admit a *deus ex machina* (at the beginning of time, if there is a beginning, or a finite time ago), I must concede that the deterministic interpretation fails; and this applies not only to ordinary "games of chance" in which the statistical dispersion is obvious, but in general to those cases where a similar dispersion of effects is revealed only by microphysical instruments.

Empirically it is a most surprising fact, which could not have been foreseen a priori, that there *are* sequences of events in harmony with mathematical random theory. This empirical discovery was already made by cavemen when they gambled for the best pieces of a slain bear. But when irreducible random is once accepted, then it is a comparatively minor point of dispute whether (*a*) each new experiment constitutes a new game of chance (as quantum theory maintains), or (*b*) random was set up *once,* a long or an infinite time ago, and random distributions observed at present are but the deterministic effects of that one initial "shuffling of the cards" (as classical statistical mechanics maintains). The difference between the two positions may be illustrated by the example of a great number of arrows laid out as radii of a circle. Each individual arrow has its definite x- and y-component, positive or negative. Suppose that the arrows are distributed over all directions in a random-like fashion, with or without the help of a demon. When viewing this ensemble through a circular glass disk, the northern half of which is transparent and the southern half opaque, one observes a statistical $50:50$ ratio between visible and invisible arrows. The same ratio of visible to invisible arrows will be observed when the disk is held in the *NE-SW*-direction or in any other direction whatsoever. The frequency ratios in all these instances are deterministic consequences of the *one* original random distribution over all directions within the circle. Also, when an individual arrow of given x- and given y-component is viewed through our glass disk held in a given orientation, then it is *predictable* whether this arrow will be found belonging to the visible or the invisible group in that particular orientation of the disk. This is an illustration of the classical situation. Since it requires random mixing at least once, it is a *soft determinism* at most.

Suppose now that our arrows are of microscopic magnitude and represent the spin directions of electrons. In this case not even a demon can lay out various spins in a variety of chosen directions simultaneously. Electronic arrows (spin directions) can only be laid out by means of a linear slit (a magnetic field). When the slit is held in the *NS*-direction the arrows will assume only the *N*- and/or *S*-direction. If the arrows are now subjected to a new orientation test by means of a slit of *NE-SW*-direction, each arrow has to *jump* from its original *N*- or *S*-direction either to the *NE*- or to the *SW*-direction. The indeterministic character of these jumps is proved, according to our former argument, by the mere fact that each new slit experiment actually yields a new statistical frequency ratio between opposite arrows that, together with averages and fluctuations, conforms with the mathematical theory of random events. In the present instance the subsequent *N* : *S* and *NE* : *SW* ratios cannot be regarded as deterministic consequences of an original random distribution over *all* directions, since each new slit experiment collects all arrows within two opposite directions only. Each new test is an independent game of chance in which it is *unpredictable* whether a given arrow will choose one or the opposite direction. This is the obvious and trivial inference from the fact, discovered by quantum physicists, that there are mutually incompatible quantities such as *x*- and *y*-components of an electronic spin vector (or an *x*-component of position and an *x*-component of momentum of any particle), so that one cannot provide an original random-like outlay of spins over all directions.

Quantum theorists, however, do not seem to cherish such simple and elementary considerations, since they always refer to J. von Neumann's proof that quantum theory has no room for concealed causal mechanisms. But what did von Neumann do to prove this result? He first introduced the whole involved apparatus of the quantum theory, thereby lifting us to a highly exalted plane. In this lofty atmosphere he carried out certain calculations, then brought his results back to earth again—when he could have stayed there all the time. Yet when von Neumann's conclusions were recently found to suffer from the fault of circularity, the determinists took heart again. Let it be said, however, that irrespective of von Neumann and irrespective of the technicalities of quantum mechanics, the mere existence of mutually incompatible quantities a and b that require statistical redistributions in consecutive a- and b-tests leaves us no other alternative than either to assume a demon who feigns pseudo-random, or to concede that the harmony between statistical fact and random theory is deterministically inexplicable.

The wide acclaim that von Neumann's (inconclusive) proof has found among theoretical physicists is symptomatic of the present vogue for considering quantum mechanics with all its subtleties, wave-particle antinomies, and bewildering mathematical prescriptions as the ultimate and irreducible ground structure, the deepest bottom of theoretical analysis. This fundamentalist dogma is quite in opposition to Bridgman's and my own view that the enigmatic quantum laws ought to be explainable as consequences of more fundamental laws having their roots in the experiences of everyday life. In order to support this view I should like to ask my determinist opponents: "Do you accept the principle, abstracted from everyday experience, that a *finite* effect calls for a *finite* cause, that a finite change of effect can never be produced by an infinitely small change of cause? If you accept this principle of continuity of Leibnitz, you have already lost your case!"

To return to our ball-knife game: If the chute is aimed at the right (left) of the knife edge, then all balls will drop to the right (left) of the knife. But suppose that the angle a of aim is *gradually* shifted from right to left. Will this lead to an *abrupt* change of effect, from all balls dropping to the right to all balls dropping to the left, at the moment when the aim passes the center? If so, it would constitute a violation of the postulate of continuity. According to this postulate there ought to be a *finite* range Δa of transition from the one extreme case to the other—a range Δa within a given angle a of aim leads to the dropping of a numerical fraction of all balls to the right and of the remaining fraction to the left. This is exactly the situation observed, discussed previously. The postulate of continuity thus leads to the same statistical situation by inference that we have accepted before simply as a strange matter of fact discovered by cavemen.

A slight variant of the game of dropping balls on a knife edge leads to a well-known phenomenon of quantum physics. Consider a stream of particles incident on a filter of some sort where they have to choose between passing and not passing. Let us define an A-filter as an instrument that passes the incident particles when they are in the state A and rejects them when they are in a state different from A. Suppose, first, that our particles are in a state A and that we now modify them to a state B differing from A by some amount, however small. Are we to expect that this infinitely small change of state will *abruptly* convert *all* passing particles into blocked partcles? According to the continuity principle there ought to be a *gradual* transition from the case $B = A$, with all B's passed, to the case $B \neq A$, with all B's rejected by the A-filter. That is, there ought to be intermediate cases of a "fractional equality," written B $\sim$ A, in which neither all B's pass nor all are blocked—cases, then, in which a "splitting" of the incident B-state particles into a passing and a blocked fraction takes place. The continuity postulate in application to the sharp contrast between equality and inequality thus leads to the same "splitting effect" by inference that quantum physicists have discovered by delicate microphysical experiments.

Let us further introduce the principle of reproducibility of the result of a measurement. In the above experiment it requires that a B-state particle that has passed the A-filter once will pass an A-filter again, the second time with certainty; that is, the B-particle must have "jumped" in its first passage to the new state A where it now remains (unless thrown into another state by a third test by means of a B- or C-filter). Similarly, a B- particle once rejected by the A-filter will be rejected again in another A-filter test; that is, it must have jumped from the state B to a state non-A, completely different from A. The observation that there is a definite statistical frequency ratio between passed and blocked particles shows, according to our previous argument, that those "quantum jumps" from B to A and/or non-A represent a true game of chance that cannot be referred to hidden deterministic causes.

One may supplement the postulates of continuity and reproducibility by a few other postulates of a simple and elementary sort and from there arrive by inference at the mathematical and conceptual schema known today as the quantum theory[2]—thereby confirming Bridgman's opinion that the roots of this theory should be discover-

---

[2] A. Landé. *Brit. J. Philos. Sci.*, **6**, 300, 1956. Also *Foundations of Quantum Theory, A Study in Continuity and Symmetry* (New Haven: Yale University Press, 1955).

able in the sphere of ordinary experience, and also confirming the statistical interpretation of Born, Heisenberg, and Bohr. When the first surprising quantum facts, such as $E = hv$, were brought to light, the theorists tried to explain them on the grounds of accepted principles of mechanics. When this attempt proved a failure, quantum theory with its various rules and prescriptions was finally accepted as not further reducible, as "fundamental." It also seemed so very convenient to listen to the positivistic siren song, that physicists should observe and describe, and not question *why* things are as they are. This negative attitude is accompanied today by ever repeated exhortations that the principle of complementarity is the most profound and sublime law of nature, applicable not only to microphysics but also to biology, psychology, and lately even to the relation between the sexes and among political power groups. In opposition to this cult it is hoped that the recently revived search for simple and general postulates *underlying* quantum theory may bring us one step nearer the goal of all scientific endeavor, which, according to a well-coined phrase of Bridgman's, is the goal of satisfying our curiosity.

4.   Determinism and the Cosmos

Dennis W. Sciama, Trinity College, Cambridge

As a physicist I have found the following working hypothesis very useful: violent controversy about a scientific problem is a sign that some simple essential consideration is missing. The polemic, as it were, tries to substitute for the missing point, but of course it never can. I think for instance that this has been so in discussions of Mach's principle of the origin of inertia, and also of the problem deducing irreversible macroscopic behavior from reversible microscopic laws.

Bridgman has reminded us that the physicists are conducting a violent controversy about the meaning of quantum mechanics. This situation is in striking contrast to that prevailing in classical mechanics; for although classical mechanics is known to be false, there is no dispute as to its meaning. It is only in quantum mechanics (which is known to be true!) that there is such a dispute. Application of the working hypothesis suggests that some simple point has still to be made. My aim in these remarks is to propose one possibility for this simple point, a proposal based mainly on the work of Dr. K. V. Roberts.

The basic way in which quantum mechanics differs from classical mechanics is the following: our inferences about the future *must* be expressed in terms of probabilities. This introduction of probability would enable us to make the calculation.

With this state of affairs in mind, let us make a new assumption. Let us suppose that in nature systems are deterministic in the sense that we can calculate the state of a system at time *t* if we know enough boundary conditions referring to times other than *t;* but let us differ from classical mechanics by supposing that nature is so constructed that, roughly speaking, half the boundary conditions *must* refer to the past and half to the future of the moment *t*. In other words, we assume that nature is such that "mixed" boundary conditions are always needed.

Presumably a system with such properties would be called deterministic. This is a matter of definition, of course; what is really important is that the behavior of the system is as well defined and intelligible as that of a system obeying classical mechanics. But now we must ask: How would a "mixed" system appear to an observer who himself is part of the system?

Now, such an observer, for reasons that cannot be elaborated here but that have to do with the second law of thermodynamics, is acquainted only with the past. Hence if he attempts to calculate the state of a system at a time *t* in his future, he will find that he cannot do so, for he does not know all the boundary conditions. His knowledge of the past boundary conditions will delimit the possibilities considerably, but it is clear that to the observer the system will appear to contain indeterminate elements.

What sort of a theory will such an observer devise? In effect he will be forced to average over all those future boundary conditions that are compatible with his present knowledge. (Of course, at first he will not realize that this is what he is doing.) That is to say, he will be forced to introduce a probability calculus to account for his observations. The suggestion is that this probability calculus is just quantum mechanics.

In this way the correctness of quantum mechanics can be reconciled with a deterministic universe. In the language of von Neumann, there are hidden variables; they escape his ban because they refer to the future.

We are now in a position to answer the question: Is quantum mechanical probability subjective or objective? We have seen that the probability arises from the observer's ignorance of some of the determining conditions. The probability is therefore subjective.

So far the discussion has been academic in the sense that no new physical results have emerged. However there is an interesting possibility in this direction. For on the view presented here quantum mechanics is no longer a primitive theory; it is a formalism that is derived from a more basic theory. Now, Planck's constant, h, is a measure of the "amount" of deviation from classical mechanics. In quantum mechanics as it stands today the numerical value of this constant is completely arbitrary. However, if quantum mechanics is deducible from a more basic theory, then presumably h, which is here a measure of our ignorance of the future, will be expressed in terms of quantities fundamental to the basic theory. Such a relation could be tested experimentally, and so the theory could be checked.

PART III   Determinism and
Responsibility in Law and Ethics

1. Legal Responsibility and Excuses

H. L. A. Hart, Oxford University

I

It is characteristic of our own and all advanced legal systems that the individual's liability to punishment, at any rate for serious crimes carrying severe penalties, is made by law to depend on, among other things, certain mental conditions. These conditions can best be expressed in negative form as *excusing* conditions: the individual is not liable to punishment if at the time of his doing what would otherwise be a punishable act he is, say, unconscious, mistaken about the physical consequences of his bodily movements or the nature or qualities of the thing or persons affected by them, or, in some cases, if he is subjected to threats or other gross forms of coercion or is the victim of certain types of mental disease. This is a list, not meant to be complete, giving broad descriptions of the principal excusing conditions; the exact definition of these and their precise character and scope must be sought in the detailed exposition of our criminal law. If an individual breaks the law when none of the excusing conditions are present, he is ordinarily said to have acted of "his own free will," "of his own accord," "voluntarily"; or it might be said, "He could have helped doing what he did." If the determinist[1] has anything to say on this subject, it must be because he makes two claims. The first claim is that it may be true—though we cannot at present and may never be able to show that it is true—that human conduct (including in that expression not only actions involving the movements of the human body but its psychological elements or components such as decisions, choices, experiences of desire, effort, etc.) are subject to certain types of law, where law is to be understood in the sense of a scientific law. The second claim is that, if human conduct so understood is in fact subject to such laws (though

[1] Earlier papers in this session will doubtless have specified the variety of theories or claims that shelter under the label "determinism." For many purposes it is necessary to distinguish among them, especially on the question whether the elements in human conduct that are said to be "determined" are regarded as the product of sufficient conditions, or sets of jointly sufficient conditions, which include the individual's character. I think, however, that the defense I make in this paper of the rationality, morality, and justice of qualifying criminal responsibility by excusing conditions will be compatible with any form of determinism that satisfies the two following sets of requirements.

A. The determinist must not deny (*a*) those *empirical* facts that at present we treat as proper grounds for saying, "He did what he chose," "His choice was effective," "He got what he chose," "That was the result of his choice," etc; (*b*) the fact that when we get what we chose to have, live our lives as we have chosen, and particularly when we obtain by a choice what we have judged to be the lesser of two evils, this is a source of satisfaction; (*c*) the fact that we are often able to predict successfully and on reasonable evidence that our choice will be effective over certain periods in relation to certain matters.

B. The determinist does not assert and could not truly assert that we *already know* the laws that he says may exist or (in some versions) *must* exist. Determinists differ on the question whether or not the laws are sufficiently simple (*a*) for human beings to discover, (*b*) for human beings to use for the prediction of their own and others' conduct. But as long as it is not asserted that we know these laws I do not think this difference of opinion important here. Of course if we knew the laws and could use them for the detailed and exact prediction of our own and others' conduct, *deliberation* and *choice* would become pointless, and perhaps in such circumstances there could not (logically) be "deliberation" or "choice."

at the present time we do not know it to be so), the distinction we draw between one who acts under excusing conditions and one who acts when none are present becomes unimportant, if not absurd. Consequently, to allow punishment to depend on the presence or absence of excusing conditions, or to think it justified when they are absent but not when they are present, is absurd, meaningless, irrational, or unjust, or immoral, or perhaps all of these.

My principal object in this paper is to draw attention to the analogy between conditions that are treated by criminal law as *excusing* conditions and certain similar conditions that are treated in another branch of the law as *invalidating* certain civil transactions such as wills, gifts, contracts, and marriages. If we consider this analogy, I think we can see that there is a rationale for our insistence on the importance of excusing conditions in criminal law that no form of determinism that I, at any rate, can construct could impugn; and this rationale seems to me superior at many points to the two main accounts or explanations that in Anglo-American jurisprudence have been put forward as the basis of the recognition of excusing conditions in criminal responsibility.

In this preliminary section, however, I want to explain why I shall not undertake the analysis or elucidation of the meaning of such expressions as "He did it voluntarily," "He acted of his own free will," "He could have helped doing it," "He could have done otherwise." I do not, of course, think the analysis of these terms unimportant: indeed I think we owe the progress that has been made, at least in determining what the "free will problem" is, to the work of philosophers who have pursued this analysis. Perhaps it may be shown that statements of the form "He did it of his own free will" or "He could have done otherwise," etc., are not logically incompatible with the existence of the type of laws the determinist claims may exist; if they do exist, it may not follow that statements of the kind quoted are always false, for it may be that these statements are true given certain conditions, which need not include the nonexistence of any such laws.

Here, however, I shall not attempt to carry further any such inquiries into the meaning of these expressions or to press the view I have urged elsewhere, that the expression "voluntary action" is best understood as excluding the presence of the various excuses. So I will not deal here with a determinist who is so incautious as to say that it may be false that anyone has ever acted "voluntarily," "of his own free will," or "could have done otherwise than he did." It will help clarify our conception of criminal responsibility, I think, if I confront a more cautious skeptic who, without committing himself as to the meaning of those expressions or their logical or linguistic dependence on, or independence of, the negation of those types of law to which the determinist refers, yet criticizes our allocation of responsibility by reference to excusing conditions. This more cautious determinist says that, whatever the expressions "voluntary" etc. may mean, unless we have reasonable grounds for thinking there are no such laws, the distinctions drawn by these expressions cannot be regarded as of any importance, and there can be neither reason nor justice in allowing punishment to depend on the presence or absence of excusing conditions.

II

In the criminal law of every modern state responsibility for serious crimes is excluded or "diminished" by some of the conditions we have referred to as "excusing conditions." In Anglo-American criminal law this is the doctrine that a "subjective element," or "mens rea," is required for criminal responsibility, and it is because of this doctrine that a criminal trial may involve investigations into the sanity of the accused, into what he knew, believed, or foresaw; into the questions whether or not he was subject to coercion by threats or provoked into passion, or was prevented by disease or transitory loss of consciousness from controlling the movements of his body or muscles. These matters come up under the heads known to lawyers as Mistake, Accident, Provocation, Duress, and Insanity, and are most clearly and dramatically exemplified when the charge is one of murder or manslaughter.

Though this general doctrine underlies the criminal law, no legal system in practice admits without qualification the principle that *all* criminal responsibility is excluded by *any* of the excusing conditions. In Anglo-American law this principle is qualified in two ways.

First, our law admits crimes of "strict liability."[2] These are crimes where it is no defense to show that the accused, in spite of the exercise of proper care, was ignorant of the facts that made his act illegal. Here he is liable to punishment even though he did not intend to commit an act answering the definition of the crime. These are for the most part petty offences contravening statutes that require the maintenance of standards in the manufacture of goods sold for consumption; e.g., a statute forbidding the sale of adulterated milk. Such offenses are usually punishable with a fine and are sometimes said by jurists who object to strict liability not to be criminal in any "real" sense. Secondly, even in regard to crimes where liability is not "strict," so that mistake or accident rendering the accused's action *unintentional* would provide an excuse, many legal systems do not accept some of the other conditions we have listed as excluding liability to punishment. This is so for a variety of reasons.

For one thing, it is clear that not only lawyers but scientists and plain men differ as to the relevance of some excusing conditions, and this lack of agreement is usually expressed as a difference of view regarding what kind of factor limits the human *capacity* to control behavior. Views so expressed have indeed changed with the advance of knowledge about the human mind. Perhaps most people are now persuaded that it is possible for a man to have volitional control of his muscles and also to know the physical character of his movements and their consequences for himself and others, and yet be *unable* to resist the urge or temptation to perform a certain act; yet many think this incapacity exists only if it is associated with well-marked physiological or neurological symptoms or independently definable psychological disturbances. And perhaps there are still some who hold a modified form of the Platonic doctrine that Virtue is Knowledge and believe that the possession of knowledge[3] (and

---

[2] For an illuminating discussion of strict liability, see the opinion of Justice Jackson in *Morisetts v. United States* (1952) 342 U.S. 246; 96 L. Ed. 288; 78 S. Ct. 241. Also Sayre, "Public Welfare Offences," 33 *Col. L. Rev.* 58; Hall, *Principles of Criminal Law* (Indianapolis: Bobbs-Merrill Co., 1947), chap. x.

[3] This view is often defended by the assertion that the mind is an "integrated whole," that if the capacity for self-control is absent, knowledge must also be absent. See Hall, *op. cit.,* p. 524: "Diseased volition does not exist apart from diseased intelligence"; also reference to the "integration theory," chap. xiv.

muscular control) is per se a sufficient condition of the capacity to comply with the law.[4]

Another reason limiting the scope of the excusing conditions is difficulty of *proof*. Some of the mental elements involved are much easier to prove than others. It is relatively simple to show that an agent lacked either generally or on a particular occasion volitional muscular control; it is somewhat more difficult to show that he did not know certain facts either about present circumstances (e.g., that a gun was loaded) or the future (that a man would step into the line of fire); it is much more difficult to establish whether or not a person was deprived of "self-control" by passion provoked by others, or by partial mental disease. As we consider these different cases, not only do we reach much vaguer concepts, but we become progressively more dependent on the agent's own statements about himself, buttressed by inferences from common-sense generalizations about human nature, such as that men are capable of self-control when confronted with an open till but not when confronted with a wife in adultery. The law is accordingly much more cautious in admitting "defects of the will" than "defect in knowledge" as qualifying or excluding criminal responsibility. Further difficulties of proof may cause a legal system to limit its inquiry into the agent's "subjective condition" by asking what a "reasonable man" would in the circumstances have known or foreseen, or by asking whether "a reasonable man" in the circumstances would have been deprived (say, by provocation) or self-control; and the system may then impute to the agent such knowledge or foresight or control.[5]

For these practical reasons no simple identification of the necessary mental subjective elements in responsibility, with the full list of excusing conditions, can be made; and in all systems far greater prominence is given to the more easily provable elements of volitional control of muscular movement and knowledge of circum-

---

[4] English judges have taken different sides on the issue whether a man can be said to have "lost self-control," and killed another while in that condition, if he knew what he was doing and killed his victim intentionally. See *Holmes v. D.P.P.* (1946) A.C. 597 (Lord Simon) and *A.G. for Ceylon v. Kumarasinghege v. Don John Perera* (1953) A.C. 200 (Lord Goddard).

[5] But see for a defense of the "reasonable man" test (in cases of alleged provocation) Royal Commission on Capital Punishment, pp. 51–56 (ss 139–145). This defense is not confined to the difficulties of proof.

stances or consequences than to the other more elusive elements. Hence it is true that legal recognition of the importance of excusing conditions is never unqualified; the law, like every other human institution, has to compromise with other values besides whatever value is incorporated in the recognition of some conditions as excusing. Sometimes, of course, it is not clear, when "strict liability" is imposed, what value (social welfare?) is triumphant, and there has consequently been much criticism of this as an odious and useless departure from proper principles of liability.

Modern systems of law are however also concerned with most of the conditions we have listed as excusing conditions in another way. Besides the criminal law that requires men to do or abstain from certain actions whether they wish to or not, all legal systems contain rules of a different type that provide legal facilities whereby individuals can give effect to their wishes by entering into certain transactions that alter their own and/or others' legal position (rights, duties, status, etc.). Examples of these civil transactions (acts in the law, *Rechtsgeschäfte*) are wills, contracts, gifts, marriage. If a legal system did not provide facilities allowing individuals to give legal effect to their choices in such areas of conduct, it would fail to make one of the law's most distinctive and valuable contributions to social life. But here too most of the mental conditions we have mentioned are recognized by the law as important not primarily as *excusing* conditions but as *invalidating* conditions. Thus a will, a gift, a marriage, and (subject to many complex exceptions) a contract may be invalid if the party concerned was insane, mistaken about the legal character of the transaction or some "essential" term of it, or if he was subject to duress, coercion, or the undue influence of other persons. These are the obvious analogues of mistake, accident, coercion, duress, insanity, admitted by criminal law as excusing conditions. Analogously, the recognition of such conditions as invalidating civil transactions is qualified or limited by other principles. Those who enter in good faith into bilateral transactions of the kind mentioned with persons who appear normal (i.e., not subject to any of the relevant invalidating conditions) must be protected, as must third parties who may have purchased interests originating from a transaction that on the face of it seemed normal. Hence a technique has been introduced to safeguard such persons. This includes principles precluding, say, a party who has entered into a transaction by some mistake from making this the basis of his defense against one who honestly took his words at face value and justifiably relied on them; there are also distinctions between transactions wholly invalidated *ab initio* (void) and those that are valid until denounced (voidable) to protect those who have relied on the transaction's normal form.

III

The similarity between the law's insistence on certain mental elements for both criminal responsibility and the validity of acts in the law is clear. Why, then, do we value a system of social control that takes mental condition into account? Let us start with criminal law and its excusing conditions. What is so precious in its attention to these, and what would be lost if it gave this up? What precisely is the ground of our dissatisfaction with "strict liability" in criminal law? To these fundamental questions, there still are, curiously enough, many quite discordant answers, and I propose to consider two of them before suggesting an answer that would stress the analogy with civil transactions.

The first general answer takes this form. It is said that the importance of excusing conditions in criminal responsibility is derivative, and it derives from the more fundamental requirement that for criminal responsibility there must be "moral culpability," which would not exist where the excusing conditions are present. On this view the maxim *actus non est reus nisi mens sit rea* means a morally evil mind. Certainly traces of this view are to be found in scattered observations of English and American judges—in phrases such as "an evil mind with regard to that which he is doing," "a bad mind," "there must be an act done not merely unguardedly or accidentally, without an evil mind."[6] Some of these well-known formulations were perhaps careless statements of the quite different principle that *mens rea* is an intention to commit an act that is wrong in the sense of legally forbidden. But the same view has been reasserted in general terms in England by Lord Justice Denning: "In order that an act

[6] Lord Esher in *Lee v. Dangar* (1892) 2 Q.B. 337.

should be punishable it must be morally blameworthy, it must be a sin."[7] Most English lawyers would however now agree with Sir James FitzJames Stephen that the expression *mens rea* is unfortunate, though too firmly established to be expelled, just because it misleadingly suggests that in general moral culpability is essential to a crime, and they would assent to the criticism expressed by a later judge that "the true translation of *mens rea* is an intention to do the act which is made penal by statute or common law."[8] Yet, in spite of this, the view has been urged by a distinguished American contemporary writer on criminal law, Professor Jerome Hall, in his important and illuminating *Principles of Criminal Law,* that *moral* culpability is the basis of responsibility in crime. Again and again in Chapters V and VI of his book Professor Hall asserts that, though the goodness or badness of the *motive* with which a crime is committed may not be relevant, the general principle of liability, except of course where liability is unfortunately "strict" and so any mental element must be disregarded, is the "intentional or reckless doing of a *morally* wrong act."[9] This is declared to be the essential meaning of *mens rea:* "though *mens rea* differs in different crimes there is one common essential element, namely, the *voluntary* doing of a *morally* wrong act forbidden by the law."[10] On this view the law inquires into the mind in criminal cases in order to secure that no one shall be punished in the absence of the basic condition of *moral* culpability. For it is just only to "punish those who have intentionally committed *moral* wrongs proscribed by law."[11]

Now, if this theory were merely a theory as to what the criminal law of a good society should be, it would not be possible to refute it, for it represents a moral preference: namely that legal punishment should be administered only where a "morally wrong" act has been done—though I think such plausibility as it would have even as an ideal is due to a confusion. But of course Professor Hall's

[7] Denning, *The Changing Law* (London: Stevens, 1953), p. 12.

[8] *Allard v. Selfridge* (1925) 1 K.B. 137. (Shearman.) This is quoted by Glanville Williams in *The Criminal Law* (London: Stevens, 1953), p. 29, note 3, where the author comments that the judge should have added "recklessness."

[9] Hall, *op. cit.,* p. 166.

[10] *Ibid.,* p. 167.

[11] *Ibid.,* p. 149.

doctrine does not fit any actual system of criminal law because in every such system there are necessarily many actions (quite apart from the cases of "strict liability") that if voluntarily done are criminally punishable, although our moral code may be either silent as to their moral quality, or divided. Very many offenses are created by legislation designed to give effect to a particular economic scheme (e.g., a state monopoly of road or rail transport), the utility or moral character of which may be genuinely in dispute. An offender against such legislation can hardly be said to be morally guilty or to have intentionally committed a moral wrong, still less "a sin" *proscribed* by law;[12] yet if he has broken such laws "voluntarily" (to use Professor Hall's expression), which in practice means that he was not in any of the excusing conditions, the requirements of *justice* are surely satisfied. Doubts about the justice of the punishment would begin only if he were punished even though he was at the time of the action in one of the excusing conditions; for what is essential is that the offender, if he is to be *fairly* punished, must have acted "voluntarily," and not that he must have committed some moral offense. In addition to such requirements of justice in the individual case, there is of course, as we shall see, a different type of requirement as to the *general* character of the laws.

It is important to see what has led Professor Hall and others to the conclusion that the basis of criminal responsibility *must* be moral culpability ("the voluntary doing of a morally wrong act"), for latent in this position, I think, is a false dilemma. The false dilemma is that criminal liability *must* either be "strict"—that is, based on nothing more than the outward conduct of the accused—or *must* be based on moral culpability. On this view there is no third alternative and so there can be no reason for inquiring into the state of mind of the accused—"inner facts," as Professor Hall terms them—except for the purpose of establishing *moral* guilt. To be understood all theories should be examined in the context of argument in which they are advanced, and it is important to notice that Professor Hall's

---

[12] "The criminal quality of an act cannot be discovered by intuition: nor can it be discovered by any standard but one. Is the act prohibited with penal consequences? Morality and criminality are far from coextensive nor is the sphere of criminality part of a more exclusive field covered by morality unless morals necessarily disapproves of the acts prohibited by the state, in which case the argument moves in a circle." Lord Atkin, *Proprietory Articles Trade Association v. A.G. for Canada* (1931) A.C. 324.

doctrine was developed mainly by way of criticism of the so-called objective theory of liability, which was developed, though not very consistently, by Chief Justice Holmes in his famous essays on common law.[13] Holmes asserted that the law did not consider, and need not consider, in administering punishment what in fact the accused intended, but that it imputed to him the intention that an "ordinary man," equipped with ordinary knowledge, would be taken to have had in acting as the accused did. Holmes in advocating this theory of "objective liability" used the phrase "inner facts" and frequently stressed that *mens rea,* in the sense of the actual wickedness of the party, was unnecessary. So he often identified "mental facts" with moral guilt and also identified the notion of an objective standard of liability with the rejection of *moral* culpability as a basis of liability. This terminology was pregnant with confusion. It fatally suggests that there are only two alternatives: to consider the mental condition of the accused only to find moral culpability or not to consider it at all. But we are not impaled on the horns of any such dilemma: there are independent reasons, apart from the question of moral guilt, why a legal system should require a voluntary action as a condition of responsibility. These reasons I shall develop in a moment and merely summarize here by saying that the principle (1) that it is unfair and unjust to punish those who have not "voluntarily" broken the law is a moral principle quite distinct from the assertion (2) that it is wrong to punish those who have not "voluntarily committed a moral wrong proscribed by law."

The confusion that suggests the false dilemma—either "objective" standards (strict liability) or liability based on the "inner fact" of *moral* guilt—is, I think, this. We would all agree that unless a legal system was as a whole morally defensible, so that its existence was better than the chaos of its collapse, and more good than evil was secured by maintaining and enforcing laws in general, these laws should not be enforced, and no one should be punished for breaking them. It *seems* therefore to follow, but does not, that we should not punish anyone unless in breaking the law he has done something morally wrong; for it looks as if the mere fact that a law has been voluntarily broken were not enough to justify punishment; the extra element required is "moral culpability," at least in the sense that we should have done something morally wrong. What we need to

[13] Holmes, *The Common Law,* Lecture II, "The Criminal Law."

escape confusion here is a distinction between two sets of questions. The first is a general question about the moral value of the laws: Will enforcing them produce more good than evil? If they do, then it is morally permissible to enforce them by punishing those who have broken them, unless in any given case there is some "excuse." The second is a particular question concerning individual cases: Is it right or just to punish this particular person? Is he to be excused on account of his mental condition because it would be unjust—in view of his lack of knowledge or control—to punish him? The first, general question with regard to each law is a question for the legislature; the second, arising in particular cases, is for the judge. And the question of responsibility arises only at the judicial stage. One necessary condition of the just application of a punishment is normally expressed by saying that the agent "could have helped" doing what he did, and hence the need to inquire into the "inner facts" is dictated not by the moral principle that only the doing of an *immoral* act may be legally punished, but by the moral principle that no one should be punished who could not help doing what he did. This is a necessary condition (unless strict liability is admitted) for the moral propriety of legal punishment and no doubt also for moral censure; in this respect law and morals are similar. But this similarity as to the one essential condition that there must be a "voluntary" action if legal punishment or moral censure is to be morally permissible does not mean that legal punishment is morally permissible only where the agent has done something morally wrong. I think that the use of the word "fault" in juristic discussion to designate the requirement that liability be excluded by excusing conditions may have blurred the important distinction between the assertions that (1) it is morally permissible to punish only voluntary actions and (2) it is morally permissible to punish only voluntary commission of a moral wrong.

IV

Let me now turn to a second explanation of the laws concerned with the "inner facts" of mental life as a condition of responsibility.

This is a Benthamite theory that I shall name the "economy of threats" and is the contention that the required conditions of responsibilty—e.g., that the agent knew what he was doing, was not subject to gross coercion or duress, was not mad or a small child—are simply the conditions that must be satisfied if the threat to punish announced by the criminal law is to have any effect and if the system is to be efficient in securing the maintenance of law at the least cost in pain. This theory is stated most clearly by Bentham; it is also to be found in Austin and in the report of the great Criminal Law Commission of 1833 of which he was a member. In a refined form it is implicit in many contemporary attempted "dissolutions" of the problem of free will. Many accept this view as a common-sense utilitarian explanation of the importance that we attribute to excusing conditions. It appeals most to the utilitarian and to the determinist, and it is interesting to find that Professor Glanville Williams in his recent admirable work on "The General Principles of Criminal Law,"[14] when he wished to explain the exemption of the insane from legal responsibility compatibly with "determinism," did so by reference to this theory.

Yet the doctrine is an incoherent one at certain points, I think, and a departure from, rather than a elucidation of, the moral insistence that criminal liability should generally be conditional on the absence of excusing conditions. Bentham's best statement of the theory is in Chapter XIII of his *Principles of Morals and Legislation:* "Cases in Which Punishment Must be Inefficacious." The cases he lists, besides those where the law is made ex post facto or not adequately promulgated, fall into two main classes. The first class consists of cases in which the penal threat of punishment could not prevent a person from performing an action forbidden by the law *or any action of the same sort;* these are the cases of infancy and insanity in which the agent, according to Bentham, has not the "state or disposition of mind on which the prospect of evils so distant as those which are held forth by the law" has the effect of influencing his conduct. The second class consists of cases in which the law's threat could not have had any effect on the agent in relation to the *particular* act committed because of his lack of knowledge or control. What

14 Williams, *op. cit.,* pp. 346–47.

is wrong in punishing a man under both these types of mental conditions is that the punishment is wasteful; suffering is caused to the accused who is punished in circumstances where it could do no good.

In discussing the defense of insanity Professor Glanville Williams applies this theory in a way that brings out its consistency not only with a wholly utilitarian outlook on punishment but with determinism.

> For mankind in the mass it is impossible to tell whom the threat of punishment will restrain and whom it will not; for most it will succeed, for some it will fail. And the punishment must then be applied to those criminals in order to maintain the threat to persons generally. Mentally deranged persons, however, can be separated from the mass by scientific tests, and being a defined class their segregation from punishment does not impair the efficacy of the sanction for people generally.[15]

The point made here is that, if, for example, the mentally deranged (scientifically tested) are exempted, criminals will not be able to exploit this exemption to free themselves from liability, since they cannot bring themselves within its scope and so will not feel free to commit crimes with impunity. This is said in order to justify the exemption of the insane consistently with the "tenet" of determinism, in spite of the fact that from a determinist viewpoint

> every impulse if not in fact resisted was in those circumstances irresistible. A so-called irresistible impulse is simply one in which the desire to perform a particular act is not influenced by other factors like the threat of punishment. . . . on this definition every crime is the result of an irresistible impulse.

This theory is designed not merely to fit a utilitarian theory of punishment, but also the view that it is always false, if not senseless, to say that a criminal could have helped doing what he did. So on this theory when we inquire into the mental state of the accused, we do not do so to answer the question, Could he help it? Nor of course to answer the question, Could the threat of punishment have been effective in his case?—for we know that it was not. The theory presents us with a far simpler conceptual scheme for dealing with the whole matter, since it does not involve the seemingly counterfactual speculation regarding what the accused "could have done." On this

15 Williams, *loc. cit.*

theory we inquire into the state of mind of the accused simply to find out whether he belongs to a defined class of persons whose exemption from punishment, if allowed, will not weaken the effect on others of the general threat of punishment made by the law. So there is no question of its being unjust or unfair to punish a particular criminal or to exempt him from punishment. Once the crime has been committed the decision to punish or not has nothing to do with any moral claim or right of the criminal to have the features of his case considered, but only with the causal efficacy of his punishment on others. On this view the rationale of excuses is not (to put it shortly) that the accused should in view of his mental condition be excused whatever the effect of this on others, but rather the mere fact that excusing him will not harm society by reducing the efficacy of the law's threats for others. So the relevance of the criminal's mental condition is purely the question of the effect on others of his punishment or exemption from it.

This is certainly paradoxical enough. It seems to destroy the entire notion that in punishing we must be just to the particular criminal in front of us and that the purpose of excusing conditions is to protect him from society's claims. But apart from paradox the doctrine that we consider the state of a man's mind only to see if punishment is required in order to maintain the efficacy of threats for others is vitiated by a *non sequitur*. Before a man does a criminal action we may know that he is in such a condition that the threats cannot operate on him, either because of some temporary condition or because of a disease; but it does not follow—because the *threat* of punishment in his case, and in the case of others like him, is useless— that his *punishment* in the sense of the official administration of penalties will also be unnecessary to maintain the efficacy of threats for others at its highest. It may very well be that, if the law contained no explicit exemptions from responsibility on the score of ignorance, accident, mistake, or insanity, many people who now take a chance in the hope that they will bring themselves, if discovered, within these exempting provisions would in fact be deterred. It is indeed a perfectly familiar fact that pleas of loss of consciousness or other abnormal mental states, or of the existence of some other excusing condition, are frequently and sometimes successfully advanced where there is no real basis for them, for the difficulties of disproof are often considerable. The uselessness of a *threat* against a given individual or class does not entail that the *punishment* of that individual or class cannot be required to maintain in the highest degree the efficacy of threats for others. It may in fact be the case that to make liability to punishment dependent on the absence of excusing conditions is the most efficient way of maintaining the laws with the least cost in pain. But it is not *obviously* or *necessarily* the case.

It is clear, I think, that if we were to base our views of criminal responsibility on the doctrine of the economy of threats, we should misrepresent altogether the character of our moral preference for a legal system that requires mental conditions of responsibility over a system of total strict liability or entirely different methods of social control such as hypnosis, propaganda, or conditioning.

To make this intelligible we must cease to regard the law as merely a causal factor in human behavior differing from others only in the fact that it produces its effect through the medium of the mind; for it is clear that we look on excusing conditions as something that *protects* the individual against the claims of the rest of society. Recognition of their excusing force may lead to a lower, not a higher, level of efficacy of threats; yet—and this is the point—we could not regard that as sufficient ground for abandoning this protection of the individual; or if we did, it would be with the recognition that we had sacrificed one principle to another; for more is at stake than the single principle of maintaining the laws at their most efficacious level. We must cease, therefore, to regard the law simply as a system of stimuli goading the individual by its threats into conformity. Instead I shall suggest a mercantile analogy. Consider the law not as a system of stimuli but as what might be termed a *choosing* system in which individuals can find out, in general terms at least, the costs they have to pay if they act in certain ways. This done, let us ask what value this system would have in social life and why we should regret its absence. I do not of course mean to suggest that it is a matter of indifference whether we obey the law or break it and pay the penalty. Punishment *is* different from a mere "tax on a course of conduct." What I do mean is that the conception of the law simply as goading individuals into desired courses of behavior is inadequate and misleading; what a legal system that makes liability generally depend on excusing conditions does is to guide individuals' choices as to behavior by presenting them with reasons for exercising choice in the direction of obedience, but leaving them to choose.

It is at this this point that I would stress the analogy between the mental conditions that excuse from criminal responsibility and the mental conditions that are regarded as invalidating civil transactions such as wills, gifts, contracts, marriages, and the like. The latter institutions provide individuals with two inestimable advantages in relation to those areas of conduct they cover. These are (1) the advantage to the individual of determining by his choice what the future shall be and (2) the advantage of being able to predict what the future will be. For these institutions enable the individual (1) to bring into operation the coercive forces of the law so that those legal arrangements he has chosen shall be carried into effect and (2) to plan the rest of his life with a certainty or at least the confidence (in a legal system that is working normally) that the arrangements he has made will in fact be carried out. By these devices the individual's choice is brought into the legal system and allowed to determine its future operations in certain areas, thereby giving him a type of indirect coercive control over, and a power to foresee the development of, official life. This he would not have "naturally"; that is, apart from these legal institutions.

In brief, the function of these institutions of private law is to render effective the individual's preferences in certain areas. It is therefore clear why in this sphere the law treats the mental factors of, say, mistake, ignorance of the nature of the transaction, coercion, undue influence, or insanity as invalidating such civil transactions. For a transaction entered into under such conditions will not represent a real choice: the individual, might have chosen one course of events and by the transaction procured another (cases of mistake, ignorance, etc.), or he might have chosen to enter the transaction without coolly and calmly thinking out what he wanted (undue influence), or he might have been subjected to the threats of another who had imposed *his* choices (coercion).

To see the value of such institutions in rendering effective the individual's considered and informed choices as to what on the whole shall happen, we have but to conduct the experiment of imagining their absence: a system where no mental conditions would be recognized as invalidating such transactions and the consequent loss of control over the future that the individual would suffer. That such institutions *do* render individual choices effective and increase the powers of individuals to predict the course of events is simply a matter of empirical fact, and no form of "determinism," of course, can show this to be false or illusory. If a man makes a will to which the law gives effect after his death, this is not, of course, merely a case of *post hoc:* we have enough empirical evidence to show that this was an instance of a regularity sufficient to have enabled us to predict the outcome with reasonable probability, at least in some cases, and to justify us, therefore, in interpreting this outcome as a consequence of making the will. There is no reason why we should not describe the situation as one where the testator *caused* the outcome of the distribution made. Of course the testator's choice in this example is only one prominent member of a complex set of conditions, of which all the other members were as necessary for the production of the outcome as his choice. Science may indeed show (1) that this set of conditions also includes conditions of which we are at the present moment quite ignorant and (2) that the testator's choice itself was the outcome of some set of jointly sufficient conditions of which we have no present knowledge. Yet neither of these two suppositions, even if they were verified, would make it false to say that the individual's choice did determine the results, or make illusory the satisfaction got (*a*) from the knowledge that this kind of thing is possible, (*b*) from the exercise of such choice. And if determinism does not entail that satisfactions (*a*) or (*b*) are obtainable, I for one do not understand how it could affect the wisdom, justice, rationality, or morality of the system we are considering.

If with this in mind we turn back to criminal law and its excusing conditions, we can regard their function as a mechanism for similarly maximizing within the framework of coercive criminal law the efficacy of the individual's informed and considered choice in determining the future and also his power to predict that future. We must start, of course, with the need for criminal law and its sanctions as at least some check on behavior that threatens society. This implies a belief that the criminal law's threats actually do diminish the frequency of antisocial behavior, and no doubt this belief may be said to be based on inadequate evidence. However, we must clearly take it as our starting point: if this belief is wrong, it is so because of lack of empirical evidence and not because it contradicts any form of determinism. Then we can see that by attaching excusing conditions to criminal responsibility, we provide each individual with something he would not have if we made the system of criminal law operate on a basis of total "strict liability." First, we maximize the individual's power at any time to predict the likelihood that the sanctions of the criminal law will be applied to him. Secondly, we introduce the individual's choice as one of the operative factors determining whether or not these sanctions shall be applied to him. He can weigh the cost to him of obeying the law—and of sacrificing some satisfaction in order to obey—against obtaining that satisfaction at the cost of paying "the penalty." Thirdly, by adopting this system of attaching excusing conditions we provide that, if the sanctions of the criminal law are applied, the pains of punishment will for each indivdiual represent the price of some satisfaction obtained from breach of law. This, of course, can sound like a very cold, if not immoral, attitude toward the criminal law, general obedience to which we regard as an essential part of a decent social order. But this attitude seems repellent only if we assume that all criminal laws are ones whose operation we approve. To be realistic we must also think of bad and repressive criminal laws; in South Africa, Nazi Germany, Soviet Russia, and no doubt else where, we might be thankful to have their badness mitigated by the fact that they fall only on those who have obtained a satisfaction from knowingly doing what they forbid.

Again, the value of these three factors can be realized if we conduct the *Gedankenexperiment* of imagining criminal law operating without excusing conditions. First, our power of predicting what will happen to us will be immeasurably diminshed; the likelihood that I shall choose to do the forbidden act (e.g., strike someone) and so incur the sanctions of the criminal law may not be very easy to calculate even under our system: as a basis for this prediction we have indeed only the knowledge of our own character and some estimate of the temptations life is likely to offer us. But if we are also to be liable if we strike someone by accident, by mistake, under coercrion, etc., the chances that we shall incur the sanctions are immeasurably increased. From our knowledge of the past career of our body considered as a *thing,* we cannot infer much as to the chances of its being brought into violent contact with another, and under a system that dispensed with the excusing condition of, say, accident (implying lack of intention), a collision alone would land us in jail. Secondly, our choice would condition what befalls us to a lesser extent. Thirdly, we should suffer sanctions without having obtained any satisfaction. Again, no form of determinism that I, at least, can construct can throw any doubt on, or show to be illusory, the real satisfaction that a system of criminal law incorporating excusing conditions provides for individuals in maximizing the effect of their choices within the framework of coercive law. The choices remain choices, the satisfactions remain satisfactions, and the consequences of choices remain the consequences of choices even if choices are determined and other "determinants" besides our choices condition the satisfaction arising from their being rendered effective in this way by the structure of the criminal law.

It is now important to contrast this view of excusing conditions with the Benthamite explanation I discussed in Part III of this paper. On that view excusing conditions were treated as conditions under which the law's threat could operate with maximum efficacy. They were recognized *not* because they ensured justice to individuals considered separately, but because sanctions administered under those conditions were believed more effective and economical of pain in securing the general conformity to law. If these beliefs as to the *efficacy* of excusing conditions could be shown false, then all reasons for recognizing them as conditions of criminal responsibility would disappear. On the present view, which I advocate, excusing conditions are accepted as independent of the efficacy of the system of threats. Instead it is conceded that recognition of these conditions may, and probably does, diminish that efficacy by increasing the number of conditions for criminal liability and hence giving opportunities for pretense on the part of criminals, or mistakes on the part of tribunals.

On this view excusing conditions are accepted as something that may conflict with the social utility of the law's threats; they are regarded as of moral importance because they provide for all individuals alike the satisfactions of a costing system. Recognition of excusing conditions is therefore seen as a matter of protection of the individual against the claims of society for the highest measure of protection from crime that can be obtained from a system of threats. In this way the criminal law respects the claims of the individual as such, or at least as a *choosing being,* and distributes its coercive sanctions in a way that reflects this respect for the individual. This surely is very central in the notion of justice and is *one,* though no doubt only one, among the many strands of principle that I think lie at the root of the preference for legal institutions conditioning liability by reference to excusing conditions.

I cannot, of course, by unearthing this principle claim to have solved everyone's perplexities. In particular, I do not know what to say to a critic who urges that I have shown only that the system in which excusing conditions are recognized protects the individual better against the claims of society than one in which no recognition is accorded to these factors. This seems to me to be enough; yet I cannot satisfy his complaint, if he makes it, that I have not shown that we are justified in punishing anyone *ever,* at all, under any conditions. He may say that even the criminal who has committed his crime in the most deliberate and calculating way and has shown himself throughout his life competent in maximizing what he thinks his own interests will be little comforted when he is caught and punished for some major crime. At *that* stage he will get little satisfaction if it is pointed out to him (1) that he has obtained some satisfaction from his crime, (2) that he knew that it was likely he would be punished and that he had decided to pay for his satisfaction by exposing himself to this risk, and (3) that the system under which he is punished is not one of strict liability, is not one under which a man who accidentally did what he did would also have suffered the penalities of the law.

V

I will add four observations *ex abundante cautela.*

1. The elucidation of the moral importance of the mental element in responsibility, and the moral odium of strict liability that I have indicated, must not be mistaken for a psychological theory of motivation. It does not answer the question, Why do people obey the

law? It does not assert that they obey only because they choose to obey rather than pay the cost. Instead, my theory answers the question, Why *should* we have a law with just these features? Human beings in the main do what the law requires without first choosing between the advantage and the cost of disobeying, and when they obey it is not usually from fear of the sanction. For most the sanction is important not because it inspires them with fear but because it offers a guarantee that the antisocial minority who would not otherwise obey will be coerced into obedience by fear. To obey without this assurance might, as Hobbes saw, be very foolish: it would be to risk going to the wall. However, the fact that only a few people, as things are, consider the question, Shall I obey or pay? does not in the least mean that the standing possibility of asking this question is unimportant: for it secures just those values for the individual that I have mentioned.

2. I must of course confront the objection the Marxist might make, that the excusing conditions, or indeed *mutatis mutandis* the invalidating conditions, of civil transactions are of no use to many individuals in society whose economic or social position is such that the difference between a law of strict liability and a law that recognizes excusing conditions is of no importance.

It is quite true that the fact that criminal law recognizes excusing mental conditions may be of no importance to a person whose economic condition is such that he cannot profit from the difference between a law against theft that is strict and one that incorporates excusing conditions. If starvation "forces" him to steal, the values the system respects and incorporates in excusing conditions are nothing to him. This is of course similar to the claim often made that the freedom that a political democracy of the Western type offers to its subjects is merely formal freedom, not real freedom, and leaves one free to starve. I regard this as a confusing way of putting what may be true under certain conditions: namely, that the freedoms the law offers may be *valueless* as playing no part in the happiness of persons who are too poor or weak to take advantage of them. The admission that the excusing conditions may be of no value to those who are below a minimum level of economic prosperity may mean, of course, that we should incorporate as a further excusing condition the pressure of gross forms of economic necessity. This point, though

valid, does not seem to me to throw doubt on the principle lying behind such excusing conditions as we do recognize at present, nor to
destroy their genuine value for those who are above the minimum
level of economic prosperity, for a difference between a system of
strict liability and our present system plays a part in their happiness.

3. The principle by reference to which I have explained the
moral importance of excusing conditions may help clarify an old
dispute, apt to spring up between lawyers on the one hand and
doctors and scientists on the other, about the moral basis of punishment.

From Plato to the present day there has been a recurrent insistence that if we were rational we would always look on crime as a
disease and address ourselves to its cure. We would do this not only
where a crime has actually been committed but where we find well-
marked evidence that it will be. We would take the individual and
treat him as a patient before the deed was done. Plato,[16] it will be
remembered, thought it superstitious to look back and go into questions of responsibility or the previous history of a crime except
when it might throw light on what was needed to cure the criminal.

Carried to its extreme, this doctrine is the program of Erewhon
where those with criminal tendencies were sent by doctors for indefinite periods of cure; punishment was displaced by a concept of
social hygiene. It is, I think, of some importance to realize why we
should object to this point of view, for both those who defend it
and those who attack it often assume that the *only* possible consistent alternative to Erewhon is a theory of punishment under which
it is justified simply as a return for the moral evil attributable to
the accused. Those opposed to the Erewhonian program are apt to
object that it disregards moral guilt as a necessary condition of a
just punishment and thus leads to a condition in which any person
may be sacrificed to the welfare of society. Those who defend an
Erewhonian view think that their opponents' objection must entail
adherence to the form of retributive punishment that regards punishment as a justified return for the moral evil in the criminal's action.

Both sides, I think, make a common mistake: there *is* a reason
for making punishment conditional on the commission of crime and
respecting excusing conditions, which are quite independent of the

16 Plato, *Protagoras,* 324; *Laws* 861, 865.

form of retributive theory that is often urged as the only alternative to Erewhon. Even if we regard the over-all purpose of punishment as that of protecting society by deterring persons from committing crimes and insist that the penalties we inflict be adapted to this end, we can in perfect consistency and with good reason insist that these punishments be applied only to those who have broken a law and to whom no excusing conditions apply. For this system will provide a measure of protection to individuals and will maximize their powers of prediction and the efficacy of their choices in the way that I have mentioned. To see this we have only to ask ourselves what in terms of these values we should lose (however much else we might gain) if social hygiene and a *system of compulsory treatment* for those with detectable criminal tendencies were throughout substituted for our system of punishment modified by excusing conditions. Surely the realization of what would be lost, and not a retributive theory of punishment, is all that is required as a reason for refusing to make the descent into Erewhon.

4. Finally, what I have written concerns only *legal* responsibility and the rationale of excuses in a legal system in which there are organized, coercive sanctions. I do not think the same arguments can be used to defend *moral* responsibility from the determinist, if it is in any danger from that source.

2.   Hard and Soft Determinism

Paul Edwards, New York University

In his essay "The Dilemma of Determinism," William James makes a distinction that will serve as a point of departure for my remarks. He there distinguishes between the philosophers he calls "hard" determinists and those he labels "soft" determinists. The former, the hard determinists, James tells us, "did not shrink from such words as fatality, bondage of the will, necessitation and the like." He quotes a famous stanza from Omar Khayyám as representing this kind of determinism:

> With earth's first clay they did the last man knead,
> And there of the last harvest sowed the seed.
> And the first morning of creation wrote
> What the last dawn of reckoning shall read.

Another of Omar's verses expresses perhaps even better the kind of theory that James has here in mind:

> Tis all a checker-board of nights and days,
> Where destiny with men for pieces plays;
> Thither and thither moves, and mates, and slays,
> And one by one back to the closet lays.

James mentioned no names other than Omar Khayyám. But there is little doubt that among the hard determinists he would have included Jonathan Edwards, Anthony Collins, Holbach, Priestley, Robert Owen, Schopenhauer, Freud, and also, if he had come a little earlier, Clarence Darrow.

James of course rejected both hard and soft determinism, but for hard determinism he had a certain respect: the kind of respect one sometimes has for an honest, straightforward adversary. For soft determinism, on the other hand, he had nothing but contempt, calling it a "quagmire of evasion." "Nowadays," he writes, "we have a *soft* determinism which abhors harsh words, and repudiating fatality, necessity, and even predetermination, says that its real name is 'freedom.' " From his subsequent observations it is clear that he would include among the evasionists not only neo-Hegelians like Green and Bradley but also Hobbes and Hume and Mill; and if he were alive today James would undoubtedly include Schlick and Ayer and Stevenson and Noel-Smith, not to mention some of the philosophers present in this room.

The theory James calls soft determinism, especially the Hume-Mill-Schlick variety of it, has been extremely fashionable during the last twenty-five years, while hardly anybody can be found today who has anything good to say for hard determinism. In opposition to this contemporary trend, I should like to strike a blow on behalf of hard determinism in my talk today. I shall also try to bring out exactly what is really at issue between hard and soft determinism. I think the nature of this dispute has frequently been misconceived chiefly because many writers, including James, have a very inaccurate notion of what is maintained by actual hard determinists, as distinct from the bogey men they set up in order to score an easy victory.

To begin with, it is necessary to spell more fully the main contentions of the soft determinists. Since it is the dominant form of soft determinism at the present time, I shall confine myself to the Hume-Mill-Schlick theory. According to this theory there is in the first place no contradiction whatsoever between determinism and the proposition that human beings are sometimes free agents. When we call an action "free" we never in any ordinary situation mean that it was uncaused; and this emphatically includes the kind of action about which we pass moral judgments. By calling an action "free" we mean that the agent was not compelled or constrained to perform it. Sometimes people act in a certain way because of threats or because they have been drugged or because of a posthypnotic suggestion or because of an irrational overpowering urge such as the one that makes a kleptomaniac steal something he does not really need. On such occasions human beings are not free agents. But on other occasions they act in certain ways because of their own rational desires, because of their own unimpeded efforts, because they have chosen to act in these ways. On these occasions they are free agents although their actions are just as much caused as actions that are not deemed free. In distinguishing between free and unfree actions we do not try to mark the presence and absence of causes but attempt to indicate the *kind* of causes that are present.

Secondly there is no antithesis between determinism and moral responsibility. When we judge a person morally responsible for a certain action, we do indeed presuppose that he was a free agent at the time of the action. But the freedom presupposed is not the contracausal freedom about which indeterminists go into such ecstatic raptures. It is nothing more than the freedom already mentioned— the ability to act according to one's choices or desires. Since determinism is compatible with freedom in this sense, it is also compatible with moral responsibility. In other words, the world is after all wonderful: we can be determinists and yet go on punishing our enemies and our children, and we can go on blaming ourselves, all without a bad intellectual conscience.

Mill, who was probably the greatest moralizer among the soft determinists, recognized with particular satisfaction the influence or alleged influence of one class of human desires. Not only, for example, does such a lowly desire as my desire to get a new car influence my conduct. It is equally true, or so at least Mill believed, that my desire to become a more virtuous person does on occasion influence my actions. By suitable training and efforts my desire to change my character may in fact bring about the desired changes. If Mill were alive today he might point to contemporary psychiatry as an illustration of his point. Let us suppose that I have an intense desire to become famous, but that I also have an intense desire to become a happier and more lovable person who, among other things, does not greatly care about fame. Let us suppose, furthermore, that I know of a therapy that can transform fame-seeking and unlovable into lovable and fame-indifferent character structures. If, now, I have enough money, energy, and courage, and if a few other conditions are fulfilled, my desire may actually lead to a major change in my character. Since we can, therefore, at least to some extent, form our own character, determinism according to Mill is compatible not only with judgments of moral responsibility about this or that particular *action* flowing from an unimpeded desire, but also, within limits, with moral judgments about the *character* of human beings.

I think that several of Mill's observations were well worth making and that James's verdict on his theory as a "quagmire of evasion" is far too derogatory. I think hard determinists have occasionally written in such a way as to suggest that they deny the causal efficacy of human desires and efforts. Thus Holbach wrote:

> You will say that I feel free. This is an illusion, which may be compared to that of the fly in the fable, who, lighting upon the pole of a heavy carriage, applauded himself for directing its course. Man, who thinks himself free, is a fly who imagines he has power to move the universe, while he is himself unknowingly carried along by it.

There is also the following passage in Schopenhauer:

> Every man, being what he is and placed in the circumstances which for the moment obtain, but which on their part also arise by strict necessity, can absolutely never do anything else than just what at that moment he does do. Accordingly, the whole course of a man's life,

in all its incidents great and small, is as necessarily predetermined as the course of a clock.

Voltaire expresses himself in much the same way in the article on "Destiny" in the *Philosophical Dictionary.*

> Everything happens through immutable laws, . . . everything is necessary. . . . "There are," some persons say, "some events which are necessary and others which are not." It would be very comic that one part of the world was arranged, and the other were not; that one part of what happens had to happen and that another part of what happens did not have to happen. If one looks closely at it, one sees that the doctrine contrary to that of destiny is absurd; but there are many people destined to reason badly; others not to reason at all, others to persecute those who reason. . . .
> . . . I necessarily have the passion for writing this, and you have the passion for condemning me; both of us are equally fools, equally the toy of destiny. Your nature is to do harm, mine is to love truth, and to make it public in spite of you.

Furthermore there can be little doubt that Hume and Mill and Schlick were a great deal clearer about the relation between motives and actions than the hard determinists, who either conceived it, like Collins, as one of logical necessity or, like Priestley and Voltaire and Schopenhauer, as necessarily involving coercion or constraint.

But when all is said and done, there remains a good deal of truth in James's charge that soft determinism is an evasion. For a careful reading of their works shows that none of the hard determinists really denied that human desires, efforts, and choices make a difference in the course of events. Any remarks to the contrary are at most temporary lapses. This, then, is hardly the point at issue. If it is not the point at issue, what is? Let me at this stage imagine a hard determinist replying to a champion of the Hume-Mill theory: "You are right," he would say, "in maintaining that some of our actions are caused by our desires and choices. But you do not pursue the subject far enough. You arbitrarily stop at the desires and volitions. We must not stop there. We must go on to ask where *they* come from; and if determinism is true there can be no doubt about the answer to this question. Ultimately our desires and our whole character are derived from our inherited equipment and the environmental influences to which we were subjected at the beginning of our lives. It is clear that we had no hand in shaping either of these." A hard determinist could quote a number of eminent supporters. "Our volitions and our desires," wrote Holbach in his little book *Good Sense,* "are never in our power. You think yourself free, because you do what you will; but are you free to will or not to will; to desire or not to desire?" And Schopenhauer expressed the same thought in the following epigram: "A man can surely do what he wills to do, but he cannot determine what he wills."

Let me turn once more to the topic of character transformation by means of psychiatry to bring out this point with full force. Let us suppose that both *A* and *B* are compulsive and suffer intensely from their neuroses. Let us assume that there is a therapy that could help them, which could materially change their character structure, but that it takes a great deal of energy and courage to undertake the treatment. Let us suppose that *A* has the necessary energy and courage while *B* lacks it. *A* undergoes the therapy and changes in the desired way. *B* just gets more and more compulsive and more and more miserable. Now, it is true that *A* helped form his own later character. But his starting point, his desire to change, his energy and courage, were already there. They may or may not have been the result of previous efforts on his own part. But there must have been a first effort, and the effort at that time was the result of factors that were not of his making.

The fact that a person's character is ultimately the product of factors over which he had no control is not denied by the soft determinists, though many of them don't like to be reminded of it when they are in a moralizing mood. Since the hard determinists admit that our desires and choices do on occasion influence the course of our lives, there is thus no disagreement between the soft and the hard determinists about the empirical facts. However, some hard determinists infer from some of these facts that human beings are never morally responsible for their actions. The soft determinists, as already stated, do not draw any such inference. In the remainder of my paper I shall try to show just what it is that hard determinists are inferring and why, in my opinion, they are justified in their conclusion.

I shall begin by adopting for my purposes a distinction introduced by C. A. Campbell in his extremely valuable article "Is Free Will a

Pseudo-Problem?"[1] in which he distinguishes between two conceptions of moral responsibility. Different persons, he says, require different conditions to be fulfilled before holding human beings morally responsible for what they do. First, there is what Campbell calls the ordinary unreflective person, who is rather ignorant and who is not greatly concerned with the theories of science, philosophy, and religion. If the unreflective person is sure that the agent to be judged was acting under coercion or constraint, he will not hold him responsible. If, however, he is sure that the action was performed in accordance with the agent's unimpeded rational desire, if he is sure that the action would not have taken place but for the agent's decision, then the unreflective person will consider ascription of moral responsibility justified. The fact that the agent did not ultimately make his own character will either not occur to him, or else it will not be considered a sufficient ground for withholding a judgment of moral responsibility.

In addition to such unreflective persons, continues Campbell, there are others who have reached "a tolerably advanced level of reflection."

> Such a person will doubtless be acquainted with the claims advanced in some quarters that causal law operates universally; or/ and with the theories of some philosophies that the universe is throughout the expression of a single supreme principle; or/ and with the doctrines of some theologians that the world is created, sustained and governed by an Omniscient and Omnipotent Being.

Such a person will tend to require the fulfillment of a further condition before holding anybody morally responsible. He will require not only that the agent was not coerced or constrained but also— and this is taken to be an additional condition—that he "could have chosen otherwise than he actually did." I should prefer to put this somewhat differently, but it will not affect the main conclusion drawn by Campbell, with which I agree. The reflective person, I should prefer to express it, requires not only that the agent was not coerced; he also requires that the agent *originally chose his own character*—the character that now displays itself in his choices and desires and efforts. Campbell concludes that determinism is indeed compatible with judgments of moral responsibility in the unreflec-

[1] *Mind,* 1951.

tive sense, but that it is incompatible with judgments of moral responsibility in the reflective sense.

Although I do not follow Campbell in rejecting determinism, I agree basically with his analysis, with one other qualification. I do not think it is a question of the different senses in which the term is used by ignorant and unreflective people, on the one hand, and by those who are interested in science, religion, and philosophy, on the other. The very same persons, whether educated or uneducated, use it in certain contexts in the one sense and in other contexts in the other. Practically all human beings, no matter how much interested they are in science, religion, and philosophy, employ what Campbell calls the unreflective conception when they are dominated by violent emotions like anger, indignation, or hate, and especially when the conduct they are judging has been personally injurious to them. On the other hand, a great many people, whether they are educated or not, will employ what Campbell calls the reflective conception when they are not consumed with hate or anger—when they are judging a situation calmly and reflectively and when the fact that the agent did not ultimately shape his own character has been vividly brought to their attention. Clarence Darrow in his celebrated pleas repeatedly appealed to the jury on precisely this ground. If any of you, he would say, had been reared in an environment like that of the accused or had to suffer from his defective heredity, *you* would now be standing in the dock. I cannot refrain at this stage from reading a poem written by the hard determinist, A. E. Housman, which Darrow recited on such occasions. Its title is "The Culprit," and it is the soliloquy of a boy about to be hanged.

> The night my father got me
> His mind was not on me;
> He did not plague his fancy
> To muse if I should be
> The son you see.
>
> The day my mother bore me
> She was a fool and glad,
> For all the pain I cost her,
> That she had borne the lad
> That borne she had.

My mother and my father
Out of the light they lie;
The warrant could not find them,
And here 'tis only I
Shall hang so high.

Oh let not man remember
The soul that God forgot,
But fetch the county kerchief
And noose me in the knot,
And I will rot.

For so the game is ended
That should not have begun.
My father and my mother
They had a likely son,
And I have none.[2]

Darrow nearly always convinced the jury that the accused could not be held morally responsible for his acts; and certainly the majority of the jurors were relatively uneducated.

I have so far merely distinguished between two concepts of moral responsibility. I now wish to go a step farther and claim that only one of them can be considered, properly speaking, a moral concept. This is not an easy point to make clear, but I can at least indicate what I mean. We do not normally consider just any positive or negative feeling a "moral" emotion. Nor do we consider just any sentence containing the words "good" or "bad" expressions of "moral" judgment. For example, if a man hates a woman because she rejected him, this would not be counted as a moral emotion. If, however, he disapproves, say, of Senator McCarthy's libelous speech against Adlai Stevenson before the 1952 election because he disapproves of slander in general and not merely because he likes Stevenson and dislikes McCarthy, his feeling would be counted as moral. A feeling or judgment must in a certain sense be "impersonal" before we consider it moral. To this I would add that it must also be independent of violent emotions. Confining myself to judgments, I would say that a judgment was "moral" only if it was formulated in a calm and reflective mood, or at least if it is supported in a calm and reflective

2 From *The Collected Poems of A. E. Housman.* Copyright, 1922, 1940 by Henry Holt and Company, Inc. Copyright, 1950, by Barclays Bank, Ltd. By permission of the publishers.

state of mind. If this is so, it follows that what Campbell calls the reflective sense of "moral responsibility" is the only one that qualifies as a properly moral use of the term.

Before I conclude I wish to avoid a certain misunderstanding of my remarks. From the fact that human beings do not ultimately shape their own character, I said, it *follows* that they are never morally responsible. I do not mean that by reminding people of the ultimate causes of their character one makes them more charitable and less vengeful. Maybe one does, but that is not what I mean. I mean "follow" or "imply" in the same sense as, or in a sense closely akin to, that in which the conclusion of a valid syllogism follows from the premises. The effectiveness of Darrow's pleas does not merely show, I am arguing, how powerfully he could sway the emotions of the jurors. His pleas also brought into the open one of the conditions the jurors, like others, consider necessary on reflection before they hold an agent morally responsible. Or perhaps I should say that Darrow *committed* the jurors in their reflective nature to a certain ground for the ascription of moral responsibility.[3]

3.   What Means This Freedom?

John Hospers, Brooklyn College

I am in agreement to a very large extent with the conclusions of Professor Edwards' paper, and am happy in these days of "soft determinism" to hear the other view so forcefully and fearlessly stated. As a preparation for developing my own views on the subject, I want

[3] *Author's Note.* This paper was written in the hope of stimulating discussion of a position which has not received adequate attention in recent years. The position was stated rather bluntly and without the necessary qualifications because of limitations of time. I hope to return to the subject at greater length in the near future, and on that occasion to present a more balanced treatment which will attempt to meet criticisms made in the discussion. (*December 1957.*)

to mention a factor that I think is of enormous importance and relevance: namely, unconscious motivation. There are many actions—not those of an insane person (however the term "insane" be defined), nor of a person ignorant of the effects of his action, nor ignorant of some relevant fact about the situation, nor in any obvious way mentally deranged—for which human beings in general and the courts in particular are inclined to hold the doer responsible, and for which, I would say, he should not be held responsible. The deed may be planned, it may be carried out in cold calculation, it may spring from the agent's character and be continuous with the rest of his behavior, and it may be perfectly true that he could have done differently *if* he had wanted to; nonetheless his behavior was brought about by unconscious conflicts developed in infancy, over which he had no control and of which (without training in psychiatry) he does not even have knowledge. He may even *think* he knows why he acted as he did, he may *think* he has conscious control over his actions, he may even *think* he is fully responsible for them; but he is not. Psychiatric casebooks provide hundreds of examples. The law and common sense, though puzzled sometimes by such cases, are gradually becoming aware that they exist; but at this early stage countless tragic blunders still occur because neither the law nor the public in general is aware of the genesis of criminal actions. The mother blames her daughter for choosing the wrong men as candidates for husbands; but though the daughter thinks she is choosing freely and spends a considerable amount of time "deciding" among them, the identification with her sick father, resulting from Oedipal fantasies in early childhood, prevents her from caring for any but sick men, twenty or thirty years older than herself. Blaming her is beside the point; she cannot help it, and she cannot change it. Countless criminal acts are thought out in great detail; yet the participants are (without their own knowledge) acting out fantasies, fears, and defenses from early childhood, over whose coming and going they have no conscious control.

Now, I am not saying that none of these persons should be in jails or asylums. Often society must be protected against them. Nor am I saying that people should cease the practices of blaming and praising, punishing and rewarding; in general these devices are justified by the results—although very often they have practically no effect;

the deeds are done from inner compulsion, which is not lessened when the threat of punishment is great. I am only saying that frequently persons we think responsible are not properly to be called so; we mistakenly think them responsible because we assume they are like those in whom no unconscious drive (toward this type of behavior) is present, and that their behavior can be changed by reasoning, exhorting, or threatening.

I .

I have said that these persons are not responsible. But what is the criterion for responsibility? Under precisely what conditions is a person to be held morally responsible for an action? Disregarding here those conditions that have to do with a person's *ignorance* of the situation or the effects of his action, let us concentrate on those having to do with his "inner state." There are several criteria that might be suggested:

1. The first idea that comes to mind is that responsibility is determined by the presence or absence of *premeditation*—the opposite of "premeditated" being, presumably, "unthinking" or "impulsive." But this will not do—both because some acts are not premeditated but responsible, and because some are premeditated and not responsible.

Many acts we call responsible can be as unthinking or impulsive as you please. If you rush across the street to help the victim of an automobile collision, you are (at least so we would ordinarily say) acting responsibly, but you did not do so out of premeditation; you saw the accident, you didn't think, you rushed to the scene without hesitation. It was like a reflex action. But you acted responsibly: unlike the knee jerk, the act was the result of past training and past thought about situations of this kind; that is why you ran to help instead of ignoring the incident or running away. When something done originally from conviction or training becomes habitual, it becomes *like* a reflex action. As Aristotle said, virtue should become second nature through habit: a virtuous act should be performed *as if* by instinct; this, far from detracting from its moral worth, testifies to one's mastery of the desired type of behavior; one does not have to make a moral effort each time it is repeated.

There are also premeditated acts for which, I would say, the person is not responsible. Premeditation, especially when it is so exaggerated as to issue in no action at all, can be the result of neurotic disturbance or what we sometimes call an emotional "block," which the person inherits from long-past situations. In Hamlet's revenge on his uncle (I use this example because it is familiar to all of us), there was no lack, but rather a surfeit, of premeditation; his actions were so exquisitely premeditated as to make Freud and Dr. Ernest Jones look more closely to find out what lay behind them. The very premeditation camouflaged unconscious motives of which Hamlet himself was not aware. I think this is an important point, since it seems that the courts often assume that premeditation is a criterion of responsibility. If failure to kill his uncle had been considered a crime, every court in the land would have convicted Hamlet. Again: a woman's decision to stay with her husband in spite of endless "mental cruelty" is, if she is the victim of an unconscious masochistic "will to punishment," one for which she is not responsible; she is the victim and not the agent, no matter how profound her conviction that she is the agent; she is caught in a masochistic web (of complicated genesis) dating back to babyhood, perhaps a repetition of a comparable situation involving her own parents, a repetition-compulsion that, as Freud said, goes "beyond the pleasure principle." Again: a criminal whose crime was carefully planned step by step is usually considered responsible, but as we shall see in later examples, the overwhelming impulse toward it, stemming from an unusually humiliating ego defeat in early childhood, was as compulsive as any can be.

2. Shall we say, then, that a person is not responsible for his act unless he can *defend it with reasons?* I am afraid that this criterion is no better than the previous one. First, intellectuals are usually better at giving reasons than nonintellectuals, and according to this criterion would be more responsible than persons acting from moral conviction not implemented by reasoning; yet it is very doubtful whether we should want to say that the latter are the more responsible. Second, the giving of reasons itself may be suspect. The reasons may be rationalizations camouflaging unconscious motives of

which the agent knows nothing. Hamlet gave many reasons for not doing what he felt it was his duty to do: the time was not right, his uncle's soul might go to heaven, etc. His various "reasons" contradicted one another, and if an overpowering compulsion had not been present, the highly intellectual Hamlet would not have been taken in for a moment by these rationalizations. The real reason, the Oedipal conflict that made his uncle's crime the accomplishment of his own deepest desire, binding their fates into one and paralyzing him into inaction, was unconscious and of course unknown to him. One's intelligence and reasoning power do not enable one to escape from unconsciously motivated behavior; it only gives one greater facility in rationalizing that behavior; one's intelligence is simply used in the interests of the neurosis—it is pressed into service to justify with reasons what one does quite independently of the reasons.

If these two criteria are inadequate, let us seek others.

3. Shall we say that a person is responsible for his action unless it is the *result of unconscious forces* of which he knows nothing? Many psychoanalysts would probably accept this criterion. If it is not largely reflected in the language of responsibility as ordinarily used, this may be due to ignorance of fact: most people do not know that there are such things as unconscious motives and unconscious conflicts causing human beings to act. But it may be that if they did, perhaps they would refrain from holding persons responsible for certain actions.

I do not wish here to quarrel with this criterion of responsibility. I only want to point out the fact that if this criterion is employed a far greater number of actions will be excluded from the domain of responsibility than we might at first suppose. Whether we are neat or untidy, whether we are selfish or unselfish, whether we provoke scenes or avoid them, even whether we can exert our powers of will to change our behavior—all these may, and often do, have their source in our unconscious life.

4. Shall we say that a person is responsible for his act unless it is *compelled?* Here we are reminded of Aristotle's assertion (*Nicomachean Ethics,* Book III) that a person is responsible for his act except for reasons of either ignorance or compulsion. Ignorance is not part of our problem here (unless it is unconsciously induced ig-

norance of facts previously remembered and selectively forgotten—
in which case the forgetting is again compulsive), but compulsion
is. How will compulsion do as a criterion? The difficulty is to state
just what it means. When we say an act is compelled in a psychological sense, our language is metaphorical—which is not to say that
there is no point in it or that, properly interpreted, it is not true. Our
actions are compelled in a literal sense if someone has us in chains
or is controlling our bodily movements. When we say that the storm
compelled us to jettison the cargo of the ship (Aristotle's example),
we have a less literal sense of compulsion, for at least it is open to us
to go down with the ship. When psychoanalysts say that a man was
compelled by unconscious conflicts to wash his hands constantly,
this is also not a literal use of "compel"; for nobody forced his hands
under the tap. Still, it is a typical example of what psychologists call
compulsive behavior: it has unconscious causes inaccesible to
introspection, and moreover nothing can change it—it is as inevitable for him to do it as it would be if someone were forcing his hands
under the tap. In this it is exactly like the action of a powerful external force; it is just as little within one's conscious control.

In its area of application this interpretation of responsibility
comes to much the same as the previous one. And this area is very
great indeed. For if we cannot be held responsible for the infantile
situations (in which we were after all passive victims), then neither,
it would seem, can we be held responsible for compulsive actions
occurring in adulthood that are inevitable consequences of those infantile situations. And, psychiatrists and psychoanalysts tell us, actions fulfilling this description are characteristic of all people some
of the time and some people most of the time. Their occurrence,
once the infantile events have taken place, is inevitable, just as the
explosion is inevitable once the fuse has been lighted; there is simply
more "delayed action" in the psychological explosions than there
is in the physical ones.

(I have not used the word "inevitable" here to mean "causally
determined," for according to such a definition every event would
be inevitable if one accepted the causal principle in some form or
other; and probably nobody except certain philosophers uses "inevitable" in this sense. Rather, I use "inevitable" in its ordinary sense
of "cannot be avoided." To the extent, therefore, that adult neurotic

manifestations *can* be avoided, once the infantile patterns have become set, the assertion that they are inevitable is not true.)

5. There is still another criterion, which I prefer to the previous ones, by which a man's responsibility for an act can be measured: the degree to which that act can (or could have been) *changed by the use of reasons.* Suppose that the man who washes his hands constantly does so, he says, for hygienic reasons, believing that if he doesn't do so he will be poisoned by germs. We now convince him, on the best medical authority, that his belief is groundless. Now, the test of his responsibility is whether the changed belief will result in changed behavior. If it does not, as with the compulsive hand washer, he is not acting responsibly, but if it does, he is. It is not the *use* of reasons, but their *efficacy in changing behavior,* that is being made the criterion of responsibility. And clearly in neurotic cases no such change occurs; in fact, this is often made the defining characteristic of neurotic behavior: it is unchangeable by any rational considerations.

II

I have suggested these criteria to distinguish actions for which we can call the agent responsible from those for which we cannot. Even persons with extensive knowledge of psychiatry do not, I think, use any one of these criteria to the exclusion of the others; a conjunction of two or more may be used at once. But however they may be combined or selected in actual application, I believe we can make the distinction along some such lines as we have suggested.

But is there not still another possible meaning of "responsibility" that we have not yet mentioned? Even after we have made all the above distinctions, there remains a question in our minds whether we are, in the final analysis, *responsible for any of our actions at all.* The issue may be put this way: How can anyone be responsible for his actions, since they grow out of his character, which is shaped and molded and made what it is by influences—some hereditary, but most of them stemming from early parental environment—that were not of his own making or choosing? This question, I believe, still troubles many people who would agree to all the distinctions we have just made but still have the feeling that "this isn't all." They have the uneasy suspicion that there is a more ultimate sense, a "deeper" sense, in which we are *not* responsible for our actions, since we are not responsible for the character out of which those actions spring. This, of course, is the sense Professor Edwards was describing.

Let us take as an example a criminal who, let us say, strangled several persons and is himself now condemned to die in the electric chair. Jury and public alike hold him fully responsible (at least they utter the words "he is responsible"), for the murders were planned down to the minutest detail, and the defendant tells the jury exactly how he planned them. But now we find out how it all came about; we learn of parents who rejected him from babyhood, of the childhood spent in one foster home after another, where it was always plain to him that he was not wanted; of the constantly frustrated early desire for affection, the hard shell of nonchalance and bitterness that he assumed to cover the painful and humiliating fact of being unwanted, and his subsequent attempts to heal these wounds to his shattered ego through defensive aggression.

> The criminal is the most passive person in this world, helpless as a baby in his motorically inexpressible fury. Not only does he try to wreak revenge on the mother of the earliest period of his babyhood; his criminality is based on the inner feeling of being incapable of making the mother even feel that the child seeks revenge on her. The situation is that of a dwarf trying to annoy a giant who superciliously refuses to see these attempts. . . . Because of his inner feeling of being a dwarf, the criminotic uses, so to speak, dynamite. Of that the giant must take cognizance. True, the "revenge" harms the avenger. He may be legally executed. However, the primary inner aim of forcing the giant to acknowledge the dwarf's fury is fulfilled.[1]

The poor victim is not conscious of the inner forces that exact from him this ghastly toll; he battles, he schemes, he revels in pseudo-aggression, he is miserable, but he does not know what works within him to produce these catastrophic acts of crime. His aggressive actions are the wriggling of a worm on a fisherman's hook. And if this is so, it seems difficult to say any longer, "He is responsible."

[1] Edmund Bergler, *The Basic Neurosis* (New York: Grune and Stratton, 1949), p. 305.

Rather, we shall put him behind bars for the protection of society, but we shall no longer flatter our feeling of moral superiority by calling him personally responsible for what he did.

Let us suppose it were established that a man commits murder only if, sometime during the previous week, he has eaten a certain combination of foods—say, tuna fish salad at a meal also including peas, mushroom soup, and blueberry pie. What if we were to track down the factors common to all murders committed in this country during the last twenty years and found this factor present in all of them, and only in them? The example is of course empirically absurd; but may it not be that there is *some* combination of factors that regularly leads to homicide, factors such as are described in general terms in the above quotation? (Indeed the situation in the quotation is less fortunate than in our hypothetical example, for it is easy to avoid certain foods once we have been warned about them, but the situation of the infant is thrust on him; something has already happened to him once and for all, before he knows it has happened.) When such specific factors are discovered, won't they make it clear that it is foolish and pointless, as well as immoral, to hold human beings responsible for crimes? Or, if one prefers biological to psychological factors, suppose a neurologist is called in to testify at a murder trial and produces X-ray pictures of the brain of the criminal; anyone can see, he argues, that the *cella turcica* was already calcified at the age of nineteen; it should be a flexible bone, growing, enabling the gland to grow.[2] All the defendant's disorders might have resulted from this early calcification. Now, this particular explanation may be empirically false; but who can say that no such factors, far more complex, to be sure, exist?

When we know such things as these, we no longer feel so much tempted to say that the criminal is responsible for his crime; and we tend also (do we not?) to excuse him—not legally (we still confine him to prison) but morally; we no longer call him a monster or hold him personally responsible for what he did. Moreover, we do this in general, not merely in the case of crime: "You must excuse Grandmother for being irritable; she's really quite ill and is suffering some pain all the time." Or: "The dog always bites children

[2] Meyer Levin, *Compulsion* (New York: Simon and Schuster, 1956), p. 403.

after she's had a litter of pups; you can't blame her for it: she's not feeling well, and besides she naturally wants to defend them." Or: "She's nervous and jumpy, but do excuse her: she has a severe glandular disturbance."

Let us note that the more *thoroughly* and *in detail* we know the causal factors leading a person to behave as he does, the more we tend to exempt him from responsibility. When we know nothing of the man except what we see him do, we say he is an ungrateful cad who expects much of other people and does nothing in return, and we are usually indignant. When we learn that his parents were the same way and, having no guilt feelings about this mode of behavior themselves, brought him up to be greedy and avaricious, we see that we could hardly expect him to have developed moral feelings in this direction. When we learn, in addition, that he is not aware of being ungrateful or selfish, but unconsciously represses the memory of events unfavorable to himself, we feel that the situation is unfortunate but "not really his fault." When we know that this behavior of his, which makes others angry, occurs more constantly when he feels tense or insecure, and that he now feels tense and insecure, and that relief from pressure will diminish it, then we tend to "feel sorry for the poor guy" and say he's more to be pitied than censured. We no longer want to say that he is personally responsible; we might rather blame nature or his parents for having given him an unfortunate constitution or temperament.

In recent years a new form of punishment has been imposed on middle-aged and elderly parents. Their children, now in their twenties, thirties or even forties, present them with a modern grievance: "My analysis proves that *you* are responsible for my neurosis." Overawed by these authoritative statements, the poor tired parents fall easy victims to the newest variations on the scapegoat theory.

In my opinion, this senseless cruelty—which disinters educational sins which had been buried for decades, and uses them as the basis for accusations which the victims cannot answer—is unjustified. Yes, "the truth loves to be centrally located" (Melville), and few parents —since they are human—have been perfect. But granting their mistakes, they acted as *their* neurotic difficulties forced them to act. To turn the tables and declare the children not guilty because of the *impersonal* nature of their own neuroses, while at the same time the parents are *personally* blamed, is worse than illogical; it is profoundly unjust.[3]

And so, it would now appear, neither of the parties is responsible: "they acted as their neurotic difficulties forced them to act." The patients are not responsible for their neurotic manifestations, but then neither are the parents responsible for theirs; and so, of course, for their parents in turn, and theirs before them. It is the twentieth-century version of the family curse, the curse on the House of Atreus.

"But," a critic complains, "it's immoral to exonerate people indiscriminately in this way. I might have thought it fit to excuse somebody because he was born on the other side of the tracks, if I didn't know so many bank presidents who were also born on the other side of the tracks." Now, I submit that the most immoral thing in this situation is the critic's caricature of the conditions of the excuse. Nobody is excused merely because he was born on the other side of the tracks. But if he was born on the other side of the tracks *and* was a highly narcissistic infant to begin with *and* was repudiated or neglected by his parents *and* . . . (here we list a finite number of conditions), and if this complex of factors is *regularly* followed by certain behavior traits in adulthood, and moreover *unavoidably* so—that is, they occur no matter what he or anyone else tries to do —then we excuse him morally and say he is not responsible for his deed. If he is not responsible for *A,* a series of events occurring in his babyhood, then neither is he responsible for *B,* a series of things he does in adulthood, provided that *B* inevitably—that is, unavoidably—follows upon the occurrence of *A.* And according to psychiatrists and psychoanalysts, this often happens.

But one may still object that so far we have talked only about neurotic behavior. Isn't nonneurotic or normal or not unconsciously motivated (or whatever you want to call it) behavior still within the area of responsibility? There are reasons for answering "No" even here, for the normal person no more than the neurotic one has caused his own character, which makes him what he is. Granted that neurotics are not responsible for their behavior (that part of it which we call neurotic) because it stems from undigested infantile conflicts that they had no part in bringing about, and that are external to them

[3] Edmund Bergler, *The Superego* (New York: Grune and Stratton, 1952), p. 320.

just as surely as if their behavior had been forced on them by a malevolent deity (which is indeed one theory on the subject); but the so-called normal person is equally the product of causes in which his volition took no part. And if, unlike the neurotic's, his behavior is changeable by rational considerations, and if he has the will power to overcome the effects of an unfortunate early environment, this again is no credit to him; he is just lucky. If energy is available to him in a form in which it can be mobilized for constructive purposes, this is no credit to him, for this too is part of his psychic legacy. Those of us who can discipline ourselves and develop habits of concentration of purpose tend to blame those who cannot, and call them lazy and weak-willed; but what we fail to see is that they literally *cannot* do what we expect; if their psyches were structured like ours, they could, but as they are burdened with a tyrannical superego (to use psychoanalytic jargon for the moment), and a weak defenseless ego whose energies are constantly consumed in fighting endless charges of the superego, they simply cannot do it, and it is irrational to expect it of them. We cannot with justification blame them for their inability, any more than we can congratulate ourselves for our ability. This lesson is hard to learn, for we constantly and naïvely assume that other people are constructed as we ourselves are.

For example: A child raised under slum conditions, whose parents are socially ambitious and envy families with money, but who nevertheless squander the little they have on drink, may simply be unable in later life to mobilize a drive sufficient to overcome these early conditions. Common sense would expect that he would develop the virtue of thrift; he would make quite sure that he would never again endure the grinding poverty he had experienced as a child. But in fact it is not so: the exact conditions are too complex to be specified in detail here, but when certain conditions are fulfilled (concerning the subject's early life), he will always thereafter be a spendthrift, and no rational considerations will be able to change this. He will listen to the rational considerations and see the force of these, but they will not be able to change him, even if he tries; he cannot change his wasteful habits any more than he can lift the Empire State Building with his bare hands. We moralize and plead with him to be thrifty, but we do not see how strong, how utterly overpowering, and how constantly with him, is the opposite

drive, which is so easily manageable with us. But he is possessed by
the all-consuming, all-encompassing urge to make the world see
that he belongs, that he has arrived, that he is just as well off as anyone else, that the awful humiliations were not real, that they never
actually occurred, for isn't he now able to spend and spend? The
humiliation must be blotted out; and conspicuous, flashy, expensive,
and wasteful buying will do this; it shows the world what the world
must know! True, it is only for the moment; true, it is in the end self-
defeating, for wasteful consumption is the best way to bring poverty
back again; but the person with an overpowering drive to mend a
lesion to his narcissism cannot resist the avalanche of that drive with
this puny rational consideration. A man with his back against the
wall and a gun at his throat doesn't think of what may happen ten
years hence. (Consciously, of course, he knows nothing of this drive;
all that appears to consciousness is its shattering effects; he knows
only that he must keep on spending—not why—and that he is unable to resist.) He hasn't in him the psychic capacity, the energy to
stem the tide of a drive that at that moment is all-powerful. We,
seated comfortably away from this flood, sit in judgment on him and
blame him and exhort him and criticize him; but he, carried along
by the flood, cannot do otherwise than he does. He may fight with
all the strength of which he is capable, but it is not enough. And we,
who are rational enough at least to exonerate a man in a situation
of "overpowering impulse" when we recognize it to be one, do not
even recognize this as an example of it; and so, in addition to being
swept away in the flood that childhood conditions rendered inevitable, he must also endure our lectures, our criticisms, and our moral
excoriation.

But, one will say, he could have overcome his spendthrift tendencies; some people do. Quite true: some people do. They are lucky.
They have it in them to overcome early deficiencies by exerting great
effort, and they are capable of exerting the effort. Some of us, luckier
still, can overcome them with but little effort; and a few, the luckiest,
haven't the deficiencies to overcome. It's all a matter of luck. The
least lucky are those who can't overcome them, even with great effort, and those who haven't the ability to exert the effort.

But, one persists, it isn't a matter simply of luck; it *is* a matter of
effort. Very well then, it's a matter of effort; without exerting the

effort you may not overcome the deficiency. But whether or not you are the kind of person who has it in him to exert the effort is a matter of luck.

All this is well known to psychoanalysts. They can predict, from minimal clues that most of us don't notice, whether a person is going to turn out to be lucky or not. "The analyst," they say, "must be able to use the residue of the patient's unconscious guilt so as to remove the symptom or character trait that creates the guilt. The guilt must not only be present, but *available* for use, *mobilizable*. If it is used used up (absorbed) in criminal activity, or in an excessive amount of self-damaging tendencies, then it cannot be used for therapeutic purposes, and the prognosis is negative." Not all philosophers will relish the analyst's way of putting the matter, but at least as a physician he can soon detect whether the patient is lucky or unlucky— and he knows that whichever it is, it *isn't the patient's fault.* The patient's conscious volition cannot remedy the deficiency. Even whether he will co-operate with the analyst is really out of the patient's hands: if he continually projects the denying-mother fantasy on the analyst and unconsciously identifies him always with the cruel, harsh forbidder of the nursery, thus frustrating any attempt at impersonal observation, the sessions are useless; yet if it happens that way, he can't help that either. That fatal projection is not under his control; whether it occurs or not depends on how his unconscious identifications have developed since his infancy. He can try, yes— but the ability to try enough for the therapy to have effect is also beyond his control; the capacity to try more than just so much is either there or it isn't—and either way "it's in the lap of the gods."

The position, then, is this: if we *can* overcome the effects of early environment, the ability to do so is itself a product of the early environment. We did not give ourselves this ability; and if we lack it we cannot be blamed for not having it. Sometimes, to be sure, moral exhortation brings out an ability that is there but not being used, and in this lies its *occasional* utility; but very often its use is pointless, because the ability is not there. The only thing that can overcome a desire, as Spinoza said, is a stronger contrary desire; and many times there simply is no wherewithal for producing a stronger contrary desire. Those of us who do have the wherewithal are lucky.

There is one possible practical advantage in remembering this.

It may prevent us (unless we are compulsive blamers) from indulging in righteous indignation and committing the sin of spiritual pride, thanking God that we are not as this publican here. And it will protect from our useless moralizings those who are least equipped by nature for enduring them.

As with responsibility, so with deserts. Someone commits a crime and is punished by the state; "he deserved it," we say self-righteously —as if we were moral and he immoral, when in fact we are lucky and he is unlucky—forgetting that there, but for the grace of God and a fortunate early environment, go we. Or, as Clarence Darrow said in his speech for the defense in the Loeb-Leopold case:

> I do not believe that people are in jail because they deserve to be. . . . I know what causes the emotional life. . . . I know it is practically left out of some. Without it they cannot act with the rest. They cannot feel the moral shocks which safeguard others. Is [this man] to blame that his machine is imperfect? Who is to blame? I do not know. I have never in my life been interested so much in fixing blame as I have in relieving people from blame. I am not wise enough to fix it.[4]

III[5]

I want to make it quite clear that I have not been arguing for determinism. Though I find it difficult to give any sense to the term "indeterminism," because I do not know what it would be like to come across an uncaused event, let us grant indeterminists everything they want, at least in words—influences that suggest but do not constrain, a measure of acausality in an otherwise rigidly causal order, and so on—whatever these phrases may mean. With all this granted, exactly the same situation faces the indeterminist and the determinist; all we have been saying would still hold true. "Are our powers innate or acquired?"

Suppose the powers are declared innate; then the villain may sensibly ask whether he is responsible for what he was born with. A nega-

---

4 Levin, *op. cit.,* pp. 439–40, 469.
5 This section of Professor Hospers' paper was not read in its present form at the conference.—Ed.

tive reply is inevitable. Are they then acquired? Then the ability to
acquire them—was *that* innate? or acquired? It is innate? Very well
then. . . .[6]

The same fact remains—that we did not cause our characters, that
the influences that made us what we are are influences over which we
had no control and of whose very existence we had no knowledge
at the time. This fact remains for "determinism" and "indeterminism" alike. And it is this fact to which I would appeal, not the specific tenets of traditional forms of "determinism," which seem to
me, when analyzed, empirically empty.

"But," it may be asked, "isn't it your view that nothing ultimately
could be other than it is? And isn't this deterministic? And isn't it
deterministic if you say that human beings could never act otherwise than they do, and that their desires and temperaments could
not, when you consider their antecedent conditions, be other than
they are?"

I reply that all these charges rest on confusions.

1. To say that nothing *could* be other than it is, is, taken literally,
nonsense; and if taken as a way of saying something else, misleading
and confusing. If you say, "I can't do it," this invites the question,
"No? Not even if you want to?" "Can" and "could" are power
words, used in the context of human action; when applied to nature
they are merely anthropomorphic. "Could" has no application to
nature—unless, of course, it is uttered in a theological context: one
might say that God *could* have made things different. But with regard to inanimate nature "could" has no meaning. Or perhaps it is
intended to mean that the order of nature is in some sense *necessary*.
But in that case the sense of "necessary" must be specified. I know
what "necessary" means when we are talking about propositions,
but not when we are talking about the sequence of events in nature.

2. What of the charge that we could never have acted otherwise
than we did? This, I submit, is simply not true. Here the exponents
of Hume-Mill-Schlick-Ayer "soft determinism" are quite right. I
could have gone to the opera today instead of coming here; that is,
if certain conditions had been different, I should have gone. I could
have done many other things instead of what I did, if some condition

[6] W. I. Matson, "The Irrelevance of Free-will to Moral Responsibility,"
Mind, LXV (October 1956), p. 495.

or other had been different, specifically if my desire had been different. I repeat that "could" is a power word, and "I could have done this" means approximately "I *should* have done this *if* I had wanted to." In this sense, all of us could often have done otherwise than we did. I would not want to say that I should have done differently even if *all* the conditions leading up to my action had been the same (this is generally not what we mean by "could" anyway); but to assert that I could have is empty, for if I *did* act differently from the time before, we would automatically say that one or more of the conditions were different, whether we had independent evidence for this or not, thus rendering the assertion immune to empirical refutation. (Once again, the vacuousness of "determinism.")

3. Well, then, could we ever have, not acted, but *desired* otherwise than we did desire? This gets us once again to the heart of the matter we were discussing in the previous section. Russell said, "We can do as we please but we can't please as we please." But I am persuaded that even this statement conceals a fatal mistake. Let us follow the same analysis through. "I could have done *X*" means "I should have done *X* if I had wanted to." "I could have wanted *X*" by the same analysis would mean "I should have wanted *X* if I had wanted to"—which seems to make no sense at all. (What does Russell want? To please as he doesn't please?)

What does this show? It shows, I think, that the only meaningful context of "can" and "could have" is that of *action*. "Could have acted differently" makes sense; "could have desired differently," as we have just seen, does not. Because a word or phrase makes good sense in one context, let us not assume that it does so in another.

I conclude, then, with the following suggestion: that we operate on two levels of moral discourse, which we shouldn't confuse; one (let's call it the upper level) is that of actions; the other (the lower, or deeper, level) is that of the springs of action. Most moral talk occurs on the upper level. It is on this level that the Hume-Mill-Schlick-Ayer analysis of freedom fully applies. As we have just seen, "can" and "could" acquire their meaning on this level; so, I suspect, does "freedom." So does the distinction between compulsive and noncompulsive behavior, and among the senses of "responsibility," discussed in the first section of this paper, according to which we are responsible for some things and not for others. All these distinctions are perfectly valid on this level (or in this dimension) of moral discourse; and it is, after all, the usual one—we are practical beings interested in changing the course of human behavior, so it is natural enough that 99 per cent of our moral talk occurs here.

But when we descend to what I have called the lower level of moral discourse, as we occasionally do in thoughtful moments when there is no immediate need for action, then we must admit that we are ultimately the kind of persons we are because of conditions occurring outside us, over which we had no control. But while this is true, we should beware of extending the moral terminology we used on the other level to this one also. "Could" and "can," as we have seen, no longer have meaning here. "Right" and "wrong," which apply only to actions, have no meaning here either. I suspect that the same is true of "responsibility," for now that we have recalled often forgotten facts about our being the product of outside forces, we must ask in all seriousness what would be added by saying that we are not *responsible* for our own characters and temperaments. What would it mean even? Has it a significant opposite? What would it be like to be responsible for one's own character? What possible situation is describable by this phrase? Instead of saying that it is *false* that we are responsible for our own characters, I should prefer to say that the utterance is meaningless—meaningless in the sense that it describes no possible situation, though it *seems* to because the word "responsible" is the same one we used on the upper level, where it marks a real distinction. If this is so, the result is that *moral* terms—at least the terms "could have" and "responsible"—simply drop out on the lower level. What remains, shorn now of moral terminology, is the point we tried to bring out in Part II: whether or not we have personality disturbances, whether or not we have the ability to overcome deficiences of early environment, is like the answer to the question whether or not we shall be struck down by a dread disease: "it's all a matter of luck." It is important to keep this in mind, for people almost always forget it, with consequences in human intolerance and unnecessary suffering that are incalculable.

PART IV   Discussion

I. "Excusing Conditions" and Moral Responsibility

Elizabeth Lane Beardsley, Lincoln University

I

Mr. Hart presents an extremely interesting justification of the use of "excusing conditions" as removing liability to legal penalties on the ground that the individual's powers of prediction and choice are thereby maximized. That is, the individual can be more confident of being able to predict and control the possibility that legal penalties will be applied to him than he could in a society that abolished excusing conditions. As I understand Mr. Hart's thesis, this consideration is deemed sufficient to justify the use of excusing conditions. But, although this line of thought seems to shed considerable light on the problem why we approve of excusing conditions, I am not quite convinced that this can be the entire truth of the matter.

It seems clear that if I lived in a society in which all liability to legal penalties was of the "strict" kind, I should stand in danger of suffering such penalties without having really chosen to commit the act that brought them upon me. Here the absence of excusing conditions is a necessary condition of my standing in such danger. The extent of the danger, however, depends also on the likelihood of my ever being in one of the conditions that in other societies would be regarded as excusing. And some of these conditions, such as mental disease and psychopathic states in general, and also ignorance, appear capable, in principle at least, of being reduced in incidence by fairly direct action.

If we now perform the kind of mental experiment so skillfully carried out by Mr. Hart, we may compare the situation in two different hypothetical societies, $S1$ and $S2$. In $S1$, all liability to legal sanctions is of the strict kind, but the chances of anyone's suffering such sanctions because of insanity or neurosis or ignorance are small, because the incidence of these conditions is low. In $S2$, on the other hand, insanity, neurosis, and ignorance are much more prevalent, but here they constitute excusing conditions. (A member of $S2$ stands in some slight danger of suffering legal penalties for acts committed when in these conditions, because of the difficulties of establishing the presence or absence of the conditions.) In both $S1$ and $S2$, the danger of suffering legal penalties for acts committed because of mental aberration or ignorance is small—let us assume that it is equally small. The reduction of this danger is certainly an achievement to which we give moral approval. But in $S1$ and $S2$ it has been accomplished by different means, and it seems to me that our moral appraisal of the methods used by the two societies is not the same. There is an element of moral value in the method used by $S2$ that is absent in what has been done in $S1$. This seems to indicate that something more than the power to maximize the individual's power of prediction and choice underlies our approval of the use of at least certain ones of the excusing conditions.

II

The thesis set forth by C. A. Campbell,[1] and Edwards, that people

1 *Mind,* 1951.

differ with regard to their reflectiveness concerning the problem of relating the concepts of cause and moral blame, is helpful. It seems to me, however, that Mr. Edwards' two-rung hierarchy is a truncated one, and that it needs to be extended at both ends. I should like to distinguish four degrees or levels of reflectiveness on this matter. On the bottom level would be persons who do not even require that the immediate causes of an act be of a certain kind, i.e., that the act be voluntary (free from "coercion"), before the agent is blamed for it. I do not know whether any such persons now exist. Perhaps they do not, even in our simplest societies, though even complex societies count among their members those who sometimes direct judgments of blame toward agents without first ascertaining that their acts were voluntary. In any case, it is certainly plausible to assume that the human race, in the evolution of its moral thinking, once passed through the stage of failing to recognize the moral significance of the distinction between voluntary and nonvoluntary acts. To point this out helps us remember that, however little reflective Mr. Edwards' "unreflective" individuals may be, it would be possible to be even less so. The individuals termed "unreflective" by Mr. Edwards occupy the second level in my proposed hierarchy. For these persons the voluntariness of an act is a condition of the blameworthiness of the agent. This means that they ask certain questions regarding the immediate causes of an act; but they do not go on to ask about the causes of those causes, nor do they feel impelled to bring into line their views about the scope of causality in general, on the one hand, and their beliefs and practices regarding moral blame, on the other.

The third degree of reflectiveness is reached by Mr. Edwards' "reflective" persons. These persons, as I interpret their state of mind, are disturbed by several considerations that do not trouble their second-level associates. The former agree that men are responsible only for their voluntary acts, but they see that the process of asking for the causal conditions of a given act can be carried much farther than is required merely to establish that the act is voluntary, or chosen by the agent; and they do not see any reason why further questions about more remote causal conditions leading to the choice itself should be ruled out in an appraisal of the blameworthiness of the agent for the act chosen. Moreover, persons at this third level of reflectiveness are aware that when these further questions are asked, the answers will very soon begin to include references to factors that are not themselves voluntary acts of the agent, and for which the agent cannot be held "responsible" from any point of view. The reaction of such persons is then to wonder how one can justify regarding any agent as blameworthy for an act, however "voluntary" it may seem after a limited inquiry, when it is clear that a further inquiry would disclose causal antecedents of the act that are not voluntary acts. It appears that persons at this level of reflectiveness make one of two drastic moves. They may feel so sure that the notions of moral blame and responsibility must be retained that they abandon the thesis that all acts of choosing have causal antecedents (Campbell's view), or they may feel so sure that all events, including acts of choosing, are caused that they abandon the notions of moral blame and responsibility (the "hard determinism" of Edwards' view).

Many moral philosophers of a determinist bent will hope that there is a still higher level of reflectiveness here, to which we may aspire. I think that there is, although I do not know how to describe its basic characteristics very precisely. But I think that such a fourth level of reflectiveness can perhaps be reached by those who see both the force and the flaws of the arguments that seem so persuasive at the third level. Such persons would see that the fact that the concepts of moral responsibility and blame have limits in their application does not mean that they have no application. That they do have limits is demonstrated by the considerations advanced at the third level. Surely these show that there are indeed some ways of feeling about other people, some acts of total rejection of their characters, some judgments of unlimited condemnation for their acts, that are wholly unjustified, no matter what monstrous things they may do. Whatever degree of condemnation would be properly reserved for a first cause of the doing of evil is certainly to be withheld from men. But this is not to say that no condemnation whatsoever is to be applied to men. Third-level theorists apparently believe that the decision not to blame the doers of acts that include factors other than voluntary acts among their causal antecedents is reached by a mere extension of the very same reasoning that leads us not to blame the doers of nonvoluntary acts; but this is not the case. The two premises, (1) that we are not morally responsible for acts unless they are voluntary, and (2) that for many of the causes of our acts we are not morally responsible, since these are not themselves voluntary acts, are not sufficient to yield the conclusion that we are not morally responsible for our voluntary acts. But those who wish to avoid this conclusion, without renouncing determinism in the process, cannot content themselves with the negative task of looking for loopholes in third-level arguments. Some rather complicated analyses of the standards that actually govern our judgments of moral praise and blame will be needed, along with much other work. The construction of a position at the fourth level of reflectiveness presents a difficult challenge; but the stimulating papers of Edwards and Hospers, as well as the spirited discussion that followed, have provided a strong incentive for continuing to try to meet that challenge.

2. Determinism and the Justifiability of Moral Blame

Richard Brandt, Swarthmore College

People often say that someone's act was "reprehensible" or "morally blameworthy" or "admirable" or "praiseworthy"; and they often have correspondingly favorable or unfavorable attitudes toward individuals on account of their acts. Furthermore, they often make very similar remarks about the character of persons, or about persons on account of their character; and again they sometimes have favorable or unfavorable attitudes toward persons on account of their character. We might sum all this up by saying that people sometimes engage in "blaming" or "praising." (A person need not say anything aloud in order to blame; it is enough if he makes a mental appraisal and takes up a corresponding attitude.)

When philosophers say that human beings are "morally responsible" for their actions, what they apparently mean—although one perhaps does them an injustice if one supposes anything specific is meant—is that it is right and proper, sometimes, to engage in blaming and praising as defined above. People are sometimes fittingly, deservedly, praised and blamed. These philosophers are not just making a *causal* statement, such as "Human volitions are sometimes uncaused beginnings of causal series," although some such causal proposition may be part of their reason for saying that human beings are "morally responsible." (Sometimes, too, when philosophers say that people "act freely" they are not asserting any definite causal proposition, but rather, simply, that those causal propositions are true about human behavior that are not inconsistent with the fittingness of blaming and praising behavior.)

A great many distinguished philosophers have held that, if determinism is a correct theory of all human psychological processes, then people are not "morally responsible" for their actions or character; viz., blaming and praising are not really fitting. I am unconvinced by their reasoning, however, and shall now explain why I think determinism is not inconsistent with moral responsibility.

It is convenient to begin by ascribing to these philosophers, who think determinism requires serious revision of ordinary moral thinking, a rather radical thesis, as follows. Traditionally, both in law and in morals, some acts have been regarded as excusable because of certain specific conditions, and other acts have been regarded as inexcusable in view of the absence of such specific conditions. Now, the radical thesis to be considered is this: that *no* actions are ever *inexcusable,* that all actions are excusable in view of their having been caused.

It would be unfair to suggest that any philosophers advocate this view in such a sweeping and unqualified form. So we must consider how this thesis should be complicated if it is to be seriously defended.

First, nobody holds that society has no need for a system of criminal justice. Moreover, given such a system with legal requirements for conduct and sanctions in case of infractions, there must be *some* actions that are inexcusable as far as the law is concerned. Everyone is agreed that misconduct must be subject to punishment, as a condition of the protection of the rights of all, as a condition of a well-ordered society where people live in security. It is also agreed, I suppose, that any acceptable system of criminal justice will excuse antisocial and forbidden behavior when it is unintentional, manifests itself under duress, etc., and that it will not excuse such behavior when it is deliberate, uncompelled—in short, when none of the standard defenses against a criminal charge apply. This distinction will stand, I think, irrespective of improvements in the system of criminal justice due to advances in psychology. So far, it is not clear that the acceptance of determinism indicates any modifications.

Second, the determinist must assent to a further utility of the distinction between excusable and inexcusable actions. It would be agreed today that up to a point it is correct to view moral criticism and accusations as an informal extension of the system of criminal justice. Moral criticism is a mild form of punishment; its occurrence is a sanction, the operation of which can warn and teach just as do criminal codes and criminal proceedings. Moral criticism, like legal sanctions, is a device for social control that is justified—at any rate, among other things—by its good effects. And, as in criminal law, it is a good thing for moral criticism to recognize certain antisocial and forbidden behavior as excusable under specific conditions similar in general type to those under which a person is not liable for his conduct before the law; and it is a good thing for moral criticism to recognize misconduct as inexcusable when none of these defenses are available. Again, then, it is not clear that the acceptance of determinism calls for modifications in the exercise of moral criticism.

If the determinist finds the above two points congenial, it is not easy to see how he will avoid going still farther. We must remember that, if we are to advocate moral criticism as a means of social control for the sake of the general welfare, we must specify the conditions necessary for the application of moral criticism. If moral criticism is to be effective it must be sincere, and if it is to be sincere the critic must be so constructed that he genuinely disapproves of the behavior or character trait he is criticizing; the capacity to be unfavorably excited toward persons who misbehave must be built in. Moreover, if, as suggested, what is wanted is a system of criticism that recognizes a distinction between excusable and inexcusable behavior, it appears we must also approve of people's recognizing in their own minds and consciences a distinction between excusable and inexcusable behavior.

In view of these considerations we may well ask philosophers who think determinism has sweeping importance for moral philosophy: What exactly is it that the truth of determinism renders indefensible? Are there some practices—of moral criticism etc.—that the consistent determinist must abandon, and if so, which? In what sense can it be said that, if determinism is true, no actions are inexcusable?

Perhaps what these philosophers are arguing is this: that whereas, even if determinism is true, praising and blaming *can* be justified to *some* extent by the above utilitarian appeal—so far the distinction between the excusable and the inexcusable stands up—nevertheless no *further* justification can be given for these practices. And it may be thought, in view of the essential point or significance of blaming or praising, some further justification *must* be given, if these practices are to be accepted as fitting and proper. I agree that the utilitarian justification is not enough, but I am unconvinced that further satisfactory justification is impossible.

Let us be clear what is considered unfitting by these philosophers: (1) that people should feel disgust, contempt, anger, etc., toward others on account of their misbehavior (instead of excusing them) and judge correspondingly; (2) that they should approve of making human beings suffer for their past deeds, when other things are equal (as they perhaps seldom are, since, for example, suffering is something to be avoided); (3) that they should feel remorseful about their own past deeds and not excuse themselves; (4) that they should take pride in having done what they think they ought when it was hard to do so; (5) that they should feel admiration or respect for others because they did what they ought when few would have been able to do so; and (6) that they should approve of rewarding people for special achievements, when they did what they ought though it was hard. Perhaps we are unfairly including too much. But what ought we to exclude, on the view proposed?

I am suggesting that the philosophers who say that determinism implies that people are not "morally responsible" are saying, in part, that the above activities, although they can be justified to some extent by their utility, cannot, in view of the truth of determinism, be justified in other respects, and that the utilitarian justification is not enough.

On what argument do these philosophers rely in order to show that, considerations of utility aside, moral criticism and the distinction between excusable and inexcusable behavior are unjustified if determinism is true? Professor Edwards argues, in effect, that a person who was convinced of the truth of determinism would (if he were disregarding the suggested utilities) never practice the various forms of moral criticism—or approve of such practice—if he were an impartial person in a calm frame of mind. I agree with him that, *if* such feelings would not occur if one were calm and impartial, they are not *moral* feelings when they do occur, and that then, if determinism is true, we probably ought not to say that people are blameworthy or admirable. (I have some qualms, though, since a person who thought of the utilities might still approve of such critical reactions. And it is conceivable—although here I would very much question whether in fact it has come about, even among "reflective" people—that "blameworthy" and "admirable" should be so used that a necessary condition for their applicability to an act or character would be that the latter be undetermined.

But is it the case that we incline to stop rendering—or approving the rendering of—moral judgments in our impersonal, nonviolent moments when we bring to mind the fact that all our behavior is determined and disregard the question of utility? Are we inclined to be less provoked with ourselves if we notice, for instance, how we have given way to an envious thought or motive—that we have been expounding a shoddy argument we should have more carefully scrutinized—when we think of the way all this was determined? Or suppose we hear reliably that one of our colleagues bears a baseless grudge against a student, that he marks the student's examinations low for no reason, that he refuses to listen to his questions, that he refuses to give him a recommendation necessary for medical school. Do we, when we reflect on the determinism in human behavior, find our indignation melted—in the way it is melted if we hear that his attitude was based on some serious misunderstanding, or even that he has been under severe emotional strain on account of personal difficulties? Or does our admiration for someone who has stood up for a principle at the risk of losing his job evaporate when we reflect that after all, given his make-up, such behavior was in the cards— as it does when we learn that our man knew from the start that his job was safe? It is not obvious that "No" is a wrong answer to these questions.

Further debate on these important issues is doubtless called for. Possibly it can be shown that a person who is unimpressed by the plea that some selfish action should be excused because it was determined somehow does not have a clear view of what it means for an action to be caused. Or again it might be shown that there is no formulable principle that will distinguish conditions under which we count misbehavior as excusable—e.g., ignorance or incapacity— from conditions under which we should refuse to regard misbehavior as excusable. (If we do not have such a principle ready, we might still decide that it is more plausible to keep on looking for a satisfactory formulation than to give up a distinction between types of cases that strike us as very different.)

My comments may be summarized as follows. First, the distinction between excusable and inexcusable misbehavior cannot be abandoned altogether. It is necessary for a desirable system of criminal law, and there are strong reasons of utility for its preservation in overt moral criticism and perhaps in the private moral thinking and feelings of mankind, irrespective of the truth of determinism. Second, it remains to be shown that "reprehensible" or "morally admirable" entails "was undetermined" in the usage of reflective people, or that the making of judgments of blame or the presence of corresponding feelings is *causally incompatible* with believing that the act in question was determined, even in a calm and impersonal frame of mind. And therefore the judgments and feelings whereby we distinguish between excusable and inexcusable behavior are not undermined as being unfitting, even if the truth of determinism is granted. My conclusion is that the implications of determinism for ordinary thinking about praiseworthiness and blameworthiness are by no means as serious as some philosophers suggest.

The above remarks have been concerned only with the consistency of judgments of praise and blame with determinism. But they bear also on the consistency with determinism of judgments of duty and obligation if, as I believe to be the case, saying that a certain action is one's duty is to say that one will be morally to blame if one fails to do it unless a valid excuse can be offered.

3. Determinism and Punishment

Percy W. Bridgman, Harvard University

At the present time there seems to be one question that looms as most important in the minds of many who are concerned with the question of punishment. This question is whether punishment is an acceptable line of conduct for society in the context provided by psychoanalysis, which pictures every single act of every individual as fully determined by factors over which he has no control. Thus stated, the problem whether to punish or not becomes a rather special subcase of the much more general problem of reconciling two patently inconsistent points of view, that of determinism and "free will." It is obviously of the utmost practical importance that we find a workable solution of this problem. Otherwise we become victims of a cancerous confusion leading to vacillation, like that of the donkey between two bales of hay.

It seems to me that we have to recognize clearly that there are two levels of operation. There is the level of daily life and social interaction, i.e., the level of "free will," and there is the deterministic level. So far as the deterministic level has concrete reference beyond the purely verbal it is the level of scientific activity. At this level, so far as present achievement goes, determinism has the status merely of a program to direct inquiry, a program applicable to the overwhelming majority of the phenomena of the world about us, including biological phenomena. It is a simple description of the attitude of many scientists to say that they can see nothing on the present horizon that would make this an impossible program, and that in many fields they regard finding methods of carrying out this program as the most promising line of scientific attack. It must be emphasized, however, that every biologist, and particularly every psychologist, would admit that at present we are fantastically far from being able to carry out such a program.

The other level is the common-sense level of everyday life, the level of "free will." On this level we have to devise a practical method of dealing with situations in which we cannot control or predict. Such situations occur predominantly in dealing with organisms. In particular, no one can find in his own consciousness or outside it factors that would enable him to predict his own future behavior. We develop a language to describe this situation, in which our inability to foresee our own future and that of our fellows is reflected in the concept of "free will," and we further develop a whole related vocabulary for situations in which we make no attempt at control or prediction. It is a mere statement of fact that there are situations in which we make no attempt at control or prediction, and any ultimate possibility of such control is disregarded. Whether or not we believe that we might at some time in the future achieve such control becomes, in this context, irrelevant.

There is, and can be, no sharp dividing line between the vocabulary of determinism and that of daily life. Use of the vocabulary of daily life is an art, and the wisdom of all ages is necessary to use it effectively.

It seems to me that much of the current unwillingness to use the instrument of punishment under conditions that would be acceptable to enlightened social opinion stems from a doctrinaire insistence that our verbal edifice be a single logically consistent unit. It is in the nature of things impossible to erect a single consistent verbal structure, logically watertight in all respects. To insist on acting as if we could is in the first place self-defeating—for by what logic can the man who argues that punishment is unjustified expect his argument to affect the actions of his opponent, when both his argument and the response to it were already rigidly predetermined? Pushed still further, the insistence that punishment is unjustified can lead only to social catastrophe. At present the only technique we have for dealing with our fellows is to act as if they were the same sort of creatures as we ourselves. We disregard determinism when dealing with ourselves—we have to disregard it, within reason, in our everyday contacts with others. Too many of us take our verbal structures with a deadly seriousness—a certain tough-mindedness and small sense of humor might provide an antidote.

4. Responsibility and Avoidability

Roderick W. Chisholm, Brown University

Edwards and Hospers hold that there is an important sense in which we may be said *not* to be morally responsible for any of our acts or choices. I propose the following as an explicit formulation of their reasoning:

1. If a choice is one we could not have avoided making, then it is one for which we are not morally responsible.

2. If we make a choice under conditions such that, given those conditions, it is (causally but not logically) impossible for the choice not to be made, then the choice is one we could not have avoided making.

3. Every event occurs under conditions such that, given those conditions, it is (causally but not logically) impossible for that event not to occur.

4. The making of a choice is the occurrence of an event.

∴5. We are not morally responsible for any of our choices.

If we wish to reject the conclusion (5)—and for most of us (5) is difficult to accept—we must reject at least one of the premises.

Premise (1), I think, may be interpreted as a logical truth. If a man is responsible for what he did, then we may say, "He *could* have done otherwise." And if we may say, "He couldn't help it," then he is not responsible for what he did.

Many philosophers would deny (2), substituting a weaker account of *avoidability*. A choice is avoidable, they might say, provided only it is such that, *if* the agent had reflected further, or had reflected on certain things on which in fact he did not reflect, he would *not* have made the choice. To say of a choice that it "could *not* have been avoided," in accordance with this account, would be to say that, even if the agent *had* reflected further, on anything you like, he would all the same have made the choice. But such conditional accounts of *avoidability* ("An act or choice is avoidable provided only it is such that, *if* the agent were to do so-and-so, the act or choice would not occur") usually have this serious defect: the antecedent clause ("if the agent were to do so-and-so") refers to some act or choice, or to the failure to perform some act or to make some choice; hence we may ask, concerning the occurrence or nonoccurrence of this act or choice, whether or not *it* is avoidable. Thus one who accepted (5) could say that, if the agent's failure to reflect further was itself unavoidable, his choice was also unavoidable. And no such conditional account of *avoidability* seems adequate to the use of "avoidable" and "unavoidable" in questions and statements such as these.

If we accept a conditional account of avoidability, we may be tempted to say, of course, that it would be a *misuse* of "avoidable" to ask whether the nonoccurrence of the antecedent event ("the agent does so-and-so") is avoidable. But the philosopher who accepts (5) may well insist that, since the antecedent clause refers to an act or a choice, the use of "avoidable" in question is *not* a misuse.

What, then, if we were to deny (3)? Suppose that some of our choices do not satisfy (3)—that when they are made they are *not* made under any conditions such that it is (causally) impossible (though logically possible) for them not to be made. If there are choices of this sort, then they are merely fortuitous or capricious. And if they are merely fortuitous or capricious, if they "just happen," then, I think, we may say with Blanshard that we are *not* morally responsible for them. Hence denying (3) is not the way to avoid (5).

We seem confronted, then, with a dilemma: either our choices have sufficient causal conditions or they do not; if they do have sufficient causal conditions they are not avoidable; if they do not, they are fortuitous or capricious; and therefore, since our choices are either unavoidable or fortuitous, we are not morally responsible for them.

There are philosophers who believe that by denying the rather strange-sounding premise (4) we can escape the dilemma. Insisting on something like "the primacy of practical reason," they would say that since we are certain that (5) is false we must construct a metaphysical theory about the self, a theory denying (4) and enabling us to reconcile (3) and the denial of (5). I say "metaphysical" because it seems to be necessary for the theory to replace (4) by sentences using such terms as "active power," "the autonomy of the will," "prime mover," or "higher levels of causality"—terms designating something to which we apparently need not refer when expressing the conclusions of physics and the natural sciences. But I believe we cannot know whether such theories enable us to escape our dilemma. For it seems impossible to conceive what the relation is that, according to these theories, holds between the "will," "self," "mover," or "active power," on the one hand, and the bodily events this power is supposed to control, on the other—the relation between the "activities" of the self and the events described by physics.

I am dissatisfied, then, with what philosophers have proposed as alternatives to premises (1) through (4) above, but since I feel certain that (5) is false I also feel certain that at least one of the premises is false.

5. Determinism, Freedom, and Responsibility

C. J. Ducasse, Brown University

Several speakers at this conference appeared to take it for granted that determinism and freedom are incompatible, and hence that the questions in need of being answered were only, first, whether, or how far and where in particular, determinism or freedom in fact obtains; and second, what bearing various answers to the first question would have on practical issues in philosophy, science, law, and ethics.

Underlying this conception of the points at issue is a tacit assumption that the concepts determinism, freedom, indeterminism, and contingency are quite clear, or at least clear enough to make possible definite answers to the questions mentioned. I believe on the contrary that this assumption is largely mistaken, and that the inconclusiveness of the present discussions, as well as of innumerable other discussions of the same questions in the past, has been due to the fact that they were engaged in without adequate preliminary analysis of the concepts employed in them. The remarks to follow will therefore attempt to distinguish among several of the senses in which the key terms mentioned are often used; to clarify each of those senses; and then to indicate what does or does not follow as regards some of the issues in discussions of which those terms are commonly employed.

1. *Determinism as theoretically universal predictability.* In science, and also in certain other contexts, determinism is employed to mean *theoretically universal predictability;* that is, it is used to signify that, on the basis of knowledge of (*a*) the state of the world at any given time and (*b*) the laws according to which its state at any time is related to its states at other times, it would be possible to infer what the state of the world was, or will be, at any earlier or later time. Laplace's famous statement formulates a determinism so conceived:

> An intelligence knowing, at a given instant of time, all forces acting in nature, as well as the momentary positions of all things of which the universe consists, would be able to comprehend the motions of the largest bodies of the world and those of the smallest atoms in one single formula, provided it were sufficiently powerful to subject all data to analysis. To it, nothing would be uncertain, both future and past would be present before its eyes.[1]

2. *Critique of Laplacian determinism.* This account of determinism, however, is open to fatal criticism on several grounds.

a. For one thing, it assumes that the physical world is the whole of the world; and this leaves out of account mental events in general

---

[1] *Théorie analytique des probabilités* (3d ed.; Paris, 1820).

and volitions in particular, unless it defines them as themselves purely physical events—e.g., as molecular events in the tissues of the brain. But so to define them is not legitimate, since it amounts to asserting that the term "mental events" does not denote the events we *do* denote by means of it, but denotes instead certain quite different events—such a contention being as paradoxical as would be the parallel one that what we intend to denote—i.e., to point at— when using the word "cabbages" is not cabbages but, say, tigers. Of course, it might conceivably be true that all mental events are *dependent* on bodily events of some sort. But to be "dependent on" and to be "identically the same as" are two different relations; the first, being at least dyadic, precludes the second, since it is monadic. Hence the physical world is not the whole world.

b. But further, determinism as conceived by Laplace assumes that observation would yield precise knowledge of the state of the physical world at the time; and this, since the days of Laplace, has been disproved. It has been shown that to observe both the position and the velocity of a particle at a given time is not simply difficult but inherently impossible, because to attempt it is automatically to alter one or the other.

c. Again, Laplacian determinism assumes that the only forces at work in the world are those of classical mechanics. But this is not known to be true, and it is dubious in particular in the case of biological processes, and still more so in the case of consciously purposive action.[2]

In addition, the determinism of Laplace ignores the possibility that some events or entities are wholly or in part *sui generis*—a possibility that would make the notion of *laws* governing their occurrence incongruous, since laws obtain with regard to events or entities only in so far as these are *instances of a kind,* but not in so far as they are *individually unique.* Indeed no event or entity is *completely* similar to any other; no matter how great may be the similarity of one to another, its being "other" means at least that its spatial and/or temporal relations are somewhat different; and this

[2] On this point interesting material is to be found in an address by H. S. Jennings on "Some Implications of Emergent Evolution," *Science,* January 14, 1927; in E. S. Russell's *The Directiveness of Organic Activities* (1946); and in recent writings of a number of other biologists.

entails that an individual residuum, unpredictable because unprecedented, is an ultimate constituent of every occurring event or existent thing.

e. The upshot, then, is that determinism *in the sense of theoretically universal predictability,* whether of all physical events only, or of events of other kinds, too—for instance, of mental events in general and of volitions or decisions in particular—is not only not known to be true, but much rather is known to be false. Hence the status of determinism in the sense of theoretically universal predictability is only that of a pious but bigoted article of scientistic faith.

3. *Freedom and determinism conceived as theoretically universal predictability.* What, now is entailed as regards freedom by the indefensibility of determinism conceived as theoretically universal predictability? Consider a given event—say, the choice a given person makes on a given occasion among the alternatives open to his choice. Obviously, the fact that the choice he makes was not certainly predictable—even perhaps by himself—does not entail that it was "free" in any sense other than "free from the possibility of being predicted"! In particular, it does not entail that the choice he made was *uncaused* in any sense of "uncaused" other than that of "unpredictable"; nor does it entail that the choice was made "freely" rather than perhaps under duress, threat, or pressure.

4. *Determinism conceived as fatalism.* Certain events, e.g., eclipses, tides, earthquakes, volcanic eruptions, etc., are beyond present or prospective control by man's will. Others, such as the movements of his limbs, and also many effects that these cause directly or indirectly under specifiable conditions, are within man's control when those conditions obtain. Fatalism, however, in effect contends that even under those conditions man's volitions are not *inherently* efficacious to their intent, but that their efficacy or inefficacy is preordained, permitted, or perhaps implemented, as man's clumsiness or resourcefulness may render necessary, by some mysterious purposeful agency called Fate, the Gods, or Destiny; and that, until its decrees are fulfilled, men—other than perhaps certain prophets—do not and cannot know what "Fate" had decreed.

No evidence, however, that would tend to show fatalism to be true is available, for when the event man attempts to cause is of a kind he is capable of causing at will under circumstances of certain kinds known to him, his failure to cause it in a given case is always explicable as resulting simply from his not having known that the circumstances then existing did in fact differ in some essential respect from those under which his action would have been efficacious to its intent. Fatalism thus arises only out of man's naïve tendency to assume, animistically, that causes which thwart or unexpectedly promote his purposes must themselves be purposive!

5. *Determinism as universality of causation.* The thesis of determinism conceived as universality of causation is that every event that occurs has some cause and has some effect. Whether this thesis is true or false, and what its truth or falsity entails as to man's freedom, depends on the nature of the causality relation.

a. Hume offers two definitions of causality—one objective and the other in part subjective. According to both our judgments that certain sequences of events are *causal* sequences mean that in our experience those sequences have been *constant,* i.e., *regular.* Hume insists, however, both after and before stating his two definitions, that both of them are "drawn from circumstances foreign to the cause . . . from something extraneous and foreign to it." But although he acknowledges that this is inconvenient, he declares that it cannot be remedied.

If, however, as some writers since Hume have done, one takes *experienced regularity of sequence* to be *all* that causality consists in, then *universality* of causation would mean that every event of kind *E* we have experienced was *in our experience* preceded by an event of kind *C* and followed by one of kind *F.* And this, of course, has not in fact been the case. Moreover, even if it had been the case, it would entail nothing about events of a kind that we have experienced no instances of; nor even about *instances* we have not experienced, of a *kind* that we have experienced some (other) instances of.

Anyway, the definition of causality simply as empirical regularity of sequence would, as Thomas Reid and others have pointed out, require us to pronounce causal certain sequences in our experience that are regular, but that we confidently deny to be causal. On the other hand, we sometimes pronounce a sequence causal without waiting to observe whether or not it is constant. That is, we pro-

nounce it causal on grounds other than constancy, which, according
to Hume's definition, alone constitutes causality.

Thus the regularity of a sequence never in itself answers, but on
the contrary always raises, the question whether the sequence is a
causal one. That a given sequence is causal entails that repetition of
its first term and of its circumstances will be regularly followed by
repetition of its second term; but regularity of a sequence does
not entail, but only suggests, that it is perhaps a causal one. To decide whether or not it is indeed causal, we need have available, and
in fact use, a different definition of causality.

b. Causality is *the relation that obtains between the three factors
of a perfect experiment;* i.e., between a given state of affairs *S* and
only two changes (whether simple or complex) in it—one a change
C at a time *T*1, and the other a change *E* at an immediately sequent
time *T*2. If this relation obtains among *S, C,* and *E,* then *C* is, by
definition, the *proximate cause* of *E* under the *circumstances S.* The
causality relation is thus not dyadic only, but irreducibly triadic: the
circumstances *S* cannot be regarded as a part of the cause *C,* because
C consists of a *change* occurring in *S.*

c. That change *C* in *S* was the proximate cause of change *E* in *S*
does not presuppose that *S, C,* and *E* ever occurred before or ever
will occur again, but only that *C* and *E* were the only two changes in
S; but it entails that, should *S,* and *C* in *S,* ever have occurred before
or ever occur again, then *E* in *S* did, or will, follow in every such
case. For in the definition of etiological sufficiency of *C* in *S* to *E* in
S, i.e., of causation of the latter by the former, no particular date
is specified, but only posteriority of the time of *E* to the time of *C.*
Moreover, what occurs in *S* upon occurrence of *C* in *S* is *an intrinsic
element of the nature of S;* hence to suppose that *S* and that *C* in *S*
recur, but that *E* in *S* does not then recur, is to suppose contradic-
torily that in the second case the state of affairs in question is, to
that extent at least, *different* from *S.*

The fact that causality is defined in terms of a *single* case of sequence (of the type specified above) entails that causal laws are
causal not because they are laws (since some laws, to wit, some
empirical regularities, are not causal) but because they are generalizations from cases each of which was in its own individual right
a case of causation; if two or more sequences of the type specified

resemble one another in that, and only in that, in each of them the state of affairs is of a certain kind S, the cause of a certain kind C, and the effect of a certain kind E, then the "method of single agreement," employed as a method of generalization by abstraction, warrants the generalization that in *any* state of affairs of kind S, an only change of kind C immediately causes a single change of kind E.

d. The foregoing analysis of causality makes evident that the canon of the so-called "method of single difference" is a *description of the causality relation itself*, not of a relation other than causality, constituting only a sign of the presence of causality. That is, the "method of single difference" is a method only in the strained sense in which the description or photograph of a person can be said to be a method by which to identify him if one happens to meet him. Causality *is, and is nothing but,* the relation between S, C, and E described in what precedes. It constitutes *etiological sufficiency* of C in S to E in S, and conversely, *etiological necessitation* of E in S by C in S.

e. From this analysis of causality it follows analytically that every event has a cause and an effect. For, given any state of affairs S and any change E that is at its time the only change in S, there is always some immediately anterior change in S that qualifies as cause of E in S, i.e., that is the only change in S at its time. This follows from the fact that without some change there is no time; and hence that to suppose either that S endured or that S changed prior to E is to suppose that some sort of "clock" was "ticking" then. And should no other change than the "ticking" of that "clock" have occurred in S prior to E, then the "ticking" itself would qualify as cause of E under the definition.

For a corresponding reason any change C in any S that is the only change in S at its time causes some effect E in S. Also, the specification that C and E be the *only* two changes in S makes it superfluous to specify that C and E are contiguous in time. Their contiguity is entailed by the specification that they are the *only* two changes in S, since, if time elapsed, i.e., if any "clock" were "ticking," between C and E, its "ticks" would constitute changes in S additional to C and E.

f. To these remarks it should be added that in the case of causality as in that of sincerity or divinity or gravitation, etc., to define its nature is one task; and to decide whether something concrete—in the case of causality, a concrete relation that we observe—is really an instance of what the definition specifies is quite another task and one that, theoretically, is never performed with complete certainty. The acceptability or nonacceptability of the decision in a given case turns on pragmatic considerations, just as the answer to the question whether the weight of a given book is exactly the same as, or is a trifle more or a trifle less than, that of the standard pound—i.e., of the piece of metal whose weight is 1 lb. by definition—turns on the purpose that governs at the time. If one's purpose is to mail the book, then the scale at the post office, and the clerk's reading of what it marks, are authoritative.

On the other hand, if in the attempt to identify empirically instances of what a definition defines, all pragmatic concerns are put aside, then one automatically rules out all possibility of success; for some pragmatic concern is the only thing that gives any empirical meaning to the question whether a proposed operation of identification and a proposed criterion of the success of the operation are absurd or on the contrary rational.

g. The conclusion, then, of the present section is that determinism, in the sense that every event has some cause and some effect, is analytically true. This, however, does not at all entail that every event is completely and certainly predictable even theoretically, i.e., even on the supposition of exact and exhaustive knowledge of the past history of the universe; for complete and certain prediction would be possible only on the basis of strict sameness of present and past data, whereas what we actually get is only similarity in varying degrees. At all times in the history of the world, an element of novelty, whether great or small, is present and accounts for what has been called the *emergence* of such novelties as "life" and "mind"; which, because novel, i.e., unprecedented, were inherently unpredictable.

To designate the sense of "determinism" considered in this section, which entails that universality of causation is analytically true and yet which has room for the occurrence of novel and therefore unpredictable "emergents," we may adopt the name by which the late biologist H. S. Jennings referred to his own conception of determinism, to wit, "radically experimental determinism."

6. *Freedom.* Freedom is more often conceived negatively, i.e., in terms of indeterminism or of exception to determinism, than in terms of a positive analysis. The same is true of the terms chance and contingency.

a. What has been said up to this point will have made clear that to say of a given event—whether physical or mental—that it was "free," or more or less synonymously, that it was "contingent" or "a matter of chance," may mean different things. For example, it may mean (1) that the event was *practically* unpredictable, i.e., unpredictable on the basis of the data we had or could get at the time; or (2) that it was unpredictable *even theoretically,* for one or another of the reasons mentioned in our critique of Laplace-type determinism; or (3) that it had no cause; or (4) that it was not *logically necessary,* i.e., that supposition of the event's nonoccurrence, or of its having been more or less different from what it was, implies no contradiction. And of course, so long as these diverse meanings of the term are not distinguished in discussions of "freedom," no possibility exists of really establishing anything.

Anyway, none of these four senses seem to correspond to the meaning "free" is intended to have in the instances people commonly offer when asked to give examples of the exercise of that "free will" they believe they have; for they usually offer illustrations such as that, at the moment, they are free to raise their arm, or not, as they will; or that, when offered a choice of, say, apple pie or cherry pie, they are free to choose the one they prefer. An analysis of the meaning of "freedom" as used on these and similar occasions is what I now submit.

b. That a person *P,* under circumstances *K,* "*can,*" or synonymously "*is free to,*" do *A* or not to do it means that volition (or, *pace* Professor Ryle, "decision") by *P* to do *A* or not do *A,* would, in those circumstances, be sufficient to cause *A* to occur or not to occur. And if it should be objected that this is only freedom to *act,* but not freedom to *will,* then the reply is that that analysis applies whether *A* is a bodily act or itself an act of will; that is, it applies irrespective of whether *P*'s present decision is, say, to raise his arm, or whether his present decision is, perhaps, to *decide tomorrow* whether to buy a house or rent one.

c. That under the circumstances that obtained *P* was, in the sense just stated, free to do or not do *A* does not presuppose that his decision had no motive or other cause; nor does the fact that neither he nor anyone else could have on that occasion predicted what his decision would be constitute any evidence that it had no cause.

d. Nor does the fact that his decision, like any other event, had some cause—causation, as defined in Section 5*b*, is universal— mean that his decision was not free but compelled; for a decision one is caused to make is not describable as "compelled" unless it is a decision to do something to which one is averse, even if less averse than to the alternatives then open to choice. The decision to hand over one's money to the holdup man who confronts one with the choice "Your money or your life" is not made freely but under compulsion; whereas the decision to choose, say, apple pie rather than cherry pie in the restaurant is—assuming that one likes apple pie— an example of what is called a free decision.

Thus the assumption that tacitly underlies most discussions of "free will" and determinism—the assumption, namely, of incompatibility between, on the one hand, determinism in the sense of universality of causation and, on the other, freedom in the sense in which man certainly does have freedom in many cases—is an altogether erroneous assumption. It arises from failure to analyze the meaning that the terms in question have in the specific contexts in which they are employed.

7. *Determinism and moral responsibility*. The final question to consider is what determinism, in the sense that every event has some cause and some effect, entails concerning moral responsibility or lack of it.

a. It is essential here to distinguish between *moral* responsibility and the *legal* responsibility that in practice may or may not go with it. Also, to distinguish between either moral or legal responsibility and merely *etiological* responsibility, which consists simply in the fact that our acts, besides the effects they aim at, have many others of which we are not aware, and which may or may not harmonize with our intention.

b. That a person *P* is *now* morally responsible for his voluntary acts—or was not so but can now be made morally responsible for his future ones—means simply that to praise or blame him or otherwise reward or punish him for some thing he now does or did *will*

*tend to cause him to act, or tend to inhibit him from acting, in a
similar manner on similar future occasions.*

c. Hence, that a person P is *not* now morally responsible for what
he voluntarily does or did means that praise or blame, or other forms
of reward or punishment, would have no such effect on him. In
other words, it means that he is not now capable of moral education,
and hence that what he needs is psychiatric treatment. In such a
case to inflict punishment for a morally wrong act is either simply
stupid or sadistic or both.

d. This analysis of what constitutes "moral" responsibility entails
that such responsibility not only is not incompatible with determinism, but on the contrary presupposes determinism. In other words,
that an agent is morally responsible presupposes that an *awareness*
on his part that something he contemplates doing would be morally
wrong or, as the case may be, morally right (his notion of what
constitutes moral rightness or wrongness is irrelevant here) *will*,
other motives being equal, *cause* him to refrain from acting, or on the
contrary *cause* him to act. Without such causation there is no moral
responsibility.

6.   Some Reflections on "The Case for Determinism"

Carl G. Hempel, Princeton University

1. *On defining determinism.* There appears to be a discrepancy
between two characterizations of determinism that Professor Blanshard offers at the beginning of his admirably lucid and stimulating
paper. In the third paragraph determinism is defined as the view that
every event A has at least one temporally later necessary consequent
B. According to this view, then, the cause A is a sufficient condition
of the effect B; and determinism asserts that every event causes some

(later) event. But clearly this assertion is by no means equivalent to the thesis that every event is caused by some (earlier) event, or briefly that "all events are caused"—a formulation by which Mr. Blanshard characterizes determinism in the second paragraph of his essay.

Evidently it is the latter assertion that gives significance to the problem of free choice, the central topic in Mr. Blanshard's discussion. For the question at issue is whether all events, including human acts of choice, are caused by antecedent events—not whether they in turn have certain necessary consequents. And indeed a deterministic thesis to the effect that every event causes some later event would be quite compatible with the "uncaused" occurrence of various phenomena, such as, perhaps, the spontaneous creation of hydrogen atoms envisaged by some contemporary cosmologists. Mr. Blanshard's thesis of determinism will therefore be construed here as asserting that for every event B there exists an antecedent event A that is a sufficient condition for the occurrence of B.

Mr. Blanshard uses the phrase "given A, B must occur" as a general characterization of the relation that obtains between an event A and a later event B if A is a sufficient condition, or cause, of B. As to the meaning of that "must," he is willing to let us make our own choice among a logical "must," a physical or metaphysical one, and a "must" that simply means universal factual association. In the brief space of his paper Mr. Blanshard certainly could not be expected to give a detailed analysis of the concept in question—this would have made it necessary, for example, to tackle the hornets' nest of problems surrounding the counterfactual conditional. But I think there is reason to feel uneasy at the sweeping claims of a determinism that is said to hold true equally for all the different interpretations of "must" that Mr. Blanshard allows us here.

Choosing the logical "must," for example, we obtain the thesis that for any event B occurring at some time t_1, there is an event A at an earlier time t_0, such that the occurrence of A at t_0 is a logically sufficient condition for the occurrence of B at t_1. But this is trivially true in all cases. For example, let the occurrence of B at t_1 consist in the onset of rain on the campus of Yale University at noon of a certain day, and let t_0 be 11:00 A.M. of the same day. Then, to show that the deterministic thesis with the logical "must" is satisfied, it suffices to choose for A the state of affairs that consists in the condition of the Yale campus exactly one hour before the onset of a rainfall. To be sure, we may not be able to ascertain that A prevailed at t_0 until the occurrence of B at t_1, but this is irrelevant to the point to be proved, namely that there is in fact a state of affairs A at t_0 that is logically sufficient for the occurrence of B at t_1.

The preceding argument shows, I think, that the deterministic thesis with its "must" construed as expressing logical necessity is of no significance for the problem of free choice: the existence of an earlier state of affairs that is a logically sufficient condition for a given act of choice surely does not mean that the act is determined in any sense that would cast doubt on the freedom of choice.

I am not clear what a metaphysical construction of "must" might come to, but I should like to add a few words concerning the interpretation of "must" by reference to physical—or, more generally, empirical—laws. On this interpretation Mr. Blanshard's deterministic thesis asserts that there exists a set of laws such that every event B is a consequent, according to those laws, of some preceding event A. But this statement, again, is always true in a trivial manner. For no matter what the sequence of events in the universe may be, it can always be represented as a mathematical function of time; and this function provides the requisite law. Suppose, for example, that we are interested only in the changes of temperature and color that occurred in the course of the history of the universe at a given place. The temperature at any time may be measured on the Kelvin scale and represented by a real number; the color can be similarly expressed by means of a number indicating a location in the color scale. The temporal succession of temperatures and colors at the given place now corresponds to an assignment to each value of the time variable of one temperature number and one color number. This determines two mathematical functions, which trivially furnish laws governing the changes of temperature and color at the given place. The argument can now be extended to apply to the changes anywhere in the universe of temperature, color, and any other characteristic. Thus the course of the universe is governed by functional laws (which may, however, be so complex as to be beyond the reach of scientific discovery), and the deterministic thesis with its "must" construed in terms of empirical laws is true.[1] In fact, the laws here referred to are so strong that every event is determined by the laws alone, without the need of recourse to antecedent occurrences.

The argument here outlined shows that determinism in the form under discussion is trivially true; thus it can have no greater significance for the freedom of choice than the truth of the deterministic thesis with its "must" construed as representing logical necessity.

Nor can the truth of determinism on the basis of this construction of "must" cheer the empirical scientist, for he is interested in the possibility of prediction; and this requires the determination by law of events by earlier ones in a stronger sense than that so far considered: the laws in question have to be of a sufficiently simple kind to permit of discovery and subsequent predictive application by human beings. (Causal laws in the technical sense of physics are required to satisfy certain conditions as to mathematical form,[2] but these need not be considered here.)

On this interpretation of "must" Mr. Blanshard's thesis is by no means trivial. In fact, despite the vagueness introduced by the requirement of formal simplicity for the laws, it makes an extremely strong and sweeping assertion. And I would suggest that the objections to determinism that Mr. Blanshard examines in his paper be construed as concerning this strong thesis. (In fact, the objections based on the character of quantum physics refer to the even stronger thesis of universal causality in the technical sense of physics.)

[1] The basic idea of this argument is set forth by Bertrand Russell in his essay "On the Notion of Cause," which is reprinted in his book *Mysticism and Logic* (London, 1921). A similar consideration is presented in Moritz Schlick's essay "Causality in Everyday Life and in Recent Science" (reprinted in H. Feigl and W. Sellars, eds., *Readings in Philosophical Analysis* [New York, 1949], pp. 515ff.) Russell's idea is discussed also in Philip Frank's *Philosophy of Science* (New York: Prentice-Hall, 1957), which, in chaps. xi and xii, presents an illuminating analysis of the concepts of causality and determinism.

The argument presented above calls for one qualifying remark, however. Not all functions of time can be represented by analytic mathematical expressions, nor even by symbolic expressions of finite length in a language using a finite or denumerably infinite set of different basic symbols. Thus, not all possible laws can be expressed in the language of science, just as not all real numbers can be represented by numerical expressions.

[2] For a discussion of these conditions, see, for example, H. Margenau, *The Nature of Physical Reality* (New York, 1950), chap. xix, and Frank, *op. cit.*, chaps. xi and xii.

2. *On the relevance of introspective evidence to determinism.* As for the first objection to determinism, which refers to a stubborn feeling of freedom of choice, I fully agree with Mr. Blanshard that it cannot count as evidence against determinism, for this kind of feeling can surely be deceptive. Indeed I think that the feeling is irrelevant to the question of causal determination. For in order to decide whether a given act of choice is causally determined we have to judge whether there is an antecedent event with which the choice is *connected by a general law* of simple form. And surely the data obtainable by introspection, especially the "stubborn feeling of freedom," have no bearing on this question. The timid man in a hypnotist's audience, for example, who gets up to make a speech, may truthfully protest a feeling of complete freedom in choosing to do so: this is quite compatible with the possibility that his choice was causally determined (via general laws concerning the effects of hypnosis) by the instructions he received earlier under hypnosis.

But it seems to me that in his defense of determinism Mr. Blanshard makes use of the very same kind of argument that he rightly rejects when it is employed by indeterminists. The use of introspection illustrated by Galton's case surely is no more suited to establishing the existence of antecedent constraints determining choices according to general laws than the feeling of freedom invoked by the indeterminists is suited to establishing the opposite. A person's introspective reflection on the motives that might have determined a certain action of his can yield quite deceptive results; surely it is not suited to establishing the existence of general laws linking the adduced motives to the action under scrutiny.

3. *On levels of causation.* In his outline of a nonmechanical kind of determinism for psychological occurrences, Mr. Blanshard refers to aesthetic, logical, and moral constraints as determining factors. Now, it would be incompatible with his view of causation to construe these constraints as abstract aesthetic ideals, logical truths, and moral principles; for these lack the temporal character that Mr. Blanshard's definition of determinism requires of all causal factors. To meet this requirement we shall have to construe the constraints in question as awareness and espousal by a given human agent of the ideas or ideals in question. In explaining the work of a given painter by reference to certain aesthetic ideals, for example, we have

to construe the constraining antecedent factor as the disposition of the painter to conform to those ideals.

There is another consideration that lends support to this way of looking at the matter. The attribution of a causal role to timeless ideals and relations not only violates Mr. Blanshard's initial definition of causal determinism: it seems to me an inherently obscure idea. Surely Mr. Blanshard must be using a metaphor—and I think a misleading one—when he speaks of an abstract, nontemporal ideal as getting hold of an artist and molding his work, or of a timeless relation serving as the condition of a temporal passage. Those timeless entities cannot be held to exert a universal causal influence, or else there would be no logical or mathematical errors, no immoral acts. And indeed Mr. Blanshard notes explicitly that man is not always guided by the proper ideals. Thus how a given person is going to act will be determined, not by an ideal standard pertinent to the action, but rather by whether or not the agent has a certain disposition, namely that of acting in accordance with the standard. For example, so far as honesty can be said to have been a causal determinant of George Washington's confessing about the cherry tree, it suffices to describe this factor as Washington's disposition to act honestly, and it would be an unnecessary, and indeed very risky, hypostatization to attribute his confession to the supervenience, from a higher causal level, of the timeless moral ideal of honesty.

Yet this avoidance of an appeal to causal determinants of a higher order involves no "mechanistic" or "materialistic" assumptions: in particular, it does not presuppose the reducibility of psychology to physics and chemistry; that is, the possibility of fully describing all psychological events in physicochemical terms or the possibility of explaining them by means of physicochemical laws.

Nor, of course, does the viewpoint here suggested imply that all psychological phenomena are causally determined either by dispositions of the kind just mentioned or by other factors. In fact, as was pointed out at the end of Section 1, above, the thesis of universal determinism is inherently vague; it is not as clear and precise an assertion as, say, a law of physics. At the same time, the thesis makes a tremendously stronger claim than a physical law, for it asserts the existence of a comprehensive set of laws sufficient to determine every event in the world of our experience. And the extent to which this claim is correct cannot be discovered by philosophical reasoning alone, nor by reference to the crude data provided by everyday experience or introspection: it has to be ascertained by means of rigorous and extensive scientific research.

7. Some Further Reflections on Moral Responsibility

Howard W. Hintz, Brooklyn College

Professor Hospers' thesis (like Professor Edwards') denies the existence of moral responsibility in any sense in which an individual can be held finally accountable or answerable for his acts. Thus, by the analysis of the term and concept of responsibility attempted by Edwards and Hospers, "responsibility" is relegated to the status of a pragmatic device by which a person may by some sort of persuasion, admonition, threat, punishment, or other social pressure be induced to pursue a course of behavior consonant with the norms approved and established by a given culture group.

What I want particularly to do in this brief criticism is not categorically to deny the validity of the Edwards-Hospers thesis but to point out what I believe its necessary corollaries and implications as far as ethical considerations are concerned. Thus I do not see how we can escape the conclusion that this thesis destroys the foundations of all prescriptive ethics except on the arbitrary-power level. If, as suggested above, the possibility of establishing moral values and standards is removed, then the basis of meaningful and purposeful living, of human dignity, and ultimately of civilized society itself is undermined. It should be further noted that the thesis is not only deterministic (despite Hospers' denial of the relevance of the determinism issue) but fatalistic, no matter how much the fact may be disguised.

Neither the Edwards-Hospers' analysis nor any other deterministic explanation has yet succeeded in refuting the fact that all individuals above the idiot level possess in some sense, however limited by internal or external compulsions, the power of choice, the power to decide and to select among a given set of alternatives, or, to follow G. E. Moore, the ability to say meaningfully, after certain types of choices have been made, "I *could* have chosen or acted differently." The inescapable truth of this is repeatedly demonstrated by the fact that on reflection and a subsequent awareness of the consequences of a choice, all of us, when a similar set of alternatives is presented to us a second or third time, choose differently because we have been dissatified with the consequences of the former choice.

The attempt to invalidate freedom and power of choice on the grounds that choices are attributable to underlying desires, to previous conditioning, and to basic qualities of character is, it seems to me, highly factitious. It is saying nothing more than that a cause and effect relationship prevails in the phenomena of human behavior as it does in other natural phenomena; it is simply to assert the principle of causality. But rather than vitiating the meaningfulness of discriminating choices and acts of will, causality itself is a primary condition of meaningful choice.

Is there any possible way—within the framework of a causal determinism rooted in the obvious psychological and naturalistic facts of human experience as outlined by Edwards and Hospers—in which we can retrieve a modicum of individual moral responsibility and hence of human dignity? I believe it is not only possible but essential that we do so by recourse to the familiar principle (constantly stressed by John Dewey) that each man is *responsible* for making the best choice available to him *within the scope of his limitations and his powers*. That these limitations and powers differ widely among men no one will deny. But to the extent that an individual acts or fails to act responsibly within the range of his capacities, whatever they may be, to that extent he is praiseworthy or blameworthy. It is only because this principle is universally recognized in everyday experience and practice that any type of social order is even possible.

Two additional points should be emphasized:

1. Hospers' thesis not only destroys moral responsibility: it also destroys all *rationality* in human experience. If we accept the proposition that a man acts *only* as previous determining and conditioning factors *compel* him to act, then I submit that the function and office of reasoning have been utterly destroyed, for the very question whether a man reasons or not is then completely dependent on the allegedly fortuitous and contingent factors that shaped his nature and character. His reasoning or nonreasoning then becomes pure accident and is therefore, by definition, removed from the area of rational choice. I do not see how Hospers can escape the logical necessity of this conclusion.

2. However emphatically Hospers may deny the relevance to his argument of the determinism-indeterminism issue, his thesis is not only deterministic: it is wholly fatalistic. My quarrel is not with determinism—at least in some of its forms—but with Hospers' denial of the relevance of his thesis to the determinism issue. How can the logic of Hospers' argument possibly escape the ultimate assertion of fatalism? If everything that a man chooses or decides or does— *including* the decisions he makes after reflection and deliberation— is *entirely* the result of the conditioning factors of his heredity and his environment, then what conceivable area of what we have traditionally called moral choice has not been *predetermined?* Wherein, then, does Hospers' position differ fundamentally from that of Jonathan Edwards, who maintained that a man may choose what he wills to do but that he has no choice about what he wills to choose? In his own explication of predeterminism and predestination Jonathan Edwards was, as has long been recognized, strictly logical, and accepted, however reluctantly, all the implications of his logical consistency. Is Hospers, I wonder, willing to do the same? Jonathan Edwards finally was driven by his own rigorous logic to concede that free will was an illusion. Is Hospers, with equal logical consistency, willing to admit the same?

Neither can I recognize the validity of the distinction Hospers makes between the so-called upper and lower levels of responsibility —which presumably is a distinction between desires on the one hand and specific choices and actions on the other. On the upper level, says Hospers, will, choice, and responsibility are meaningful; on the lower level of desires they are not. But if my underlying desires are the wellspring of my volitions and my actions, how can the upper level of responsibility be disengaged from the lower level? In point of fact the two levels are constantly interacting—so that the choices I make and the acts I perform today on an upper-level volitional basis affect in large measure the *desires* I shall have tomorrow. At this juncture the two levels would seem to merge indistinguishably. The individual choices of the present are not only causative agents of future events and future acts: they are also generating and modifying agents of new desires and altered character structures.

It is now widely recognized among moral philosophers that, no matter how irrefutable the logic of absolute psychological or naturalistic determinism may be, sane and rational human beings in order to retain their sanity, their rationality, and their purposefulness in living still stubbornly insist on deciding, choosing, and acting as though they were autonomous, dignified, and free individuals. This is the phenomenon, above all, that still needs to be explained, and—herein lies the crux of my argument—the explanation is not to be found in the Edwards-Hospers thesis. I suspect that the most disturbing and serious weakness of this thesis lies in the fact that it is based on a groundwork of completely unproved and possibly unprovable assumptions. If it represents a form of determinism, as I have insisted, it is not a scientific determinism, but a rationalistic determinism differing in no essential respects from Calvinistic fatalism as far as its hypothetical assumptions and practical implications are concerned. Hospers is right in divorcing his thesis from the conclusion of empiricists like Hume, Mill, and Schlick. There is indeed nothing empirical about his position.

For the fact is that scientifically and empirically we are at the present moment far from having a complete knowledge of the meaning and dimensions of human character structure, of the complexity of the forces that create, modify, or alter this structure or, most significantly, of the degree to which the human organism contains *within itself* the autonomous power to alter, to originate, to create, and thus to overcome previous conditioning. It has yet to be demonstrated, empirically and scientifically, that acts of will, choices and decisions, and *new* conditioning forces may not radically alter character structure itself.

We might well be reminded at this point of Whitehead's conception of origination and creativity as the distinguishing marks of an "actual entity" or of the life principle itself.

8. Necessity, Indeterminism, and Sentimentalism

Sidney Hook, New York University

I

If the criterion of a necessary statement is that its denial is self-contradictory, then none but logical statements or those declared true in virtue of their form alone are strictly necessary. "Every effect has a cause" is a necessary statement. "Every event has a cause" and "Every event is a cause of another event" are not necessary statements. If determinism is the belief that all events have causes and are themselves causes of other events, its denial is not self-contradictory. The only evidence we can have for belief in the validity of determinism is empirical: the success of our predictions.

Nonetheless, "predictability" and "determinism" are not by any means interchangeable terms although they are related. Indeterminism entails unpredictability in respect to a character or event assumed to be undetermined. In a chance world God might be able to foresee any or all specific, fortuitous events; but if successful guesses are ruled out as predictions, men in such a world could make no genuine predictions. Unpredictability, however, does not entail indeterminism, since it is compatible with the existence of a theoretically determined system of such vast complexity that it is beyond human power to make correct predictions. This raises a problem that I attempted in vain to get the speakers and participants in the Institute to address themselves to: viz., What is the pragmatic difference between asserting that a system or state of affairs is undetermined and asserting that the system is so complexly determined that no predictions can be reliably made?

If one must choose between these two assertions, it is reasonable to defend the assertion that the apparently undetermined system is actually a complexly determined one on *heuristic* grounds. If we act on the assumption that a system is determined, then it is more likely that we shall discover laws and make successful predictions about the future than if we assume that chance reigns. But can anything more than this be said for the belief in determinism? It does not carry us beyond Peirce's observation that determinism is a postulate, and a postulate is something we *hope* is true. Obviously, to say that all events are caused, that determinism holds not only in this or that area, but *universally,* is always to say more than we definitely know at any actual time, even if we have a right to say it—a right that is contested by scientists who assert that the advance of scientific knowledge no longer depends on it in every domain. We can definitely reject indeterminism as false if it asserts that nothing is determined, because we know that some things are; but if it asserts merely that not everything is determined, it cannot be rejected out of hand. The issue must be joined in the field where the sway of determinism is disputed. Operationally, however, the only *evidence* one can have for the belief that a state of affairs is determined, as distinct from the reasonableness of the hope and faith that it is, is measured by the degree to which we can control, predict, construct, and, to use Professor Black's phrase, "make things happen."

If I understand Professor Blanshard, he overstates the case for determinism by interpreting causality in the realm of cognitive mental events, with some overtones that in the end this is true for all events, as a relation of necessity. He assimilates, although he does not completely identify, the necessities of aesthetic and moral thinking to logical thinking, which itself is partly under the constraint of objective logical necessity in the subject matter thought about. I see no valid reason for interpreting determinism in this way when applied to thinking in any or all of its forms. According to his conception of determinism, an event, "thinking," whether it is thinking about music or mathematics or anything at all, is said to be determined if some other event, or set of events, is a sufficient condition of its occurrence. The same is true whether the event in question is "dreaming" or "hoping," "creating" or "deducing." It still remains true whether the event is "thinking correctly" or "thinking incorrectly." If determinism is valid as applied to the realm of mind, an incorrect answer to any question is just as much determined, just as "necessary" in Professor Blanshard's sense, as a correct answer. This does not wipe out or call into question in any way the difference between a correct and an incorrect answer. It indicates only that what makes the difference between the objectively correct and objectively incorrect answer, especially if interpreted as the enduring presence of objective, timeless truths, is irrelevant in answering the question whether, given the mental event *B,* whatever its character, true or false etc., there exists another event, or set of events, *A,* such that *A* is a sufficient condition of *B.* If over and above *A,* it is necessary to invoke the compulsion of timeless *truths* to explain *B* when *B* consists in the thinking of a *correct* answer, why is it not necessary to invoke the compulsion of timeless *errors* or *falsities* to explain *B* when *B* consists in the thinking of an *incorrect* answer?

Empirically I am not at all convinced that the musician, for example, of whom Professor Blanshard speaks, who adds one bar to another in the process of composition always does so because he feels that it is an aesthetically required necessity, and that his feeling so is either a necessary or sufficient condition for the mental event that consists in the composing of the bar. He must sound the bar before he can judge or feel whether it is aesthetically required. If it is determined it must be determined by a previous event. A musician might have the feeling of aesthetic necessity for any one or even a number of quite different ways of completing a musical phrase, and a critic might say that the musician was mistaken in his judgment or feeling about each variant. In general, whether anything is required in a creation or not cannot be ascertained independently of a purpose, aim, or goal—whether of artist, critic, or spectator. Once this is given, the question of what is required permits of an objective and relative solution. We sometimes say that a goal, plan, or purpose determines the occurrence of an event. But this is an ellipsis. It is the *thought* or *desire* of the goal, a psychic or physicopsychic event, that determines, *if* determinism operates in the realm of mind.

There is one curious feature in Professor Blanshard's brilliant essay. He begins by denying that the content of consciousness, "the stubborn feeling" of being free and undetermined, is sufficient to disprove the fact of determinism. But before he concludes he cites with approval the plain man's stubborn feeling of absurdity or incredulity at the idea that the determinism to which he has no objections "as applied by physicists to atoms, by himself to machines, or by his doctor to his body," can be applied by anyone "to his reflection and will." No matter how strong the feeling, it seems to me no more decisive in assessing the validity of the claim that such a determinism can be applied to man than in appraising the claims of indeterminism. As evidence this feeling is not to be ignored or dismissed; but it is less weighty than the "medical evidence" (I use the expression as a summary term for all the scientific evidence) that willing and reflecting, like all other mental processes, are in manifold ways, too numerous to mention here, dependent on the brain and other conditions of the human body and human society. Undoubtedly it goes beyond the evidence to say that all willing and reflecting are dependent on earlier events in the history of the acculturated organism that is man. But it is less unreasonable to believe it than any other alternative. We have more evidence for it today than a hundred years ago. If we have still more evidence for it a hundred years from now, it will be an even more reasonable belief, unless there is better evidence for some other alternative.

II

Normally I should be reluctant to speak of the principle of indeterminacy in the presence of physicists, but having recently read what eminent physicists have written about philosophy I feel absolutely shameless. In addition, the interpretation of the principle of indeterminacy presented by both Professors Bridgman and Landé obviously raises no specific questions in physics but treats of matters, as Professor Munitz points out, traditionally considered in the philosophy of science. I have no "emotional commitment" to the view that every individual event in the area investigated by quantum theory as well as in the macroscopic world is causally determined. Nor do I regard the principle of causality as a logical principle applicable of necessity to everything. Even if it is considered a presupposition to understanding anything, it does not follow that everything can or will be understood. Since we did not create the world we ought to be able to recover from our surprise at its ways. So far as I can understand, no one challenges the truth of the experimental findings of the quantum physicist but only his way of talking about them. When he says that there is a pattern of statistical regularity for the swarm of haphazardly moving photons that enables us to make predictions about their aggregate behavior, there is no problem. When he says that the individual photon is not causally determined and that, by the very nature of our attempt to investigate and describe it, it cannot be, the bewilderment begins. In scientific inquiry the language of common sense is notoriously misleading and must often be abandoned in the interest of clarity, precision, and fruitfulness. But sometimes there is a needless paradox-and-puzzle-making quality in the talk of physicists reporting or interpreting their findings in common-sense terms. This was very fashionable in the early years of relativity theory. Assuming that the idiom of determinism is the language in which common sense understands the behavior of things, must it necessarily be abandoned at some point in the study of microphysical phenomena? I am quite willing to leave this question to the community of physicists, especially since new scientific knowledge is being won independently of the language habits and thought ways of plain men and professional philosophers. My doubts arise only when the quantum physicist offers an explanation and, far from insisting on the uniqueness of the microphysical situation, claims that it is familiar in ordinary situations in which until now there seemed no need to abandon the concepts of causality and determinism.

"It is to be expected," says Professor Bridgman, "that the roots of the difficulties revealed to us by quantum theory are already present in the sphere of ordinary life and should be discoverable by acute enough analysis." With this, Professor Landé cordially agrees. The two classes of phenomena in ordinary life that presumably illustrate in an analogical way the principle of indeterminacy are (1) games of chance (of which Landé's game of balls dropped through a chute onto a knife edge may be considered an ideal case) or games of insurance in which, although statistical frequencies of mortalities are predictable, individual deaths are not, and (2) measurement that "interferes" with the state of the physical situation investigated.

1. I venture to suggest that if ordinary games of chance or insurance are the analogues of the principle of indeterminacy, then no special language is required to describe the behavior of photons; nor is it necessary to abandon the principle of causality. In a clear and legitimate sense it is possible for the insurance actuary to say that, although his knowledge of statistical regularities does not enable him to predict on the basis of this kind of data whether and when any individual, *x,* will die, it would be the sheerest dogmatism to assert that no matter what *other* data were available to a *physician* or *biologist* such a prediction could not be made. For the fact is that sometimes such predictions are made with remarkable accuracy, and there is every reason to believe that their accuracy will increase. Similarly, if the values of the different variables that affect the fall of a particular ball were known, the laws of classical mechanics could supply a reliable answer as to where a particular ball would fall. It may be difficult to discover the values of some of these variables, but the difficulty is not of the kind that makes it impossible to specify simultaneously the position and velocity of a subatomic particle. For in learning the values of some of the variables affecting the fall of the ball we are not thereby of necessity precluded from learning the values of the other variables, as is allegedly the case with subatomic particles.

Professor Landé retorts that as far as his illustration of the falling balls is concerned this type of criticism is only a backhanded way of recognizing randomness and the absence of causality by pushing it farther back. Once "irreducible random" is accepted, he tells us, it is a comparatively minor matter whether "(*a*) each new experiment constitutes a new game of chance (as quantum theory maintains), or (*b*) random was set up *once,* a long or infinite time ago, and random distributions observed at present are but the deterministic effects of that one initial 'shuffling of the cards' (as classical statistical mechanics maintains)."

This seems to me to assume that in a deterministic system *everything* is to be explained. But a deterministic system is one whose state at any future time we can predict if the initial conditions and its laws are known. It is not the less determined because we cannot derive the initial conditions and laws from some other system. Suppose we could: the same thing would hold for that system. Any "basic and irreducible" set of initial conditions set up "a long or infinite time ago" would be a "random" distribution. What would be an "unrandom" distribution? Something that could be derived from a previous distribution? If so, then the term "random" is actually being used synonymously with "underived" by Professor Landé. Unless I radically misunderstand him, all he is really calling attention to is the fact that every determined system must start from some initial conditions of material distribution before our laws can be used to make specific predictions. This is a logical truth about the nature of any material system: some data must at some point be given as basic and irreducible. It is not a discovery but a tautology. If it constituted an objection to the possibility of "a deterministic system," the expression would be meaningless. Even a mathematical system has some undefined terms and undemonstrable propositions.

2. That the subject investigated is affected by the instruments and methods of investigation is an important point. I am in wholehearted agreement with Professor Bridgman about it. But its implication is—so it seems to me—to call into question not the principle of causality but the "spectator theory" of knowledge. Sometimes the interaction produced by the use of instruments and techniques makes it difficult to predict accurately the outcome of an investigation. Sometimes, however, these reactions are foreseeable. A surgeon can allow for the effect of his probe or knife on the organism; a psychologist, for the resistance his question arouses in his subject; a public opinion expert, for the effect of the publication of his poll on behavior at the election polls. If the extent to which the immersion of a thermometer in a solution raises the temperature of the solution is not detectable at present, this by itself is not a sufficient reason to assert that it will always remain undetectable.

I am prepared to grant that every act of inquiry into matters of fact involves the use of our body and its organs as instruments, and that the process of inquiry is one in which some actual change in the structure of the situation to be known takes place. To the extent that this is true, it is true whether the objects investigated are large or small. I can see that sometimes it makes sense to say that "a small instrument can find out more about a large object than a large instrument can find out about a small object." But I can see that sometimes the contrary makes sense too: for example, when we bring to bear on a microcellular organism a high-powered microscope that magnifies it many times over. What could we learn about such an organism with an instrument smaller than itself? Perhaps it is true that a large instrument produces greater changes in a small object than a small instrument in a large object, but I should have imagined that not the size but the relevance and significance of the change is the point at issue where prediction is concerned. I therefore cannot see why it should make more sense to say, merely because of the facts of instrumentation, that causality should fail for small objects than that it should fail for large, especially since a large object can sometimes be considered an organized system of small objects. I could believe the contrary just as well. My only difficulty is that I cannot see any reason why we must believe one or the other, or change the idiom of our talk as we go from one to the other. I conclude, therefore, with the observation that although "the Heisenberg uncertainty relation does not outrage my feeling of what makes sense" I have not been convinced, by anything Professors Bridgman and Landé have said about ordinary experience, that it is necessary to interpret the uncertainty relation as entailing a denial of the relation of causality.

III

The fatal error in the papers of Professors Hospers and Edwards, as read, is that they alternate between two conceptions of "moral responsibility"—one, a conception of moral responsibility as *empty* but meaningful, and the other as *vacuous* and meaningless. On the first conception, although it may be true *in fact* that no one is morally responsible, we can state the conditions under which one might be. We can differentiate between the two states. On the second, there are no possible conditions under which anyone can be declared "morally responsible." The expression has no intelligible opposite and thus makes no sense.

The force of most of their arguments, which gives them an air of high moral concern, is based on the assumption that under certain circumstances individuals are being *improperly* considered responsible. Hospers actually says that "frequently persons we think responsible are not properly to be called so," and Edwards implies the same thing. They explicitly appeal against the injustice of improperly blaming the morally innocent who, because their desires are determined, are the victims, not the agents, of misfortune. We eagerly await the description of the set of conditions under which an individual is properly held responsible, under which he is not a victim of circumstances. It then turns out that even if his desires were undetermined, even if circumstances were completely different, he would still not be responsible, would still be a morally innocent victim. The *empty* conception of moral responsibility becomes completely *vacuous*. This makes the whole procedure of Professors Hospers and Edwards methodologically self-defeating, and particularly their expressions of concern about the injustice of blaming the morally innocent. For to be morally innocent of having committed an evil deed entails that one is not responsible for its commission, and to be morally guilty entails that one is. *If moral responsibility is a vacuous expression, then moral innocence and guilt are too.* Were Hospers and Edwards consistent they could not plead for the innocent or condemn the guilty. Edwards in places suggests that a person would be responsible if he could *ultimately and completely shape or choose his own character.* But this is explaining an obscure notion by a still obscurer one. Since every decision to shape or choose one's character, to be responsible, must be one's own, and therefore already an indication of the kind of person one is, the notion that one can ultimately and completely shape or choose one's character is unintelligible. C. A. Campbell, to be sure, tries to distinguish between a choice that is the expression of a *formed character,* and therefore determined, and a choice of a *self.* But on Hospers' and Edwards' argument what is true of character must be true of self. Either the self has the power to mold character or it has not. In either case it cannot be held responsible for having or not having such a native power. And the same is true if we bring in a Self to explain the powers of the self and a Great Self to explain the powers of the Self, etc.

It is true that the notion of moral responsibility is often ambiguous and not clearly defined in ordinary experience. But if we follow Professor Hart's illuminating procedure, we can recognize certain actions in which we clearly admit the presence of excusing conditions—infancy, insanity, paralysis, duress, coercion, etc.—and actions in which we do not. We then try to formulate the principle we recognize in this distinction and apply it to more complicated and borderline cases. We find that we tend to hold individuals responsible for their voluntary or uncoerced actions, for knowingly doing or not doing what it was in their power to do or leave undone. All these terms are vague and need further specification. There are difficulties in ascertaining in particular instances what it was in one's power to do or leave undone. Nonetheless, no one can live in human society without learning to recognize the distinction between the actions he holds others and himself responsible for and the actions he does not.

For all its vagueness there is more agreement about how the distinction is to be applied than about the grounds of the distinction. No one blames a crawling infant who overturns a kerosene stove that starts a fire. Almost everybody would blame a man who, normal in every other way and by all known tests, insures a house beyond its value and then sets fire to it without even giving its occupants a chance to escape. If we make a list of the circumstances behind actions for which we hold individuals responsible and those for which we do not, we shall find that as a rule the first class consists of those in which evidence exists that praise and reward, blame and punishment, tend to influence the future conduct of those involved and/or those tempted. This is not the whole story. Campbell objects[1] that animals are not held responsible for their actions even though we can re-educate their desires and impulses by punishment. This is true, but it is also true that the higher the animal in the scale of intelligence, the more likely we are to blame it. If we believed that an animal could think like a man we would blame it like a man. The behavior of infants, too, is modifiable by appropriate reward and punishment even though we do not hold them morally responsible. But as the age of rationality approaches we gradually do. This suggests that in addition to susceptibility to reward and punishment, we

[1] *Mind*, 1951.

attribute responsibility where there is a tendency to respond to valid reasons, to behave rationally, to respond to human emotions in a human way. Perhaps a third element involved in the attribution of moral responsibility to voluntary action is the assumption that voluntary action is *approved* action. A man is morally responsible for an action he commits to the extent that he *approves* of it. If he sincerely disapproves of his action, regards it as wrong and condemns it as wrong, but still commits it we tend to regard him as ill, as acting under "compulsion." It is some such consideration as this that lies behind our extenuation of certain kinds of apparently voluntary action (as when we say: "He didn't mean to do it"), especially where ignorance is present.

There may be other elements involved in the complex notion of moral responsibility, but the foregoing explains an interesting phenomenological fact. Sickness, accident, or incapacity aside, one feels lessened as a human being if one's actions are always excused or explained away on the ground that despite appearances one is really not responsible for them. It means being treated like an object, an infant, or someone out of his mind. Our dignity as rational human beings sometimes leads us to protest, when a zealous friend seeks to extenuate our conduct on the ground that we were not responsible (we didn't know or intend what we were doing, etc.), that we really *are* responsible and that we are prepared to take the consequences of our responsibility. As bad as the priggishness of the self-righteous is the whine of the self-pitying.

The so-called "hard" determinism professed by Professors Hospers and Edwards, especially in the popular form defended by Darrow, whom Edwards so extravagantly praised, often leads to sentimentality, to so much pity for the criminal as a victim not of a special set of particular circumstances but of any circumstances in general (referred to as heredity and environment, the sway of the law of causality) that there is not sufficient pity or concern left for the criminal's victims—not only for his past victims but his future ones and the victims of others his actions may inspire. To blame and to punish, of course, are two distinct things logically (except where blame is considered a form of punishment), but psychologically there is a great reluctance to punish if one believes there is no blame. Darrow as a "hard" determinist argued on a priori grounds that everyone was blameless and often won acquittals not on the evidence but despite it. If needless pain and cruelty are evils, then punishment that prevents or deters human beings from committing actions likely to result in much greater pain and cruelty than it imposes is sometimes the lesser evil.

It is argued by Professor Edwards that "hard" determinism, which, according to him, entails the belief that no one is morally responsible because no one ultimately shapes his own character, leads to the abandonment of retributive punishment. Even if this were so, it would not make the doctrine of "hard" determinism any more intelligible. But historically it is not so. From Augustine to Calvin to Barth the torment of eternal damnation is assigned and approved independently of moral responsibility. It is not related of the oft-quoted Puritan who piously observed to his son when they saw a man being led to the gallows, "There but for the grace of God go I," that he opposed retributive punishment. Nor can Edwards consistently with his own theory assert that "hard" determinists *should* repudiate retributive punishment, or morally blame them or anyone else, as he freely does, for approving of retributive punishment. For has he not told us that a man can't help having the character he has, no matter what kind of a character it is? Further, if retributive punishment is the enemy, there seems to me to be no necessary logical connection between a belief in moral responsibility and approval of retributive punishment. Certainly, "soft" determinists who assign responsibility to actions only when there is reason to believe that blame or punishment will modify future conduct are hardly likely to defend retributive punishment.

Why, after all, is retributive punishment evil? Not because the wrongdoer "ultimately did not shape his own character"—whatever that may mean—but simply because the pain inflicted on him gratuitously adds to the sum total of suffering in the world without any compensating alleviation of anybody else's sufferings. Even if an individual were considered able "ultimately to shape his own character" and were held morally responsible for an evil act, punishment that would be purely retributive and that did not contribute to deterring him or others from evil doing, or did nothing toward rehabilitating him, would still be morally wrong. This is quite evident in situations in which the "hard" determinist who is not a fatalist, if there be any such, admits that a man is to some extent, not ultimately but proximately, responsible for some change in his character —for example, when his desire to gamble leads him to steal a beggar's portion. In such situations retributive punishment as such would be regarded as morally wrong. Directed only to the past, it would not give the beggar back his portion or wipe out his pain, and therefore the new sufferings it inflicts are futile and needlessly cruel. If one can oppose retributive punishment when one believes a person is proximately responsible for his action, one can oppose it even when one believes a person is ultimately responsible, whatever the cognitive content of that belief turns out to be. If retributive punishment is the target of their criticism, Hospers and Edwards are training their guns in the wrong direction.

Far from diminishing the amount of needless cruelty and suffering in the world, I am firmly convinced that the belief that nobody is ever morally responsible, in addition to being false, is quite certain to have a mischievous effect and to increase the amount of needless cruelty and suffering. For it justifies Smerdyakov's formula in *The Brothers Karamazov:* "All things are permissible." One of the commonest experiences is to meet someone whose belief that he can't help doing what he is doing (or failing to do) is often an excuse for not doing as well as he can or at least better than he is at present doing. What often passes as irremediable evil in this world, or inevitable suffering, is a consequence of our failure to act in time. We are responsible, whether we admit it or not, for what it is in our power to do; and most of the time we can't be sure what it is in our power to do until we attempt it. In spite of the alleged inevitabilities in personal life and history human effort can redetermine the direction of events, even though it cannot determine the conditions that make human effort possible. It is time enough to reconcile oneself to a secret shame or a public tyranny after one has done one's best to overcome it, and even then it isn't necessary.

To say, as Professor Hospers does, that "It's all a matter of luck" is no more sensible than saying: "Nothing is a matter of "luck"— assuming "luck" has a meaning in a world of hard determinism. It is true that we did not choose to be born. It is also true that we choose, most of us, to keep on living. It is not true that everything that happens to us is like "being struck down by a dread disease."

The treatment and cure of disease—to use an illustration that can serve as a moral paradigm for the whole human situation—would never have begun unless we believed that some things that were did not have to be, that they could be different, and that *we* could make them different. And what we can make different we are responsible for.

9.   Punishment as Justice and as Price; On Randomness

Abba Lerner, Roosevelt College

I

Regarding the problem of personal responsibility, it seems to me that Professor Edwards' argument, with which I am in close agreement, does not really depend on a demonstration that nobody makes his own character any more than it depends on the arguments and examples brought forth by Professor Hospers on the importance of subconscious drives and compulsions in criminal activity. Professor Edwards' position really seems to rest on the rejection of the axiom that it is desirable or just that a person who has committed a crime should be made to suffer. This axiom does not depend at all on who, if anyone, is responsible for the bad character of the bad man who performs the bad act. There is thus no suggestion that he should be punished for having a bad character if he did not commit the crime or even for having chosen to have the bad character or to make it for himself. If making a bad character is a crime in itself that is another crime. It may raise the question whether whoever was responsible for making the bad character should be punished for it, but that is a different question. The rejection of the axiom that crime must be atoned by the suffering of punishment leaves punishment without justification unless some other justification is found, such as the protection of society through the provision of a deterrent to antisocial behavior. The history of how the criminal became a bad man is then irrelevant, even though it may induce jurors to direct acquittals. The relating of such history does not constitute a logical argument against carrying out any particular punishment, but it may lead to the rejection of the axiom that justice is done when crime is balanced by the suffering of punishment.

II

I should like to comment on Professor Hart's treatment of the conditions for excusing punishment on the same footing as conditions for the invalidation of contracts, as if punishment were a price. His argument is that it is good to be able to measure the punishment against the satisfaction one may get from committing a crime. This increases freedom by permitting the exercise of rational choice in committing the crime only where the satisfaction is greater than the punishment-price. Any contract-crime not freely and responsibly entered into is then invalidated and the price-punishment is canceled.

I was particularly interested in this because I have been doing almost exactly the opposite in economics—not treating punishment as a price, but treating price as a punishment. The price of a commodity is a deterrent to the consumer; it deters him from consuming the product. Ideally, the magnitude of the price should correspond to the amount of damage that the consumer does to the rest of society by consuming the product and thereby making it unavailable for others to consume. The individual will then choose to consume if the satisfaction he gets is greater than the price and therefore greater than the loss to the rest of society. And since by the payment of the price he completely compensates the rest of society, society as a whole (including our consumer) benefits from his decision to commit the consumption. Furthermore, the complete compensation of the rest of society (by the price that he pays) leaves it without reason for wishing to interfere with his freedom of choice. The proper price, therefore, leads to the maximization of welfare and of freedom.

This kind of maximization does not, however, apply to the punishment of crime because the suffering of the punished criminal is not balanced by a benefit to the rest of society (except where the punishment takes the form of a money fine and does operate just like a price). The committing of a crime does not mean that society as a whole (including our criminal) benefits. Even if the criminal enjoys a net benefit after punishment, his punishment does not compensate the rest of society for the damage done them by the crime. On the contrary, the rest of society suffers further losses from the costs involved in providing justice and keeping the man in prison. In the case of the price mechanism, if the consumer decides to consume the commodity and suffer the purchase price, the price system is performing its function of ensuring maximum welfare and freedom perfectly. But if the criminal decides to commit the crime and then pay the punishment, the punishment system has failed in its function of preventing the crime.

III

A point that intrigued me particularly was Professor Landé's treatment of randomness. His argument seemed based on the idea that a random distribution is a special kind of order that in a determinate universe must have been planned by some demon. The question that remains is only whether there is a demon operating at every point where an apparently random distribution exists—or perhaps in every subatomic particle—or whether there was some super-demon who arranged all these random distributions at the creation. I don't find myself tempted by either form of demonology because I have always thought of random distribution as precisely the opposite of order, on the assumption that randomness is the mark of the absence of order and that as long as any distribution is random no amount of study or observation of it will give any information as to the probabilities of the next throw. But I am not very happy about my position. I think I should look into the philosophical and perhaps mathematical treatments of randomness to see if what I am saying does not involve an elementary blunder.

10. Some Notes on Determinism

Ernest Nagel, Columbia University

Whether the occurrence of every discriminable event is determined, whether for every event there is a unique set of conditions without whose presence the event would not take place, and whether if conditions of a specified kind are given an event of a certain type will invariably happen, are variant forms of a question that cannot be settled by a priori arguments. Nor do I think the question can be answered definitively and finally, even on the basis of factual evidence; for, as I shall presently suggest, the question is best construed as dealing with a rule of procedure for the conduct of cognitive inquiry, rather than with a thesis concerning the constitution of the world. I am therefore not convinced by Professor Blanshard's acute argument attempting to show that an answer to the question other than an affirmative one is indefensible, if not unintelligible. Moreover, his assertion that even in deductive thinking and artistic invention each step is necessitated by the logical and aesthetic relations that exercise a power over the mind seems to me untenable— if it is admitted as relevant to his major contention. For his assumption that logical and aesthetic relations (as distinct from *apprehensions* of such relations) may be said to engage in causal action attributes causal efficacy to something that, in no recognizable and identifiable sense of the phrase, can exercise such agency.

Nevertheless, the belief in determinism is not unfounded; and it would be just silly to maintain that in no area of experience can we rightly affirm that anything is caused or determined by anything else. It seems to me the special merit of Professor Black's paper that it indicated at least one identifiable class of contexts in which the words "caused," "determined," and their derivates have an unquestionable and important use. In these contexts involving human action it is simply nonsense to deny that events have causes or effects, in senses of these words appropriate to these contexts. Black has also made plain that the conditions under which "caused" and "determined" have significant uses, in those situations where men initiate actions and are responsible for the occurrence of events, require the presence of identifiable contingencies and the absence of just such "necessities" as those for which Blanshard argues.

But it does not follow from Black's analysis that the only sense that can be attached to "cause" and "determined" is the sense they manifestly do have in the indicated contexts—any more than it follows that, because the word "number" is undoubtedly used in situations involving the counting of objects, the meaning of the word in statements about such irrational magnitudes as the area of a circle with a unit radius must also involve reference to counting. There are, to be sure, historical continuities and important analogies between the use of these words in contexts of human action and their use in discussions about, say, the "indeterminism" of electrons. But it is patently a mistake to construe the meanings of those words in this latter context in terms of the "paradigm" for their use in situations where men are correctly identified as causal agents. Although Black does not explicitly guard himself against the suspicion that he does take his paradigm as basic for all uses of "caused," it is unlikely that he would commit himself to such a position. On the other hand, it does seem to me that Professor Bridgman (and perhaps even Professor Landé) commits a somewhat similar mistake when he suggests that the "indeterminacy" of quantum theory can be explicated in terms of familiar facts "in the sphere of ordinary life."

In the voluminous literature on the "indeterminism" of microphysics, one point stands out clearly: whatever the issue may be, it is generated by the theoretical interpretations that are placed on the acknowledged data rather than by any disagreement as to what those data are. Thus no one disputes that when a beam of light passes through appropriately arranged slits and strikes a zinc sulphide screen, scintillations occur that fall into a definite pattern; or that quantum theory accounts admirably for the occurrence of this pattern; or, finally, that there is no known law of physics that accounts for the occurrence of each individual scintillation. Problems arise, however, when the structure of quantum theory is analyzed with a view to showing why it is that this theory cannot account for individual scintillations. But the problems are generated because answers to the question are proposed in terms of familiar facts "in the sphere of ordinary life" rather than in terms of the structure of the theory itself.

It is a commonplace that quantum theory employs a distinctive way of "describing" the state of a physical system with which the theory can deal. This state description (the psi function) is such that, given its value for some initial time, and assuming an appropriate set of boundary conditions for the application of the theory, the theory makes it possible to calculate the value of the function for any other time. In this respect quantum theory is as "deterministic" as are the dynamical theories of classical physics. It differs from these in that, while the state description of the latter can be construed as representing magnitudes associated with certain individual elements that constitute the physical systems in question, its state function can be construed as representing only a statistical property of the individual elements making up the physical system. In short, the state description of quantum theory is a statistical parameter. So far nothing could be more straightforward or less puzzling. The puzzle begins when reasons are offered why the state function of quantum mechanics is a statistical parameter.

The reason Professor Landé appears to give is that any given value assigned to the psi function constitutes the initial conditions for the application of the theory to a concrete situation, and that since initial conditions constitute a brute and underived fact they represent an inherently chance or random feature of the world. I doubt very much whether I have understood Professor Landé's presentation of his views, and my comments may be entirely irrelevant to his real intent. But as I understand him, he has not made clear what he set out to clarify. For every theory—not only quantum mechanics—requires initial conditions that at some point or other in an investigation into concrete subject matter must be accepted as underived and therefore as representative of a "random" feature of the world, as are the initial conditions for quantum theory. This attempt to assimilate the "indeterminacy" of microphysics to facts "in the sphere of ordinary life" is not a successful one.

Professor Bridgman seeks to explain the statistical aspect of the psi function by invoking the general principle that whenever measurements are made the instruments employed interact with the things measured and thereby introduce changes into the latter. His contention is that, although such alterations are practically negligible when we measure things that are sufficiently large, the changes cannot be ignored when the minute "particles" of microphysics are measured with the relatively large instruments at our disposal, so that the psi function inevitably represents only statistically significant magnitudes associated with the elementary particles of quantum physics. Now, the general principle Professor Bridgman invokes is undoubtedly sound. The difficulty in his explanation, however, is that though the principle is sound it does not, in other areas of inquiry, prevent us from calculating the effects of measuring instruments on the things measured and so making corresponding allowances in assigning magnitudes to the objects under investigation. Why should the situation be inherently different in quantum physics? I find it difficult to escape the impression that Professor Bridgman has put the cart before the horse. For it seems to me that the alleged effect of measurement on microphysical "particles" must be assumed as at best a consequence that follows from the acceptance of quantum theory, rather than that the theory is based on independently ascertained facts concerning the alterations made by instruments of measurement on microphysical "particles." At any rate, I do not think Professor Bridgman has convincingly shown that the "indeterminism" inherent in the structure of quantum theory is but another illustration of a familiar feature "in the sphere of ordinary life."

Although quantum theory is not deterministic in the precise sense in which the dynamical theories of classical physics are deterministic, and although quantum theory (or, for that matter, any other available theory of contemporary physics) does not account in detail for such occurrences as the individual scintillations mentioned previously, it of course does not follow that there really are no precise conditions for the occurrence of those events that quantum mechanics does not explain, or that a theory that can account for these things is impossible. The assumption that there always are such precise conditions for every event, even if we continue to remain permanently ignorant of them, is the assumption of a universal determinism. As I have already indicated, determinism so understood is capable neither of decisive proof nor disproof. I think, nevertheless, that determinism can be regarded as a fruitful maxim or regulative principle for inquiry. It does not express a necessity of thought, for it can be abandoned. But if it is abandoned, then inquiry in certain directions is, at least temporarily, brought to a halt. In an important sense, therefore, the deterministic maxim is explicative of what is generally understood to be a goal of the scientific enterprise.

I want to conclude with a brief comment on the contention of Professors Edwards and Hospers that, if determinism supplies a true account of the nature of things, it does not make sense to hold anyone morally responsible for his actions or to offer moral praise and blame. Under what conditions do we hold a person morally responsible for an action? Consider an example. I engage the services of a student as baby sitter on the assumption that she is capable of doing certain things. Her ability to do them depends on a number of conditions, including the state of her body, her education, and her previous experience with children of a certain age. If she does indeed satisfy these conditions and also agrees to perform certain tasks that are compatible with her abilities, she is morally responsible for performing them. The fact that she did not create her own body, or that she did not choose the education she received, are not relevant considerations for judging whether she is morally responsible for some event that may take place during my absence from home. On the other hand, if during my absence burglars enter and tie up the student, or if she becomes unconscious for causes not within her control, she is not morally responsible for what may befall my children. The point is obvious. Moral responsibility is correctly ascribed to individuals who possess certain capacities; and it is correct to make the ascription for the sufficient reason that this is just the way the phrase "morally responsible" is used. The fact that possessing these capacities is contingent on a variety of conditions, most of which are perhaps beyond the control of an individual, is irrelevant to the analysis of what we do mean by the phrase as well as to the grounds on which the ascription is rightly made. To maintain the contrary is in effect to maintain that no property can be correctly predicated of an object if the property is causally dependent on anything either in the composition or in the environment of the object. Such a view makes all predication impossible. But in any event Professors Edwards and Hospers can sustain their thesis only by radically altering the customary conception of what it means for anyone to be morally responsible.

11. Causation, Determinism, and the "Good"

F. S. C. Northrop, School of Law, Yale University

I

Professor Bridgman has suggested that there is much more agreement among physicists concerning the status of the concept of causality in quantum mechanics than appears superficially from quotations pulled out of context. There are reasons for believing that this agreement is more unanimous even than Professor Bridgman has indicated.

One difficulty is that mechanical causation in modern physics has a stronger and a weaker meaning, and as yet there is no convention among physicists and informed philosophers of science as to which of these two meanings the expression "mechanical causation" is to have. Some physicists use these words in the stronger sense, others in the weaker sense. Since with respect to quantum mechanics what holds for the weaker meaning does not hold for the stronger meaning, physicists often appear to differ about the status of causality in quantum mechanics, when in fact there is complete agreement. Furthermore, there was no difference of opinion between Einstein and quantum physicists concerning the status of mechanical causality and determinism in quantum mechanics. It is precisely because Einstein agreed with them about what the theory requires that he objected to quantum theory. It can be shown, however, that according to Einstein's own theory of the relation between theoretical concepts and experimental evidence, his objection is untenable. The situation becomes clear when the weaker and stronger meanings of mechanical causality are precisely defined. As understood by physicists, determinism is equivalent to the stronger of the two types of mechanical causation. This is probably also what a man with common-sense knowledge means by determinism, even though he is rarely, if ever, clear about what this meaning is.

In the paradigm that marked Professor Black's approach to the problem of determinism, by the method of contemporary British analytic philosophy, common sense was again followed. In order to relate his conclusions to the concept of determinism as understood in mathematical physics, two things must be noted: (1) the ambiguities in his paradigm and in the method of British analytic philosophy generally; (2) the difference between the definition of cause in his paradigm and the concept of cause in mathematical physics.

The ambiguities of Professor Black's paradigm, as of British philosophical analysis generally, arise from the fact that such philosophical analysis, so-called, never makes explicit which one of several possible epistemological meanings the words convey in their common-sense contexts. The result is a surreptitious shift from assertions true for only one possible epistemological meaning to conclusions valid, if at all, only for different epistemological meanings. As a result, British analytic philosophy confuses more than it clarifies, as the following analysis of Professor Black's paradigm shows.

In the sense in which this paradigm "stands on its own feet," as Professor Black maintained it did, it must be taken in its radical empirical, nominalistic meaning. But in this sense, as Hume showed, there is merely temporal succession and no relation of necessary connection, or causality, of any kind. Professor Goodman's remark that causality is a tautology is interesting in this connection. It is the inevitable consequence of any attempt, after the manner of Professors Quine and Goodman, to rear mathematics and mathematical physics on nothing but nominalistic, radical empirical epistemological meanings. Then not merely mechanical causality in either the weaker or the stronger form—to be defined in the sequel—but most of the other concepts of mathematical physics become similarly either meaningless or trivial.

When one takes Professor Black's paradigm in its naïve realistic epistemological meaning, as he suggests in using the word "object" and conceiving of causality as a relation between objects, then, to be sure, perhaps a bit more than Hume's mere temporal succession is obtained, but in this case, as Professor Weiss points out, the paradigm does not stand on its own feet, and the conclusion Professor Black draws about the compatibility of determinism and freedom fails to follow. Certainly, interpreted as naïve realistic epistemological material objects, the things described by the paradigm may well be subject to mechanically antecedent causes.

The latter consideration suggests that the paradigm becomes relevant to the problem of causality—to say nothing about its relation to mechanically causal determinism—only if a third surreptitious epistemological shift occurs in the interpretation of it, in which the person who "causes something to happen" is not viewed from without but is instead viewed as purposefully acting from within. But again, if this is the meaning, the causality is teleological, and the difficulties raised by the mechanically causal determinism of modern physics are not touched. Furthermore, if the causality is purposeful and teleological, may not the individual's choice of this purpose have been mechanically determined? Again we see that so far as the paradigm has any relevance to the problem of determinism it does not stand on its own feet. Like British philosophical analysis generally, the so-called clarification of the problem of determinism that Professor Black's common-sense paradigm is supposed to give is so shot through with epistemological ambiguities and surreptitious shifts in the epistemological meanings of the words used that it is, like this method generally, philosophically useless.

In any event, Professor Black doesn't touch the problem of determinism, which arises only when one thinks of causality as modern physicists do: not, after the manner of Professor Black, as a relation between objects but as the relation between the states of the same object, or the same system of objects, at different times. Mechanical causation affirms, in either its weaker or its stronger meaning, that this temporal relation between the states of a system at different times is a relation of necessary connection.

Since, as Hume showed, we do not observe any relations of necessary connection, two things follow: (1) The concept of mechanical causation in modern physics cannot be attained merely by direct inspection of a common-sense example or by so-called "analysis" of the grammar of an Englishman's description of such an example; only temporal succession will be found by such a method. (2) Physical systems obeying mechanical causation can therefore be known only by deductively formulated, axiomatically constructed, indirectly verified theory. To determine, therefore, what the status of mechanical causality is in modern physics, one must do more than examine the inductive, radically empirical sensible operations— important as these are—by means of which the speculatively proposed, axiomatically constructed theory is verified indirectly. This type of examination will give one merely operational, theory-of-errors probability, which is present in any experimental testing of any theory and hence is quite insufficient to distinguish quantum mechanics from previous modern physics with respect to the status of mechanical causation and, more particularly, its stronger form, determinism. Operational probability enters into all scientific theory. This type of probability and chance is frequently referred to as epistemological probability and chance, since it has its basis in the finiteness and errors that accompany the scientist's attempt to relate himself in knowledge to the object. To understand the unique conclusion of quantum mechanics with respect to mechanical causation and its stronger form, determinism, one must concentrate attention on the speculatively introduced, axiomatically constructed postulates of the modern theories of mathematical physics, with particular reference to the presence or absence of the concept of theoretical probability—i.e., probability introduced *in principle*—in the postulates. Since such probability, if it occurs, refers to the object of scientific knowledge, it is appropriately called ontological probability or chance.

Two factors in any deductively formulated theory of modern

physics must command the focus of one's attention. These two factors are (1) the definition of the state of the system at any given moment of time and (2) the definition of the time relation between states of the system at different times.

Let us concentrate on the latter relation first. There are three major possibilities. One is instanced by any merely inductive empirical observations of the changes of the system through time without any speculatively introduced, axiomatically constructed theory. By plotting these changes from the earlier to the later state of the system, a curve can be obtained. For every curve, as Professor Philip Frank and others have noted, there is a formula or law. Such a lawfully defined relation between the earlier and later states of a system is not, however, regarded by modern physicists as constituting a truly mechanically causal system. The reason for this conclusion is that such a law or formula cannot be given until after one has seen the system pass from its earlier to its later state. Thus it has no predictive power. As Professor Frank noted, it merely affirms that what happens happens and in this sense, again, is little more than a trivial tautology so far as causality is concerned.

There is a second possibility with respect to the nature of the time relation between states of an isolated system. The relation may be one of necessary connection characterized by a repetition of constant time relations that hold true not merely for past and present but also for future cases; but it is a relation such that in any first observed instance, given the initial state of the system, one cannot predict the future state until one has observed the present state passing into the future or final state in at least one instance. The physical system in which the initial state is that of the acorn and the final state that of the oak constitutes an example. Such a relation of necessary connection, since a knowledge for prediction of future states of the system depends on a knowledge of what the future state is, is called teleological causality.

There is a third possible form that the time relation between the states of a scientifically determined system may possess. In this third type, as in the second, the relation is one of necessary connection, but the relation of necessary connection has the following properties: (1) There exists a speculatively introduced, axiomatically constructed set of postulates of an indirectly and experimentally confirmed, deductively formulated theory. (2) The postulates of this theory specify a very small number of independent variables necessary and sufficient to define completely the state of a system at any specific moment of time t_1. (3) Given the operationally determined, concept-by-intuition values of the independent variables of this definition of the state of the system at an earlier time t_1, (a) all the other properties of the system at that time t_1 can be deduced, and (b), without any observation in a present or past instance of the future state of a similar system, the empirical values of the independent variables of the physical system at the later time t_2 can be deduced by solving a second-order differential equation that the postulates and theorems of the theory provide. When the foregoing conditions are satisfied, the causality of the system, i.e., the relation of necessary connection between the states of the system at different times, is mechanical causality in the aforementioned weaker meaning of this term. More concretely, this means that the deductively formulated theory provides a time equation such that, by feeding the operationally determined empirical values of the concept-by-postulation, theoretically introduced independent variables of the state function into the equation, the values of these variables for a specific later time t_2 are completely determined by solving the equation for that time t_2.

Note that causality in this sense is not a trivial tautology. It is, instead, a relation of necessary connection such that, given the postulates of the theory and given the determination of the independent variables in any present state of the system, a completely novel future state, never before observed in any past instance, can be deduced. Furthermore, a large number of other properties of the system in the initial state and in the final state can also be deduced.

What is the role of the foregoing type of mechanical causality in the weaker meaning of these two words in any theory of modern physics in which such a relation of necessary connection between the earlier and later states of a system is present? The answer to this question is unequivocal. In the postulates of the theory the concept of probability does not enter into the definition of the time relation between the states of any system. The first important thing to note about quantum mechanics is that, as for Newton's mechanics, Maxwell's electromagnetics, and Einstein's special and general theories of relativity, mechanical causality in the weaker meaning holds. This is the case for two reasons: First, the concept of theoretical probability does not enter into its definition of the time relation between the states of a subatomic physical system. Second, it provides the Schrödinger time equation, which has the aforementioned property of enabling one, given the operationally determined empirical values of the present state of the system *as defined by the theory,* to deduce the future state of the system, as so defined, at any specified later time t^2 merely by solving this equation.

But if mechanical causation in the weaker meaning of the words holds for quantum mechanics just as it did for Newton's mechanics, Maxwell's electromagnetics, and Einstein's special and general theories of relativity, why, then, has it been affirmed by physicists that quantum mechanics alters the status of causality—and more particularly of determinism—in modern physics? The answer to this question will become clear if one shifts attention from the definition of the time relation between states to the definition of state in the modern theories. The novelty of quantum mechanics consists in this, and solely in this, that theoretically, and hence in principle, it has found it necessary in order to account for the experimental data to introduce the concept of theoretical probability into the definition of state of a subatomic physical system. In Newton's mechanics, Maxwell's electromagnetics, and Einstein's special and general theories of relativity, the concept of theoretical probability was not introduced either into the definition of state or into the definition of the time relation between states. Hence in these four theories mechanical causality in the stronger sense of absolute determinism held. There was, in other words, no ontological chance or probabilty in the object of empirically verified, theoretically designated scientific knowledge. Thus, according to these four theories, causality is not merely mechanical, but it is also unqualifiedly deterministic. Whatever probability existed belonged merely to the experimental, operational side and hence was merely epistemological. It was precisely because Einstein's own theory required, and because he consequently believed, that probability in physical science should have a merely epistemological, theory-of-errors, operational status that he objected to quantum mechanics. Thus there was no disagreement between Einstein and quantum physicists about what quantum mechanics affirms with respect to the existence of ontological chance and probability. The answer, therefore, to Professor Quine's question whether probability in quantum mechanics is merely epistemological is unequivocally "No."

For this reason also Professor Blanshard's and Sir David Ross's contention that quantum mechanics provides no evidence against causal determinism is erroneous. Professor Blanshard was quite right when, quoting Sir David, he noted that epistemological probability and chance do not imply ontological probability and chance. But the novelty of quantum mechanics consists precisely in the fact that, unlike previous modern scientific theories in which probability and chance are merely epistemological, quantum physicists have found it impossible, when faced with experimental findings on black-body radiation, to accept mere epistemological or operational, theory-of-errors probability and have been forced to introduce instead the concept of probability in principle at the theoretical level into the specification of the type of causality governing the object of scientific knowledge itself. This is the case because in quantum mechanics' definition of state the postulates in principle prescribe not merely the specification of the two independent variables, position and momentum, for each object of the system, but also a packet of such numbers with each one accompanied by its respective probability number. Furthermore, because the probability is introduced in principle, the determinism is not, as Professor Williams has suggested, restored by including the experimental apparatus within the object of scientific knowledge. Also, the Compton effect provides experimental evidence to the same conclusion.

Nevertheless, given a state of a subatomic system defined in terms of a packet of position and momentum numbers for each object in the system, accompanied by their corresponding probability numbers, the postulates of the theory are such that future state of the system defined in terms of position-momentum numbers and probability numbers can be deduced by recourse to the Schrödinger time equation. Consequently, in quantum mechanics causality in the weaker sense still holds, but mechanical causality in the stronger sense of determinism does not hold.

It remains to be shown why (*a*) Einstein's objections to quantum mechanics and (*b*) the interpretation of it suggested in this conference by Professor Williams are untenable. When Einstein came to the conclusion that it is possible to reconcile the results of the Michelson-Morley experiment with the basic theoretical assumptions of modern mechanics and electromagnetics only by modifying a basic postulate introduced by Newton and assumed by Maxwell concerning space and time and the simultaneity of spatially separated events, Einstein himself tells us that he was faced with a methodological and epistemological difficulty. Newton, having asserted that he introduced no hypotheses and deduced the concepts of his theory from the experimental data, left the impression—like Professor Williams in his attempt to derive the concepts of modern physics from the experimental data—that the experimental data entailed the concepts. Einstein saw that if this were so he could not meet the difficulty raised by the Michelson-Morley experiment by modifying Newton's theoretical assumptions. For the experiments performed by Newton can certainly be repeated today with the same results. Hence, if the experiments entail Newton's theory, Newton's theory must still be retained. Consequently, Einstein conducted a fresh examination of the relation between the experiments of the experimental physicist and the theoretical concepts of his science. In this essentially epistemological investigation Einstein had no difficulty showing that the simultaneity of spatially separated events, which is the same for all observers on the same Galilean frame of reference, is not directly sensed but is instead a speculatively introduced, indirectly verified hypothesis. Hence it followed that it was not necessary to specify the relation between space and time in the manner introduced by Newton. This opened the way for Einstein to account for all the experiments in accord with Newton's theory and the Michelson-Morley experiment without contradiction in the theoretically novel manner of Einstein's special theory of relativity. This means that there is no a priori reason knowable ahead of time why the causality of a physical system must be of the stronger mechanical type. Hence there is no epistemological justification, on Einstein's own analysis of the epistemology of modern physical knowledge, for his objection to the introduction of the theoretical concept of probability into the definition of the state of a subatomic physical system in quantum mechanics.

Furthermore, there are experimental reasons, exactly analogous to the Michelson-Morley experiment, demonstrating that the concept of probability cannot be kept out of the definition of state for subatomic systems. Before Planck introduced his quantum concept the traditional experimentally verified, speculatively proposed theories prescribed in principle that the positions and momenta of subatomic, as of molar, scientific objects were determinable and behaved without reference to chance or probability. In short, the theory of subatomic systems was strictly deterministic, introducing the concept of probability into neither the definition of the time relation between states nor the definition of state. When, however, the latter theory of the type of causality governing subatomic scientific objects was pursued mathematically to its deductive consequences, certain experiments on black-body radiation, exactly analogous to the Michelson-Morley experiment with respect to motion in electromagnetic systems, were performed, and these experiments did not give the result that the assumption of no probability in the definition of the state of subatomic systems requires. It was to meet this difficulty that Planck introduced his constant. Later Heisenberg showed that Planck's constant entails the uncertainty principle. It is this entailment, necessary to reconcile the experimental findings on black-body radiation with physical theory, that forces the introduction of the concept of probability in principle into the definition of state in quantum theory. Thus the very same epistemology and logic of the experimental situation that drove Einstein, following the Michelson-Morley experiment, to the modification of Newton's assumption concerning space and time, drives the subatomic physicists, on the basis of the experiments on black-body radiation, to the modification of the definition of state and the strict determinism of previous physical theories. Hence, on his own theory of the epistemology of mathematical physics and its methodology, Einstein's objections to quantum mechanics are invalid. We have no alternative but to hold that for subatomic systems, mechanical causality in the weaker sense of the words still holds, but determinism or mechanical causality in the stronger sense does not hold. In short, quantum mechanics does not introduce the concept of theoretical probability into the definition of the time relation between states but does introduce it into the definition of state. In other words, quantum mechanics, as Professor Bridgman's paper suggested, introduces ontological and not merely epistemological chance and probability.

By way of contrast it may be relevant to note a theory of modern physics—namely, thermodynamics in its statistical interpretation —in which the concept of probability is not introduced into the definition of state but is introduced into the definition of the time relation between states. Thus, in determining the state of such a thermodynamic system at any given time, merely the values of the independent variables—temperature, energy, etc.—need be specified and no probability numbers need be attached. But given these operationally determined values of the independent variables in the state function, the future state of the system, again described completely without probability numbers, is predicted only with a high, specified degree of probability. The time relation between states is one, therefore, not of necessary connection, but merely of highly probable connection. This is why such scientific theories are called statistical and noncausal theories.

II

Two questions may be asked of Professors Edwards and Hospers. The question to be put to the former is, "What is the meaning of the word 'good' when you say that it would be better if people did not pass moral judgments of praise and blame on what others do, but accepted the 'objective' truth that they cannot help themselves? If everything is absolutely determined and there is no moral responsibility, what is the meaning of 'better' and 'worse' as the words are used at the end of your paper?" The question addressed to Professor Hospers is, "If all theories obtained by rigorous scientific methods are rationalizations in the vicious sense of this word, how can you be sure that the Freudian theory in which you have so much confidence—whose scientific methods still remain misty and unclarified —is not also a vicious rationalization?"

May I suggest a possible answer to the questions addressed to Professor Edwards. Implicit in his use of the word "better" in his assumption that "good conduct" is conduct in accord with empirically verified scientific theory concerning the status of human deeds with respect to causal determinism. This implicit assumption is equivalent to saying that "good" is not an undefinable concept, as G. E. Moore maintained, but is instead to be defined in terms of theory that is scientifically verified as true. There are other reasons for supporting this analysis of the meaning of the word "good" and of the words "morally better" and "morally worse." Clearly, facts merely are; they are not true or false, good or bad. This being so, it seems difficult to escape the conclusion that goodness and badness, like truth and falsity, must be a function of propositions about fact. But if this analysis of the meaning of the word "good" is to be significant, then human behavior and human choice must be, in part at least, a function not merely of fact, but of the theory, true or false, that people hold about facts and on which they act.

The following question takes one, then, to the heart of the problem of moral responsibility: Do theories matter in human acts? Empirical cultural anthropology has shown that what people do in a given culture is a function of the mentality they share, i.e., the propositions they explicitly and implicitly believe. There is experimental evidence that the theory of "trapped universals" of McCulloch and Pitts makes it meaningful to say that the motor response of the nervous system (i.e., what a person does) is a function not merely of the sensory impulses (i.e., the purely inductively given facts affecting the nervous system) but also of the symbolic trapped universals in the cortex that integrate and interpret the input stimuli, thereby to a significant extent specifying the form of the motor response.

Hence, quite apart from the scientific evidence that determinism does not hold even for subatomic inorganic systems in quantum mechanics, there is evidence that scientific knowledge is quite compatible with moral responsibility and the rejection of the reductionism of judgments of right and wrong to causally deterministic antecedent factors. This conclusion is confirmed even by Professor Edwards, since at the end of his paper, notwithstanding his scientifically questionable affirmation of absolute determinism, he does not avoid passing a judgment of "morally worse" on those who do not accept, and of "morally better" on those who do accept, his thesis in judging human conduct.

12.   Determinism, Freedom, Moral Responsibility, and Causal Talk

Arthur Pap, Yale University

It is the contention of the philosophers whom William James, as reported by Professor Edwards, called "soft determinists" (a most inappropriate name, I think, in its suggestion of "soft-headed") that determinism is compatible with the occurrence of free actions, since what distinguishes free from unfree actions is the mode of causation, not the absence of causes. Some of them further explain the appearance of incompatibility as the result of an equivocation, a confusion of the meanings of "compelled" and "caused." Now, I still think that this diagnosis is correct and that the "problem" of freedom and determinism can be resolved by careful analysis of such slippery key expressions as "unavoidable," "having a choice," "could have acted differently," etc.

Professor Blanshard tries to explain how we can feel free although our actions and the silent decisions preceding them are uniquely determined by antecedent events and laws. Now, on whatever grounds a philosopher feels sure that our decisions, like all events, are "necessitated," I fail to see why our "feeling free" calls for explanation if one believes in determinism. Innumerable times in the past I have verified that my decisions were followed by the actions I decided to perform; hence I ascribe to myself the *power* "to do as I please." That I feel free just means that I believe, on good grounds that—within limits, of course—I can do as I please. But this does not even *seem* incompatible with a causal determination of one's decisions unless it is fallaciously assumed that a determined (caused) decision *eo ipso* ceases to be a decision; in other words, that "caused decision" is a contradiction in terms. It seems to me that what requires explanation is not the feeling of freedom but the fallacious belief that a caused decision is not really a decision. And I think I can supply this explanation.

Suppose I were an omniscient psychologist engaged in predicting scientifically what I was going to decide to do a short time later—say, that after five minutes I would decide to scratch my forehead. Could I really make a decision *while* predicting it silently; that is, while thinking that I was going to make it? I doubt it. Making a decision and predicting that decision are mental states that exclude each other in the same mind, since making a decision implies, by the very meaning of the term, uncertainty as to what one is going to do. But it is fallacious thence to conclude that my decision is not *predictable* by another mind. From the fact that "predicting my own decision while making the decision" is meaningless it does not follow that "predicting a decision" is meaningless or that "predicting my own decision *before* making the decision (and being at the time of deciding oblivious of my prediction)" is meaningless. We may also note that, if to a set of antecedents that make the occurrence of a decision *D* highly probable we add the antecedent expressed by "He predicts *D* on the basis of those antecedents" or "He knows that someone else has predicted *D*," we get a set that may well reduce the probability of *D* to improbability or even impossibility. But this is no contradiction. In particular, knowledge of some determinist's pretensions to be able to predict my decision may well produce in me the desire to falsify his prediction, but of course if I falsify the prediction deliberately I have not thereby refuted determinism: "same cause, same effect" is compatible with "different cause, different effect!"

Professors Blanshard and Edwards seem to be agreed—whatever their differences on other points—that the definition of a free act as one that is caused by the agent's own choice (i.e., as an act that would not occur unless the agent willed it) leaves the real problem untouched; which is, in Professor Blanshard's words, "not whether we can do what we choose to do, but whether we can choose our own choice, whether the choice itself issues in accordance with law from some antecedent." Professor Edwards seems to mean roughly the same by the words "choosing his own character—the character that now displays itself in his choices and desires and efforts." But I cannot attach any meaning to the expression "choosing my own choice." I understand what is meant by "I choose to read this book" but not what is meant by "I choose to choose to read this book." And what could be meant by "I chose my own character"? One

gathers that by "character" Professor Edwards means a set of dispositions, including dispositions to make such-and-such choices
in such-and-such situations. Now, surely it would sound queer to
say, "I chose to acquire the habit of smiling broadly at my boss
whenever I should meet him." It does make sense to say that what
was at first a deliberate, conscious effort eventually became an auto-
matic response. But then the object of one's choice, in the usual
sense of the word, is still a specific act ("I chose to put on a smile
though I can't stand him"), not a disposition to act or to decide to
act in a specific way in such-and-such a situation.

Indeed I still maintain that when people, be they philosophers or
not, ask whether one's choice itself is free or constrained they confuse determination with constraint (or compulsion). If by the assertion that the choice itself is not free—though the overt act is free
in the "soft" determinists' sense—one means, in Professor Blanshard's words, that "the choice itself issues in accordance with law
from some antecedent," then one means simply that the choice is
determined; but from its being determined it does *not* follow that
it is *compelled* in the ordinary sense of "compelled." "I was compelled to choose between death and poverty (by the gangster)"
means that either alternative, surrendering the money or not sur-
rending it, had unpleasant consequences. On the other hand, we call
a choice free if the agent has no reason to believe that both alternatives, doing *A* or not doing *A,* are intrinsically unpleasant or have
unpleasant consequences; in other words, if it is empirically possible
to choose in accordance with one's desire. The usual counterargu-
ment is that, nevertheless, if all events are strictly determined, then *I
could not* have made any other choice than the one made; therefore
the freedom of choice is a mere illusion. But what does "could"
mean? "I went to the movies, but I could have gone to the concert instead" clearly means that if I had preferred to go to the concert I
should have gone (contrast this familiar statement with the equally
familiar one: "Even if I had preferred to go to the concert, I should
not have gone, because it was sold out").

Now, certain philosophers and psychologists are not satisfied
with the common-sense distinction between avoidable and unavoidable *acts;* they ask whether the mental preference itself is avoidable.
But if "avoidable" has the same meaning in this new context, then

"My preference for the movies that night was avoidable" means "If I had preferred not to prefer the movies to the concert, I should not have preferred them"; and this, I submit, is the same meaningless iteration as "choosing to choose to read this book." If, on the other hand, "I could not have preferred anything else" means that the antecedents uniquely determined that preference, then those who deny freedom of choice on the ground of determinism are simply asserting the tautology that determinism is incompatible with indeterminism, not the interesting but false proposition that determinism is incompatible with freedom of action and freedom of choice in any usual sense of these expressions.

Implicit in the above is my reaction to the conclusion of Professor Edwards' paper that there is a sense of "moral responsibility"—indeed, this is alleged to be the sense in which the expression is used *reflectively*—in which determinism entails that one is never morally responsible for anything. Professor Edwards, following Professor C. A. Campbell, tells us that for some people the statement "*X* is morally responsible for doing *A*" entails, "*X* made (or chose) his own character." Now, if "choosing my own character" is meaningless, as it is relative to the ordinary use of "choose" (just as much as "eating my own character"), then Professor Edwards has attempted to deduce a meaningful and startling conclusion from a meaningless definition of the expression "morally responsible." Suppose, on the other hand, that "I did not choose my own character" means "My character is the product of environmental and hereditary factors that came into existence quite independently of my will." I think Professor Edwards is right in saying that many who believe in determinism refuse to hold people "ultimately" responsible for their actions on the ground that they did not choose their own character in this sense. But I think the *reason* why such determinists take this attitude is primarily that they fail to distinguish clearly between determination and compulsion; that is, they think it follows from the premise that one's actions are causally determined that they are neither right nor wrong because they fallaciously and unconsciously substitute for this premise the far different proposition that we are always compelled to act the way we act, that all our actions are unavoidable.

Professor Blanshard agrees with the "soft" determinists that de-

terminism is compatible with moral criticism. But he sides with the
indeterminists in holding that moral actions, actions inspired by a
sense of moral duty, for example, are not "necessitated" in the same
way as habitual and impulsive acts. This may be so, but I am not
clear what the distinction between causation (or necessitation) on
different levels comes to exactly. Professor Blanshard discusses deductive inference to bring out the difference. My deducing "All *A*
are *C*" from "All *A* are *B*" and "All *B* are *C*," he seems to maintain,
is not simply an example of association; the implication itself necessitates the transition of thought from premises to conclusion.
Now, it seems to me that if implications have such causative force—
directing the movement of thought the way a river bed directs the
flow of water—they must have it whether the thinker sees them or
not. Yet it is notorious that we may think of a set of premises and not
see what follows from them or draw the wrong conclusion from
them. One may counter that one would see the entailed conclusion
if one clearly grasped the *meanings* of the premised statements. But
this is either empirically false or else an unexciting tautology—the
latter if the stipulated definition of "grasping the meaning of *p*" is
that one know all the necessary consequences of *p*. At any rate, this
is not a definition of "knowing the meaning of *p*" that Professor
Blanshard could accept consistently with his well-known view that
there are synthetic entailments. I admit that where the entailment
is fairly simple—syllogistic, for example—there is a considerable
probability that thinking of the premises will make one think of the
valid conclusion. Suppose that "If *p* and *q*, then *r*" expresses such
an entailment, where *r* is not a component of the premises (it must
not be a *modus ponens* entailment, for example). Then we are justified, I presume, in making the corresponding causal statement:
other things being equal, thinking of *p* and *q* will cause a mind to
think of *r* (the "other things" are such factors as being "minded" to
draw a conclusion from the premises). But I fail to see why "cause"
in this context should have a different meaning from the one it has
in the context "If a man has frequently witnessed that the striking of
a match is followed by a flame, then a perception of the first event
will cause a thought (an expectation) of the second event"—which
I suppose is an example of what Professor Blanshard would call
mere association. I suspect that from the difference in the kind of

implication corresponding to the causal sequence of mental events—
necessary implication in one instance, contingent regularity in the
other—Professor Blanshard erroneously deduces a difference in the
kind of causation. But it is surely not logically necessary that, where
p and q entail r, the thought of p and q should be followed by the
thought of r. Otherwise we should all be perfect logicians.

In its semantic insights Professor Black's paper impressed me as
the highlight of the New York University Institute. I agree completely with nearly everything in it, especially with the argument
that to deduce from the proposition that an act is caused that it is not
free is to be guilty of what amounts to self-contradiction; that free
acts like lifting a glass of beer to one's lips are just the sort of events
with reference to which "cause" is ostensively defined in the first
place. There is only one point Professor Black made that leaves me
unconvinced. Regularity of sequence, he says, is presupposed rather
than asserted by a singular counterfactual like "If he had not lifted
the glass, it would have remained motionless." Whatever the exact
definition of the assertion-presupposition distinction may be, I am
sure that Professor Black, like Strawson, so uses "presupposition"
that the falsity of a presupposition does not entail the falsity of the
assertion that presupposes it. For example, if while pointing at Mr.
X, I say, "That American is very rich," I presuppose—do not assert
—that Mr. X is an American; for if it turned out that he was not an
American but very rich, the proposition I asserted would not be refuted; it is just that a false assumption about Mr. X led me to describe him incorrectly.

Now, let the relevant generalization that according to Professor
Black is presupposed, not asserted, by a person uttering the counterfactual "If he had not lifted the glass, it would have remained motionless" be: in situations like that one (or perhaps in all situations
whatever) a glass does not move toward a man's lips unless someone
—usually that very man—*makes* it move that way. Is it really true
that no amount of disconfirmation of this generalization would lead
us to retract the counterfactual as false as long as we saw the man's
clasping of the glass followed by the approach of the glass to his
lips? I very much doubt it. If I experience repeatedly that after I
clasped a glass an invisible force pushed the glass to my mouth
though I made no effort whatever, and other people reported similar

experiences, I should say to myself: Perhaps it was the same way in that case! Perhaps he made no effort at all; and even if he did make an effort, perhaps the same effect would have taken place if he had made no effort. Professor Black may reply that, if the generalization is indeed implicitly asserted when we utter the counterfactual, it is inexplicable how we can be as certain of the truth of the counterfactual as we normally are. But I think that this high degree of certainty can be accounted for without difficulty by one who stands by the regularity analysis of singular causal statements. We usually apply the terms "cause" and "effect" to *changes* that somehow catch our attention. And we use these terms in such a way that only a change can be said to cause a change. Hence it is analytic to say that only *a,* preceding or simultaneous, change can have caused the observed movement of the glass; for example, the drinker's passage from a state of indifference toward the beer to a state of desiring it. At once, then, factors that remained constant are ruled out: the movement of the glass could not, for example, have been caused by anybody's perception of it, for it was perceived all along before it moved, etc. True, many other changes preceded the effect: thus, someone near-by laughed shortly before it moved. But as we know of many instances when similar changes were not followed by a similar effect, they are likewise ruled out as possible causes. My point is that the very regularity analysis of the meaning of "cause" justifies an instantaneously and unconsciously performed *eliminative induction* that bestows a high probability on the singular causal statement.

13.   Some Equivocations of the Notion of Responsibility

Alfred Schutz, New School for Social Research

Our discussion of the problem of responsibility was mainly concerned with the question on what grounds a person might be held answerable or accountable by law or from a moral point of view for something he did or omitted to do. The consequence of responsibility, in this sense, is the infliction of punishment, if we take this term in a sense broad enough to include reprehension, criticism, and censure. But even in this sense the notion "to be responsible" may mean two different things: on the one hand, a man is responsible *for* what he did; on the other hand, he is responsible *to* someone— the person, the group, or the authority who makes him answerable.

This distinction between "being responsible *for*" and "being responsible *to*" becomes of particular importance if another equivocation of the notion of responsibility is taken into account, namely that between its use in terms of the third (or second) person and in terms of the first person. It is submitted that the notion of "responsible" is an entirely different one if used in a proposition of the type "This person is responsible for this and that" and in a proposition of the type "I feel responsible for this and that (e.g., for the proper education of my children)." It is further submitted that these two notions of responsibility cannot fully coincide and that any philosophical analysis of the problem of responsibility must remain incomplete without taking into account its subjective aspect.

In using the expression "the subjective aspect" about the notion "feeling responsible" in terms of the first person, we adopt an unfortunate, but by now generally accepted, terminology of the social sciences, which distinguishes between the subjective and the objective meaning of human actions, human relations, and human situations. It was Max Weber who made this distinction the cornerstone of his methodology. Subjective meaning, in this sense, is the meaning that an action has for the actor or that a relation or situation has for the person or persons involved therein; objective meaning is the meaning the same action, relation, or situation has for anybody else —a partner or observer in everyday life, the social scientist, or the philosopher. The terminology is unfortunate because the term "objective meaning" is obviously a misnomer in that the so-called "objective" interpretations are in turn relative to the particular attitudes of the interpreters and therefore, in a certain sense, "subjective."

To elaborate on the difference between the subjective and the objective meaning of responsibility would require a rather lengthy analysis. We have to restrict ourselves to some scanty remarks. If I feel merely subjectively responsible for what I did or omitted to do without being held answerable by another person, the consequence of my misdeed will not be reprehension, criticism, censure, or another form of punishment inflicted on me by someone else, but regret, remorse, or repentance—or, in theological terms, contrition and not attrition. The resulting states of grief, anguish, or distress are marks of the true sense of guilt that is phenomenologically something entirely different from the "guilt feeling" in psychoanalytic terminology. It is the outcome of the feeling of being responsible for something done or left undone and of the impossibility of restoring the past. Orestes in Aeschylus' *Eumenides* was not redeemed before the goddess had reconciled the Furies, although the judges of the Aeropagus had placed an equal number of white and black balls into the urn. In our times we find certain eminent scientists suffering under a deep-rooted sense of responsibility for having co-operated in the production of atomic weapons, in spite of the honors bestowed on them by a grateful government. On the other hand, the law might hold me answerable for an act that my personal sense of responsibility motivated me in performing (Antigone's conflict is an example). And here the distinction between being responsible for something and being responsible to someone appears in a new light. I may agree with the other's verdict that I am responsible for a particular state of affairs but maintain that I feel accountable for my deed merely to God or my conscience but not to my government.

These are merely examples for the complicated underlying dialectic of the subjective and the objective meaning of responsibility. But the same dialectic underlies the meaning of a norm for the normgiver and the norm-addressee. Any law means something different to the legislator, the person subject to the law (the law-abiding citizen and the lawbreaker), the law-interpreting court, and the agent who enforces it. Duty has a different meaning as defined by me autonomously and as imposed on me from outside. The whole question of determinism in law and ethics will have to be answered in a different way if formulated in subjective or objective terms.

The distinction between the subjective and the objective meaning of laws, values, morals, and responsibility merely from the point of view of the individual can also be made on the level of group relations. Adopting Sumner's classical distinction between in-group and out-group, it can be said that responsibility, for example, has a different meaning if an in-group acknowledges responsibility for its acts and holds some of its members responsible, or if an out-group makes the in-group and its members responsible for misdeeds. It is one thing if, in the Nuremberg trials, the Nazi leaders were held responsible by the Allied Powers, and quite another thing if they were held answerable by the German people.

14. Observations

Dennis Sciama, Trinity College, Cambridge University

I

Professor Blanshard raised the question of our feeling that we have free will. He suggested that we are under an illusion and mentioned some psychological reasons for our mistake. I agree that we may be under an illusion, but I should like to suggest that the reasons may be logical rather than psychological. I have in mind the fact that a computing machine, for instance, cannot know all about itself for the usual self-referential reasons. Similarly a brain cannot know all about itself and may therefore be unaware of some of the factors determining its behavior. This might then lead to the illusion that we have free will—an illusion that no amount of introspection could dispel. (Professor Feigl told me that this idea has been elaborated by Karl Popper in an article in the *British Journal of the Philosophy of Science*[1]—an article I have not seen.)

II

Professor Munitz raised the question: What is knowledge? Perhaps a scientific comment on this question might be useful. If you

[1] "Indeterminism in Quantum Physics and Classical Physics" (1950), I.

walk into a laboratory and find a bar of metal that is much hotter at one end than the other, you infer that the bar must have been heated at one end. (The problem of justifying this inference is interesting, but I cannot go into it here.) In other words, the bar carries some information about the past. In a specialized sense the bar can be said to "know" something about the past. To put it more abstractly: a macroscopic system that is substantially far from equilibrium carries information about the past and can be said, in a specialized sense, to "know" something about the past.

Of course we usually want to mean something more than this when we use the word "knowledge." We want the system to know that it knows. This can be achieved with the human brain if we follow those theorists who suppose that inside the brain there is a neural circuit that partially maps the state of the brain as a whole. The brain then carries information by being far from equilibrium, and this information is mapped onto the special circuit, whose deviation from equilibrium enables the brain to know that it knows.

III

Professor Landé raised the question how we are to understand the existence in nature of random or nearly random processes. Professor Frank suggested that one need only suppose that fields of force are sufficiently complicated. This is the conventional answer, but I agree with Landé that there is more to it than that. I do not know the answer, but I should like to mention some of the relevant considerations.

As we trace back in time the world line of each atom partaking of the random motion, we seek some moment at which we can say: the randomizing element is introduced here. This forces us to consider the cosmological problem concerned with the state of the universe a long time ago. Two possibilities are usually discussed in this connection. The first is that there was a singular moment about five billion years ago when all the material in the universe was crowded together at an infinitely high density. One must then assume that there was the required amount of randomness present at that time, a procedure that is perhaps somewhat *ad hoc*. The second possibility is that the universe has the same large-scale appearance at all times, the dilution arising as the expansion of the universe is compensated by the continual creation of new matter. On this view, when one traces back the world line of an atom one comes to the point where it first appeared. Have we the right to say that this appearance is a random process? We cannot answer this question in the absence of a detailed theory of the process of creation, but it seems to me that this is the question that must be answered (or the corresponding one for the high-density singularity) before Landé's problem will be solved.

15.   Determinism and the Theory of Agency

Richard Taylor, Brown University

I shall neither prove nor disprove determinism. Instead, I shall (1) give a precise statement of it, as I think Edwards and Hospers understand it, (2) show that it does, as they maintain, entail that men have no moral responsibilities, (3) elicit the defects of the usual answers to this claim, (4) indicate how a simple indeterminism supplies no better basis for responsibility, and (5) sketch a theory of agency that I think anyone insisting on moral responsibility must be driven to.

Determinism. Determinism is the thesis that whatever occurs occurs under conditions given which nothing else could occur. Indeterminism is simply the minimum denial of this, viz., that at least some things occur under conditions given which something else could occur instead. But these statements need to be made precise.

The modal term "could" expresses causal contingency, which I shall define in terms of causal or nomical necessity. There is, that is to say, a clear and common sense in which, for example, a man who has been decapitated *necessarily* dies, or *can* not go on living; or, for another example, water heated to a certain point under certain conditions *has* to boil, though no logical necessities are here involved.

Given, then, this sense of necessitation, we can define the other modal words in terms of it and reformulate determinism and indeterminism accordingly. Thus:

e is impossible $=$ $-e$ is necessary,
e is possible $\quad=$ $-(-e$ is necessary$)$,
e is contingent $=$ $-(e$ is necessary$) \cdot -(-e$ is necessary$)$,

where e stands for any event whatever, and $-e$ for any event incompatible with e. These definitions show that the possible and the contingent are not coextensive.

Determinism, then, is the thesis that in the case of any true statement of the form "e occurs" the event whose name or description replaces "e" is causally necessitated, never contingent. Indeterminism is the thesis that in the case of some true statement of that form, the event named or described is contingent.

Responsibility. Edwards and Hospers believe that determinism is incompatible with responsibility and obligation on the basis, I believe, of the following argument. It is assumed (a) that responsibility and obligation, in their strictly ethical sense, if they have any application at all, figure only in the context of human conduct, not in that of the behavior of animals, and (b) that a necessary (not sufficient) condition for ascribing this responsibility to a man for what he has done, or obligation for what he has yet to do, is that he could have done, or could do, something else; that is, that the occurrence for which he is responsible or obligated is contingent. But (c) this condition is never fulfilled. Hence (d) no man has ever been morally responsible for anything he has ever done, or will ever be morally obligated to do anything else. A corollary of this is that the notions of "ought" and "ought not" have no application to human conduct in any sense in which they do not equally apply to the behavior of animals.

"Soft determinism." Determinists unwilling to accept this conclusion have tried several rejoinders, of which I shall cite, and reject, the four most common.

1. It is said that, even assuming determinism, the necessary condition for responsibility is often fulfilled, for to say that an agent could have done otherwise means only that he would have done otherwise had he chosen to.

But this neglects the fact that, if determinism is true, he could not have chosen otherwise. Indeed, by this kind of argument, one could say that, though a man has died of decapitation, he did not *have* to die, that he *could* have lived on—meaning only that he *would* have lived had he somehow kept his head on! And this is hardly the sort of contingency we want.

2. Again, it is said that a *sufficient* condition for ascribing moral responsibility is that an agent act from deliberation with knowledge of the consequences, and that this condition is often fulfilled.

But this presupposes the necessary condition for such responsibility that according to determinism is never fulfilled, for, as Hart reminded us (citing Aristotle), it makes sense to deliberate only about things that are, or are believed to be, contingent. This point becomes clear if we remind ourselves that, according to determinism, not only is a man's behavior causally necessitated (among other things, by the course of his deliberations), but so *also* is every step and detail of his deliberations, and so *also* are his beliefs (true or false) about the future, and *hence* his beliefs concerning the effects of his actions. Under these conditions one can no more ascribe moral responsibility to a man than to a robot who "deliberates," and then "acts," in response to our pushing various buttons (labeled "deliberate" etc.), every step of the chain then following by causal necessity.

3. Determinists sometimes say that we are, after all, responsible only for our *acts,* not our intentions, choices, or decisions. A man is not punished or rewarded for deciding to do something unless he then goes ahead and does it, and since even advocates of "free will" concede that our acts are causally determined (by our choices or "wills," for instance), there is evidently no absurdity in being held responsible for what is determined.

But an indeterminist is not likely to concede that all our acts are causally determined. Moreover, this view conceives of responsibility only in terms of reward and punishment, confusing moral responsibility with corrigibility. What I am referring to as *moral* responsibility comes out more clearly if we consider cases in which no questions of law, no questions of benefiting or harming others, and no questions of reward, punishment, or retribution are at all involved. If, for instance, an intelligent man studies what is in fact a valid philosophical argument, understands it, accepts the premises as true and the reasoning as valid, and yet refuses to accept the conclusion, there is no philosopher, save those who deny obligation altogether, who would not say that he *ought* to accept the conclusion. But here no overt act is involved, but only a decision, and no question of reward, punishment, or retribution comes into the picture, much less one of legality. It cannot be true, therefore, that men have no responsibilities or obligations with respect to their decisions, unless it should turn out that they have no responsibilities or obligations whatever.

4. Finally, many determinists have said that moral responsibility consists only in amenability to a change of behavior through the force of real or anticipated rewards or punishments; in other words, that responsibility simply consists in corrigibility—a view that not only is compatible with determinism but presupposes it.

This definition of responsibility, however, violates what was assumed at the outset—namely, that lower animals have neither moral obligations nor responsibilities. The behavior of almost any sentient thing—rodents and fish, for instance—is alterable by the stimulus of reward or punishment. Moreover, this queer conception of moral responsibility and obligation, in addition to applying to situations to which moral concepts do not apply, fails to cover cases of the sort we just considered. For when one says that a man *ought* to accept a conclusion, in the light of probative evidence known to him, he does *not* mean merely that he can be *induced* to do so by threat or reward; indeed, the obligation might hold when this condition does not.

I regard it as reasonable, then, that if determinism is true no man has ever been morally responsible for anything he has ever done, and no man ever will be under any obligation to do anything. This is a painful conclusion to accept, particularly in view of the fact that, if one does accept it, one can try to persuade others to do so only by threats, blows, or arguments, but can never say that they *ought* to accept it, even if it is proved. But the conclusion may well be true nonetheless, for it seems to be entailed by what most philosophers regard as obviously true, viz., determinism.

Indeterminism. The denial of determinism, however, seems no more compatible with moral judgment than determinism, for it would seem to rob human actions, in Liebnitz's phrase, of any "rhyme or reason." Since this thought is fairly familiar I shall not elaborate it but only illustrate it.

Suppose an agent so constituted that his actions are determined by the numbers that turn up on a roulette wheel, and suppose, further, that the wheel obeys no causal laws whatever, so that its behavior is unpredictable in principle. Now, it would be plainly irrational to consider an agent so constituted morally responsible for those acts or obligated to perform others, since they are obviously utterly beyond his control; yet this situation corresponds exactly, so far as moral judgment is concerned, to that of an agent whose acts are quite undetermined.

Agency. To salvage moral responsibility one must resort to certain odd metaphysical notions that have long since been out of fashion and that are admittedly most difficult to comprehend clearly. What is needed, that is, is a view according to which (*a*) there is a reason for everything that happens, but (*b*) some such happenings —viz., some human acts are contingent. The only way of satisfying these seemingly incompatible requirements is to suppose that an act for which an agent is responsible is performed by him, but that he, in turn, is not causally necessitated to do it. Now, this does, I think, accord with what men take themselves to be—namely, *agents* (cf. Latin *agere*) or beings that *act* rather than things all aspects of whose behavior are the causal consequences of the way they are acted upon. It now remains to elicit just what this theory involves, and see whether it is compatible with responsibility.

First, then, it involves the conception of a self or person (i.e., an agent) that is not merely a congeries or series of states or events, for on this view it is an agent who performs certain acts (i.e., who acts) rather than states or events in his history that causally determine them—these states or events being, presumably, if not things done by himself, then simply the causal consequences of other states or events, whether of his own history or that of other things.

Second, it involves an extraordinary conception of causation, according to which something that is not an event can nevertheless bring about an event—a conception, that is, according to which a "cause" can be something other than a sufficient condition; for if we say that a person is the "cause" of his act, we are not saying that *he* is a sufficient condition for its occurrence, since he plainly is not. We must accordingly not speak of an agent as *causing* an act, since "being a cause" ordinarily just means "being a sufficient condition," but rather of his originating it or, simply, of his *performing* it—in a manner in which things in the physical world, so far as we know, are never done or brought about. And this is evidently the conception of Aristotle, who spoke of living things as "self-moved." It is also what later philosophers, like Thomas Reid, meant by "active power," viz., the power to act without being acted upon, and it may be what Kant meant when he obscurely spoke of a "noumenal" self that is free.

Now, both of these conceptions—that of an *agent* as distinct from the states or events of his history, and that of *performing* as distinct from being a sufficient condition—are certainly odd and hard to conceive of clearly. Indeed, a philosopher could not be accused of stubbornness if he preferred to give up moral responsibility to embracing these two notions. But I am sure that only by accepting them can one *also* accept the notions of moral responsibility, obligation, and what Professor Hook referred to as "dignity."

It still remains to see, however, whether this conception of agency is compatible with responsibility. To show that it is, it needs to be shown that *on this view* (*a*) some human acts are contingent, in the sense defined; (*b*) animals are not rendered morally responsible; and (*c*) acts do not arise "without rhyme or reason," i.e., are not capricious.

With regard to the first point: some acts *are* contingent on this view, for they are not simply the causal consequences of antecedent conditions. Now, it will be tempting to say that there *must* be sufficient conditions for an agent's doing just what he does, but this simply begs the question, being just what the theory denies. There are certainly always conditions under which any event occurs, but such conditions do not in all cases necessitate just that event to the exclusion of any other; otherwise there would be no such thing as an *act*, nor would anything ever be *done*. We may further assume that for any act that is performed, there are reasons why it is performed; but such reasons need not be causal conditions. Rather, they may be, for example, motives or purposes, which are not sufficient conditions. To say, for instance, that an agent acted in a certain way in order to achieve a certain purpose is to give an explanation, but not a causal one, for his conduct. And if it is now insisted that there must, in any case, be conditions sufficient for an agent's having just such purposes and motives as he has, this may or may not be true (I think it is not); it is in any case irrelevant, for it would mean that only his purposes and motives—but not thereby his acts—are causally determined.

Secondly, as to the question whether this theory would render animals morally responsible: it evidently would not. If animals are "self-moving," as Aristotle thought, they do indeed satisfy a necessary condition for responsibility; but it does not follow that they satisfy any sufficient condition for it, and, in fact, they evidently do not.

Finally, as to the question whether this theory avoids capriciousness in human acts: it plainly does not, *if* by "capricious" *nothing more* is meant than "contingent." That is, it does deny that there are conditions sufficient for the occurrence of all events that occur. But it does not deny that there is an explanation or reason for every event, as we have just seen, for there are ways of explaining a man's conduct otherwise than by a recitation of causal conditions. The concept of agency, then, is quite unlike that of a thing whose behavior is arranged to coincide with the random selections of a roulette; for, assuming the wheel to be causally undetermined, there is *no* ultimate explanation for the roulette's behavior, whereas there is for the agent's. Moreover, saying of an agent that *he* acts makes sense; but we cannot conceive of a wheel—no agent at all—as "deciding" what is to be "done."

Conclusion. I do not claim to have proved a theory of agency, but I believe I have shown that, if it is intelligible, it renders moral responsibility possible. The conditions of moral responsibility can thus be elicited, in terms of agency, as follows.

Consider a situation in which some object O grasps a knife and cuts off a man's hand. Now assume: (1) there were no conditions sufficient for this event—i.e., it was contingent; (2) O is an agent, e.g., a man; (3) the event described is an act of O's and not, for example, a reflex; (4) O realized, while contemplating the act, what it consisted in, and (5) he knew what its consequences would be, and that they would be evil.

A. Each of these assumptions can be true, and they can all be true together; that is, there is no proposition known to be true with which the conjunction of these five is causally or logically incompatible.

B. If (1) were false, *O* would not be morally responsible for the event described.

C. *Hence* neither (2), nor (3), (4), nor (5) is a sufficient condition for responsibility; nor are these four together sufficient, except as they may presuppose (1).

D. But (1), (2), (3), (4), and (5) are each a necessary condition for moral responsibility for this event, and

E. Together they are sufficient.

If one denies *E* one must, I believe, either deny *B*, as Edwards and Hospers do not, or else deny *A*, which would seem arbitrary and implausible.

16.   Common Sense and Beyond

Paul Weiss, Yale University

A good deal of contemporary discussion of the problem of determinism and freedom rests on a number of unexamined but rather dubious assumptions. Not until these are brought to the fore, and either modified or replaced, can there, I think, be much hope of progress toward the solution of this perplexing basic issue. One of the conspicuous virtues of Mr. Blanshard's and Mr. Black's papers is that they so evidently make these assumptions. Despite their apparent difference in outlook and conclusion, the two are substantially in accord. Their quarrel is an intramural one; the basic issue is blurred and avoided by both with equal success.

I

A surprisingly large group of thinkers today suppose that untutored common sense is beyond legitimate criticism. Many of those who make this assumption deny that philosophy has any problems of its own. There is, according to them, only the problem of understanding how it is that philosophers should think there are problems. Mr. Blanshard and Mr. Black are happily free of this folly, but they, like the others, are in accord in their acceptance of the testimony of untutored common sense. But it is surely the case that there is no single coherent, consistent body of common-sense truth. The common-sense man, whether don or plain citizen, mixes shrewd observation and practical wisdom with folly, superstition, prejudice, and convention. Men of good common sense today believe in the efficacy of individual prayers, in the wisdom of having ministers of warring nations look to God for aid, in mental telepathy, in a double sexual standard, in thrift, in the agreement and profundity of scientists, and so on. It is good common sense to claim that chalk is white because it is seen to be so. But when twilight comes and the chalk appears grayish it is also good common sense to insist that the chalk remains white, though it is seen not to be. The statemen "If I don't wear rubbers when it rains, I'll catch cold" is for many a robust common-sense man as root and firm as any other and could be treated as a paradigm.

Any view that wholly abandons common sense is at best a fiction or a fantasy. Any view that refuses to examine it is at best uncritical and dogmatic. Reflection and reason require one to stand somewhere between these two extremes. Taking into account whatever else needs explanation, one should try to forgo accounts that do maximum justice to what is daily experienced. This maximum justice is consistent with the abandonment of this or that phase of common sense if it is in conflict with a larger body of coherent, clarified knowledge. We ought to begin with some such simple fact as that a man acts or, more specifically, that certain events ensue upon his behaving in certain ways and, as experience shows, do not ensue when he does not so act. We will then not know yet whether the act was freshly initiated and freely carried out. To achieve this knowledge we go beyond common sense in order to obtain more abstract, consistent, and comprehensive accounts than common sense can provide.

It is good common sense to say that whatever occurs is determined, and it is good common sense to say that men act freely. Were a systematic treatment of man in his diverse enterprises and an understanding of time, motion, causation, mathematics, and science to make determinism the most coherent and illuminating outlook, we should have to conclude that, though common sense often says that a man acts freely, this would have to be understood merely as shorthand for the remark that he is the occasion, or the most proximate source, of an energy expended for the transformation of some objective combination of facts. On the other hand, if a satisfactory account of man and these other matters required an acknowledgement of an element of chance, novelty, or freedom in the universe, we should have to conclude that the frequent common-sense assertion that all acts are determined reflects the failure of common sense to make use of fine discriminations, its refusal to pursue reflections, and its incapacity to reason in the precise fashion that is necessary if subtle truths are to be grasped.

The contention that men are determined and the contention that they are free seem opposed. They are not. Determinism applies to what has happened when all the conditions are already present and fulfilled. Freedom applies to what is happening and will happen; it concerns the creation of new conditions and thus of consequences that until then have not been necessitated.

II

Most discussions of freedom do not distinguish among (1) freedom *from,* (2) freedom *to,* (3) freedom *for,* and (4) freedom *with.*

1. Whenever men are subject to unusual or unconventional restraints we think of them as being compelled; when those constraints are removed we think of them as freed, and speak of them as free. Thus we say that the released slave is a free man.

2. Freedom *to* is the power to act either inwardly as a being of

intent or outwardly as one who can publicly express his wishes or carry out his obligations. Thus we say that he who wishes to take drugs, and can, is free to take them; and that he who ought to pay his debts and has the money to do so is free to pay them.

3. Freedom *for* is the power to commit oneself to an end and to work to bring it about. This end may be set by society or the state; one's commitment to it might be a function of heredity and training. But the capacity to put oneself in a position to focus on this end and engage in activity to bring it about is to have a freedom *for*. Thus we say that men are at their best when they have been made free for a civilized life of leisure.

4. Finally, we are men in a society and men in a cosmos, and whatever freedom we may express is largely futile or frustrated if it does not intermesh with that exercised by others. Thus we say that we are genuinely free only when we are in harmony with equally free fellow men.

Each of these types of freedom has a number of distinct cases. Most interesting perhaps are those that fall under the second and third types, for these are most germane to questions of morality and ethics. It is most helpful, I think, to distinguish among freedom of *preference,* of *choice,* and of *will.* Freedom of preference refers to the selection of some means to an accepted goal, good or bad. Freedom of choice concerns the formation of a single unity of means and end, where the end promises to make good whatever loss in value the means involve. Freedom of will, finally, is related to the adoption of a final prescriptive good in such a way as to require a fresh approach to whatever means there are. Freedom of preference allows for a determinism dictating which among a number of goals will be found most agreeable, and which means most appealing; it is a freedom connected with the joining of goals and alternative means, with a consequent mutual alteration in their import and a possible substitution of means. Freedom of choice allows for a determinism dictating which means will be favored; but it also requires a freedom through which a compensating end is adopted and the means previously favored re-evaluated and perhaps rejected. Finally, freedom of will allows for a determinism that dictates why, and perhaps even when, the will should be exercised, while leaving free the exercise of the will in this way or that, with this or that consequence.

There are surely other meanings of freedom besides these. But enough has been indicated, perhaps, to show that we cannot settle the problem of determinism and freedom until we have decided just what type of freedom, and thus what antithetical sense of determinism, we wish to consider.

III

It is commonly assumed that prediction and determinism are either equivalent or identical, or that one follows necessarily from the other. But none of these suppositions are correct. Prediction is a prediction, a saying in advance what is to ensue. In the ideal case it consists in the deduction, through the agency of mathematics and logic, of the nature of the effect that rationally follows from the given condition. Now, all deductions are in terms of generalities, of expressions that lack the completeness and concreteness characteristic of actual occurrences. Predictions thus relate only to a phase, an aspect, of the world, to something generic, to be instanced by what in fact occurs. The occurrence of the instance is not encompassed in the prediction; it could have been deterministically produced, though in that case we should not have been able to say anything about it in advance, or even perhaps when it occurred. Conversely, predictability is compatible with freedom. Predictability, since it concerns only kinds of things, the generic features, the merely possible, allows for the free occurrence of this or that particular instance.

Most thinkers confuse the problem of prediction with that of determinism because they are phenomenologists in doctrine or in intent, and suppose that what scientists affirm to be real, or what common sense observes, is all there is in the universe. Yet a scientific account that requires the acknowledgment of determinacies or indeterminacies in the world tells us nothing about the nature of things, but only about that phase of existence isolated and pursued in common ways by a community of thinkers. In the end we have no right to say that anything completely beyond all knowledge is real. But it does not follow that what is beyond the reach of scientific instruments, scientific needs, scientific procedures, and scientific tests is beyond the reach of all cognition and outside the pale of meaningful and illuminating discourse. The concurrence of these is required if we are to know whether determinism or freedom holds sway in this world.

A scientific indeterminism is compatible with an ontological determinism; a scientific determinism is compatible with an ontological indeterminism. The wise scientist makes no claim that he is able to deal with or to know anything about the universe outside the scope of his language, instruments, experiments, or criteria. More often than not it is the philosopher who hurries to convert a laudable scientific methodological caution into an unwarranted claim that what science does not know is either not knowable or nonexistent, and who makes the uncritical contention that what science treats as a desirable supposition or a genuine fact is to be urged as a solid and unquestionable basic truth.

IV

The importance of the problem of ethical responsibility makes most thinkers attend to the question of freedom only as it relates to man. Almost all writers in the western world today are clearly, and sometimes even outspokenly, anthropocentric. Confident that the world of nature is thoroughly determined (except perhaps in the region of quanta phenomena), they insist that man, at least if ethics is to have any meaning and responsibility a locus, is somehow free. But their position involves the cutting off of man from nature. It is a view that is incompatible with the theory of evolution, and in the end it deals with man as though he were "a kingdom in a kingdom." To be sure, man is different from other beings; he has and can exercise powers denied to them. But the powers that they do have must fall under categories comprehending his, if both he and they are to be parts of the same cosmos.

V

The nature of causation has been oversimplified to make it seem as if there were only two factors to consider, the cause and the effect. As a consequence the discussion of causation has been riddled with paradox.

A cause must precede its effect. That is why history can cover an extensive stretch of time. This means that the cause cannot necessitate the effect. If it did, the effect would exist when the cause did. What is normally termed a cause is only an antecedent condition. The nature of the effect is defined by it, and can often be predicted in the light of what we know of it. But the cause does not produce the effect that in fact ensues. The actual effect comes about as the result of an activity that, taking its start with the cause, ends by producing an instance of the predictable effect. The causal situation, then, has not two but three components: the cause, the process of production, and the effect. Since freedom is the doing of something beyond the determination by a cause, the process of production is evidently free. An actual effect is freely produced inside a frame that necessarily binds together an antecedent cause and a predictable type of effect.

These observations, it is hoped, may suffice to indicate that we ought not to be content with uncriticized common sense, with the hypotheses or conclusions of the sciences, or with the traditional philosophic formulations of the problem of determinism. We ought to take our start with common-sense items, examine them critically, and then move on to what they presuppose; that is, to a systematic account encompassing man and nature and whatever else there is. If we are willing to make provision for every facet of being and knowledge, we shall soon find that no untutored common sense, no rationalism, no anthropocentrism, no simple empiricism or positivism, no theory of a radical opposition between determinism and freedom, will do justice to the facts or to the need to get a coherent explanation of them.

17.   On Causation

H. Van Rensselar Wilson, Brooklyn College

I

There are two kinds of problems connected with causation: epistemological problems and ontological or metaphysical problems. Although they are interrelated in various ways, it is possible for purposes of analysis to keep them relatively distinct, and in my opinion it is important that confusion between them be avoided so far as possible. It therefore strikes me as unfortunate to speak (as Professor Barrett does) as though predictability (an epistemological concept) were synonymous with causal necessity (an ontological concept). Lack of causal necessity would certainly entail lack of predictability; but I see no reason to assume that lack of predictability entails lack of causal necessity. The fact that the epistemological difficulties in sociological, psychological, and many biological situations preclude our *knowing* what all the specific relevant causal factors are in a particular case does not warrant the conclusion that there are none. Present inability to specify the values of a variable can hardly be construed as evidence that no such values exist.

Professor Black used a very brief illustration that has a bearing on this point. He remarked that when a penny is tossed into the air it has to come down, but it does not have to come down tails. Now, I have no quarrel with this remark if it is simply meant to assert two epistemological propositions: (1) knowing only that the penny was tossed up, but not knowing in what precise direction, with what precise force, with what kinds of spin, how it lay in my hand beforehand, what kind of surface it will strike, and so on, we are warranted in asserting (without specifying when, where, or how) that it has to come down; but (2) in the absence of fuller information neither the statement "It has to come down heads" nor the statement "It has to come down tails" is a warranted assertion. But in the context of a discussion of causal determinism one tends to construe Professor Black's remark as denying that there is causal necessity in a particular case of the penny's coming down tails, which is a very different matter. The difficulties of measuring even approximately the momentum and spin of a tossed penny—to say nothing of doing so precisely enough for safe prediction—are obvious. But surely this does not alter the fact that, irrespective of anyone's knowledge or lack of it, the penny *has* a specific momentum and spin, and that if all the data were precisely known it would be clear that the penny "has to" come down the way it does.

The fact that five hundred years ago no one could have computed the penny's trajectory even if precise data had been available, whereas today we can, is beside the point, of course. If the trajectory is admittedly necessitated by computable causal factors today, then similiar trajectories were always necessitated. The unavoidable analogy between (1) a fifteenth-century physicist in relation to today's physicist and (2) today's neurologist (let us say) in relation to an imaginable twenty-fifth-century neurologist needs no elaboration. The analogy proves nothing, to be sure; but it should give us pause, restraining our tendency to equate absence of *knowledge* of precise data and formulas with absence of *existence* of precise states of affairs and objective correlations in fields where they are not currently specifiable.

Causal necessity in a particular case, I would contend, is *holistic* with respect to the relevant controlling factors rather than fragmental with respect to those factors; that is, causal necessity is a concept that is meaningful only as a function of *all* the relevant causal factors (material, formal, and efficient), whether known or unknown, taken collectively. Fragmentally (i.e., when not even one relevant factor is taken account of) neither assertion nor denial of causal necessity in a given case would be warranted, although one could certainly form hypotheses, for conceivable future testing, about what sorts of currently unavailable data would need to become available in order to complete the picture. A basic heuristic postulate for determinism is that it is worth while *without limit* to formulate and (as it becomes possible) to test experimentally such hypotheses regarding currently missing causal factors, since (the determinist assumes) every instance of apparent lack of causal necessity is an instance of fragmental knowledge of the relevant causal factors. The pragmatic effects on the future development of science of proceeding (without proof) *as if* this assumption were true and of proceeding *as if* it were false are quite evident.

Professor Blanshard's suggestion that there are levels of causation is one with which I agree, if I may construe it as referring primarily to the levels of complexity of the relevant causal factors in various types of situation, and secondarily to the levels of concomitant epistemological difficulty in ascertaining without error or omission (1) what *all* the relevant factors are about which specific information is needed before we can specify the holistic causal necessity in such situations, (2) the specific formulas that would adequately formulate the relevant causal laws, and (3) the precise value of the variables to be substituted in the relevant formulas in a particular case. For the tossed penny most of the data that would be relevant at a more specific level are irrelevant when we only wish to assert nonspecifically that it must come down sometime, somewhere, somehow. We may therefore ignore such data and still assert causal necessity without using the concept (at this level) fragmentally.

When we assert that there is holistic causal necessity in the penny's coming down tails in a specific case, the domain of relevance is much vaster and the epistemological difficulties far greater, but the relevant formulas and data are still theoretically within the scope of current physics and current observability. In asking, however, whether the tosser "had to" decide to toss the penny one enters a level of complexity and difficulty where only fragmental consideration of the relevant factors is currently possible, and from fragmental consideration no specifiable necessity can emerge, any more than it could from a fragmental consideration of the factors in the penny's trajectory. This being the case, the pertinent questions would seem to be not those about current knowledge and predictability but rather the frankly speculative, as yet untested, hypotheses and assumptions about the factors that still elude us, entailing a projected program of further inquiry that is believed (without proof, but equally without disproof) to be worth pursuing in the hope of gradually reducing our ignorance. In these terms I agree with Professor Blanshard (as I understand him) that to assume, for animate and human and societal cases as for inanimate cases, that holistic causal necessity exists, as a function not merely of some or most but collectively of *all* the relevant causal factors involved (regardless of their complexity and our current inability to specify them exhaustively), makes more sense than it does to assume, as indeterminists do, that no such causal necessity exists even as a function of all the relevant causal factors, known and unknown, or to assume (as Professor Barrett appears to do) that absence of specifiable causal necessity in terms of a fragmental consideration of those factors that happen to be currently *known* is to be equated with absence of causal necessity altogether.

II

We would all agree, I suppose, that the verb "to determine" has two independent meanings which are not to be confused: (1) to *ascertain,* or obtain information about; and (2) to *necessitate,* or to be related to a dependent variable in such a way as to render all but one of its values impossible. "Currently ascertainable" is surely not synonymous with "existing in a definite state," nor is "epistemologically determinable" synonymous with "ontologically determinate." And yet we seem to find ourselves speaking at times almost as if "having no currently measurable difference" were synonymous with "having absolutely no difference," and even as if "present human inability to determine (ascertain) the state of affairs" were synonymous with "ontological indeterminacy of the state of affairs."

Possibly the trouble arises from an unfortunate semantic assumption that meaningful terms include only those for which operational tests are *currently performable* and exclude those for which such tests are conceived only and not currently feasible to perform. But so to restrict meaning is disastrous to theoretical speculation. To forbid, by arbitrary semantic fiat, hypothetical discussion of situations that currently preclude our ascertaining precise values for the relevant variables, or for which we have not yet been able to formulate any applicable differential equations, would seem to exhibit a defeatist attitude that is utterly foreign to the history of science.

When Professor Landé speaks about dropping ball bearings from a chute onto a knife edge, he seems to make the tacit assumption that the several occurrences are *mathematically identical,* except for the random falling to left and right. He would undoubtedly agree, however, that the most that could be validly asserted about the objective state of affairs is that the actual differences (if any) among the occurrences are too slight to be detected by available measuring devices. But does this justify the assumption that there *are* no differences? Someone has suggested performing the experiment in a vacuum to avoid stray currents of air. I agree. But that is not sufficient. Slight but definite deviations from mathematical sphericity or from absolutely homogeneous density, even if undetectable by available instruments, would presumably affect the results, and even if such factors were completely controllable, the knife edge itself would lose a few molecules of material each time a ball struck it and the next ball would therefore strike a knife edge of slightly different shape. Unless one insists on equating "below the threshold of detectability with currently available instruments" with "mathematically infinitesimal," there is no relevance to the objection that infinitesimal differences in the conditions could not account for finite differences in the outcome. I see no logical inconsistency in positing the hypothesis that in such an experiment there is no randomness in the outcome of really *identical* events, but varying behavior under varying conditions in accordance with perfectly definite formulas—a hypothesis that will become progressively testable as measuring techniques become progressively more refined. No new or "hidden" variables are here involved, but merely slight, uncontrolled differences in the values of the familiar variables.

These slight, uncontrolled differences in the conditions are, I suppose, the "phantom knife edge suspended above the actual knife edge," to which Professor Landé alluded. But I see no other way out without a quite needless retreat from essential scientific attitudes. A basic programmatic decision is involved. One alternative is to accept "inherent randomness of nature" as an *explanation* of the observed facts, in which case no program of further experimentation and theoretical refinement is called for, since one already has the "explanation," such as it is. The other alternative is to act upon a heuristic postulate that construes the phenomenon of apparent randomness, wherever observed and quite unconditionally, as a challenge to the experimenter to refine his measurements or his theory or both until determinate orderliness replaces the randomness—*assuming* that eventually it will, if he and his successors persist. Instead of interpreting this assumption (as Professor Munitz seems to do) as implying a belief that the universe is like a humanly constructed "puzzle" that one assumes to have a "solution" merely because puzzles are always constructed that way, I would interpret it as inextricably involved in the basic attitude of scientific curiosity itself, without which there would never have been any science and in the absence of which further scientific advancement would stop cold. Without celestial mechanics the places where successive solar eclipses are visible give every appearance of randomness. Without meteorology the weather has every appearance of randomness. Is it not scientific defeatism to assume that contemporary types of randomness are more invincible than these?

At the risk of appearing utterly stupid to the experts in quantum mechanics, I must still ask, How does anyone *know,* beyond all doubt, that every photon is identical with every other photon? Not long ago we thought that every hydrogen atom was identical with every other, but then we discovered deuterium and tritium. Is there any logical absurdity in the hypothesis that when and if we reach a higher degree of precision we shall find (as so often in the past) our current instances of apparent randomness exhibiting determinate order after all?

Of course we might then discover new instances of apparent randomness at the new level, and thus be faced with the same choice again—either admit defeat and accept "inherent randomness of nature" as the answer or act again on the former heuristic postulate. But this should not surprise us. The "erratic" orbits of Uranus and then of Neptune were not treated as instances of randomness but as challenges. If sometime, with more precise measurements, we find that Pluto too is behaving in random fashion, would we quit or proceed as before? Determinists and indeterminists might appear to sanction opposite answers to such a question.

III

I make only two very brief comments on the papers of Edwards and Hospers.

1. There may be some danger of mistakenly supposing that an actual cause of an effect is somehow *less* a cause if it can be shown to have prior causes of its own. But this would be like supposing that I am somehow less the father of my children because I in turn have a father. If I am really the cause of my decisions, I am no less so after it is shown that, *in addition* to being the cause of these and other effects, I am also the product of earlier causes. Whatever moral responsibility I have for my decisions, I have as their *proximate* cause, and the responsibility is not diminished by showing that responsible selves (as well as irresponsible selves) have causes.

2. The relation of one's "self" or character to one's decisions and actions is sometimes such that (*a*) a modification of the self *would* result in a modification of future behavior in similar situations, and the self *is modifiable* by praise, blame, and other manifestations of approval and disapproval from other persons (including courts of law) and from one's own conscience; while at other times it is such that (*b*) either the self *is not thus modifiable,* or such modification *would not* result in modified future behavior. In ordinary language we call the person "responsible" in case *a* and "not responsible" in case *b*. If Professors Edwards and Hospers are asserting that all human actions come under category *b*, then I think the empirical facts are clearly against them. On the other hand, if they agree that there are actions that come under category *a* but simply refuse to call such actions "responsible," then I think linguistic usage is against them. Also, I think they would then be under obligation to introduce some new terms of their own as a translation of the quite essential distinction between *a* and *b*, which otherwise seems to disappear.

INDEX

233

Carnap, R., 10
Cassirer, E., 54
Causality: and anthropomorphism, 22ff, 128; and constant conjunction, 11ff, 25–6, 151ff, 190ff; and "making something happen," 15ff; definition of, 20ff, 118, 151ff, 184, 189ff, 204–6, 224, 225ff; language of, 28–30; levels of, 11ff, 135ff, 161–2, 227; mechanical, 190; mental, 11, 106ff, 114ff, 155–6, 164, 213; metaphysical, 24, 215ff; physical, 7ff, 20ff, 45ff, 69, 70ff, 151ff, 198ff; proximate, 152; related to choice, 22, 97–8, 106ff, 136–7, 164; related to punishment, 95, 144–5; teleological, 190ff
Causal laws, 11, 44ff, 64, 82, 110, 152, 159–60, 215, 227
Chance: in history, 38; in physics, 52–3, 69–71, 172, 185, 191
Change, 28; as criterion of responsibility, 119; in definition of "cause," 152–3, 206; in definition of "event," 3
Chisholm, R. W., 145
Choice: and disposition, 201; efficacy of, as maximized by law, 96ff; freedom of, 5, 82n, 107ff, 114ff, 145–7, 155–7, 160, 164ff, 175ff, 201ff, 220ff; meaning of, 5; system of, in criminal law, 96ff. *See also* Freedom
Coleridge, S. T., 36–7
Collins, A., 107, 110
Common sense, 171; criticism of, 219ff
Complementarity, principle of, 47–8, 76
Completeness and incompleteness: in mathematics, 33–4; of physical knowledge, 148ff
Compton effect, 195
Consumer, 181–2
Continuity: postulate of, 74–5; continuous creation of matter, 211
Contradiction, in mathematics, 34
Counterfactual conditionals, 24, 94, 158, 205–6
Creativity, 167; in art, 36–7; in mathematics, 34–5

Darrow, C., 105ff, 127, 177
DeBroglie, L., 44, 53, 58
Deduction, 57, 193, 204, 222
Definition: and undefinability, 199; by stipulation, 18, 204; formal and informal, 19; in quantum theory, 68–

9, 77, 192ff; ostensive, 205; paradigmatic, 18ff, 189–90; pragmatic criteria of, 154
Denotation, 149
Determinism: meaning of, 4, 30, 33–4, 69, 77, 148ff, 157ff, 191ff, 211ff; "soft" and "hard," 104ff, 113ff, 177–8, 200ff, 212ff. *See also* Necessity; Causality; Predictability
Dewey, J., 31, 164
Difference, method of, 153
Dignity, as basis of moral responsibility, 177, 216
Dilemma, of moral responsibility, 146–7,
Dispositions, as causes of moral actions, 162
Ducasse, C. J., 147

Economy of threats, doctrine of, 93ff
Eddington, A., 7, 9
Edwards, Jonathan, 105, 165
Edwards, P., 104, 113, 120, 135ff, 141, 163ff, 174ff, 180, 187–8, 199, 200ff, 211–2, 218, 231
Einstein, A., 7, 43–4, 51, 64ff, 189, 193ff
Electron: definition of, 60; position and velocity of, 7–8, 60–1, 67, 73, 149, 172
Emergence, 154
Entailment: analytic and synthetic, 204; in defining causality, 152, 204; of a theory, 196
Epistemology, 189ff, 225ff
Erewhon, 103–4
Event: definition of, 3; mental, 11, 149, 168; physical, 6, 149, 170, 183ff, 229; probability of, 53; uniqueness of, 149
Evidence: for determinism, 168–70; for fatalism, absense of, 150; introspective, 161–3; of causal efficacy, 16; of voluntary action, 100, 131
Excusing conditions: distinguished from invalidating conditions, 87; in law, 81ff, 133ff, 138ff, 176ff, 181

Fatalism, 31, 108, 150, 165–6
Feigl, H., 160n, 209
Frank, P., 160n, 192, 210
Freedom: and indeterminism, 4, 148ff, 220ff; as absence of constraint, 22, 106–7, 135, 155–6, 200; as quality of action, 23; as rational control, 14–5, 176–7; feeling or sense of, 5–7, 14, 161, 170, 200, 209; of will, 9,